A HOMEOWNER'S GUIDE
WIRING

A HOMEOWNER'S GUIDE

WIRING

STEVE CORY

The Taunton Press

The Taunton Press
Inspiration for hands-on living®

The Taunton Press, Inc., 63 South Main Street, Newtown, CT 06470-2344
Email: tp@taunton.com

Editor: Peter Chapman
Copy editor: Seth Reichgott
Indexer: Jay Kreider
Cover design: Barbara Cottingham
Interior design: Sandra Salamony
Layout: Barbara Cottingham, Lynne Phillips
Cover photographers: Steve Cory and Diane Slavik
Illustrator: Mario Ferro unless otherwise noted on p. 261

The following names/manufacturers appearing in *Wiring: A Homeowner's Guide* are trademarks:
Adobe™, Amazon Alexa™, Hulu®, Nest®, Netflix®, Roku®, Romex®, Spotify®, Tech Lighting®, Uber™,
WarmlyYours®, YouTube®

Library of Congress Cataloging-in-Publication Data

Names: Cory, Steve, author.
Title: Wiring : a homeowner's guide / Steve Cory.
Description: Newtown, CT : The Taunton Press, Inc., [2019] | Includes index.
Identifiers: LCCN 2019004415 | ISBN 9781641550031
Subjects: LCSH: Electric wiring, Interior--Amateurs' manuals. |
   Dwellings--Maintenance and repair--Amateurs' manuals.
Classification: LCC TK3285 .C753 2019 | DDC 621.319/24--dc23
LC record available at https://lccn.loc.gov/2019004415

Printed in the United States of America
10 9 8 7 6 5 4 3 2 1

About Your Safety: Working with electricity is inherently dangerous. Using hand or power tools improperly or ignoring safety practices can lead to permanent injury or even death. Don't try to perform operations you learn about here (or elsewhere) unless you're certain they are safe for you. If something about an operation doesn't feel right, don't do it. Look for another way. We want you to enjoy working on your home, so please keep safety foremost in your mind.

IN MEMORY OF STEVE CORY

It was with great sadness that we learned of the death of author Steve Cory late in the production process for this, his last book. Builder, remodeler, author, photographer, editor, Steve was truly a Renaissance man and jack of all trades.

Over the course of his long, prolific career, Steve wrote more than 60 do-it-yourself books on topics ranging from decks and carpentry to wiring, plumbing, and kitchen remodeling. I had the privilege of working with Steve on 6 titles for The Taunton Press since 2012, and he was an editor's dream of an author: his knowledge of construction was exhaustive, his text impeccable and invariably on or ahead of schedule, and he always had ideas for his next book simmering in mind. And he was one funny guy.

His long-time friend and fellow author Dave Toht graciously agreed to step in to see this book through the last stages of production. Another consummate professional, Dave remembers Steve in his own words: "He was not only a great how-to writer, but also one of the mellowest and kindest people I had the pleasure of knowing. In the more than 60 years I knew him, I literally cannot think of one mean-spirited thing he ever said or did. Steve was the genuine item."

We all mourn his passing.

Peter Chapman
Executive Editor

Contents

Introduction

Your home's electrical system can seem scary—and a certain amount of fear is healthy. After all, your home's many wires, devices, and fixtures carry current that when "live" can cause harm, and in rare cases even death if safety measures are not followed. However, following a few simple practices will keep you completely safe as you replace, repair, or add electrical service. And I'll guide you, step by step, through the process for each of the projects in this book so you always work with dead wires and devices.

Most wiring projects can be accomplished with a few easy-to-learn skills. Whether you are replacing a fixture or device, or installing boxes and running cable for new service, with an hour or so of practice you can run and connect wiring that is every bit as safe and durable as work done by a professional electrician. (The most difficult task is to run new cable inside finished walls and ceilings.)

Projects You Can Do, and Projects Best Left to the Pros

Let's start with a few do's and don'ts. First, do not have any dealings with the wires that enter your house from the utility company. Leave that to the pros.

Most household wiring carries 120 (or 115 or 125) volts. However, your house also probably has appliances or receptacles that use 240 (or 250) volts. This level of voltage is, of course, far more dangerous than 120-volt service. You can work on 240-volt service, but take extra-special care to ensure that power is off when you do so.

Replacing a fixture or a device where one already exists is certainly a homeowner DIY project. Installing a new service panel is best left to the pros. In between are a good number of projects that you can certainly consider doing, as long as you learn techniques and take the time to understand the steps needed.

As a general rule, do not tackle an installation unless you fully understand what you will be doing. If you feel unsure, reread the project instructions or the descriptions of how household power works in Chapter 1. If you're still wavering, refrain from plowing ahead anyway; hire a professional electrician, at least for a consultation.

Hiring a pro

After reading the relevant portions of this book, you may choose to hire a professional electrician, at least for the "rough-in"—installing boxes, connecting to the service panel, installing new circuits, and running cable into the boxes. The electrician may allow you to install devices and fixtures yourself so you can save some money. But many pros will insist on doing all the work—and for good reason, since their work must be inspected and since they are held responsible for the safety of the final installations. See p. 145 for advice on hiring a professional.

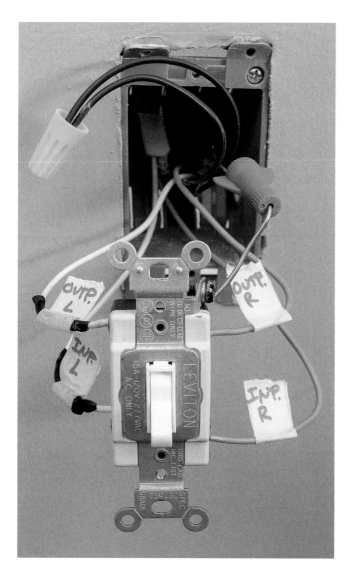

How This Book Is Organized

This book begins with an explanation of basic electrical concepts and an overview of your home's electrical system. Understanding this basic background information will be helpful for almost any wiring task, so I recommend that you spend some time reading Chapters 1 and 2. The rest of the book can be consulted on a project-by-project basis; you need read only what pertains to your specific needs.

All the projects described in Chapters 3 through 5 can be accomplished with a surprisingly modest set of tools (described in Chapter 2) and some basic testing, stripping, and connecting skills (also covered in Chapter 2). In these chapters, you will learn how to upgrade various types of lights and fans, as well as switches and receptacles. You'll also learn how to tackle the most common household electrical repairs. For many readers, these will be the only chapters they need consult. None of these projects calls for running new cable or installing new circuits, so they are DIY-friendly.

The second half of the book is more DIY-challenging. It shows how to install new electrical service where there was none before. This may mean extending an electrical circuit to add a new receptacle or fixture or two, or it may involve installing a new circuit. I encourage you to read most or all of Chapter 6, which will help you plan the job, and then decide whether or not you need to hire a pro.

Chapter 7 describes installing new boxes and running new electrical cable of various types, as well as conduit with wires. Chapters 8 and 9 show how to install new devices, fixtures, and appliances. Chapter 8 also shows how new circuits, as well as new service panels, are installed—projects for which you may want to hire a professional electrician. And in Chapter 10 you will find out about the latest installations for data, security, "smart home," television, and other low-voltage hookups.

Whenever you run new service, be sure to get a permit from your building department. They may allow you to do the work; if so, consult the section on inspections and codes on pp. 152–154. Or they may require that you hire a pro for everything.

Another possibility: a professional may agree to let you do the work, while for a fee he or she will inspect and sign off on it. This would likely take place after the rough-in and after the finished installations—just before the inspector from your building department does an inspection.

Being Safe and Understanding Your System

WITH MINIMAL KNOWLEDGE, you might be able to jump right into many home improvement projects that involve simple carpentry; any mistakes you make will probably be correctable. The same is *not* true for electrical work. There is serious power running through wires and into devices and fixtures, and the better part of caution requires that you learn some things about your home's wiring system before you open anything up. Please read through this chapter carefully, and do further reading or consulting (with your building department or an electrician) if necessary before you start work.

This chapter shows how to work safely with your electrical system. It shows some of the most common wiring configurations to help demystify the wires you will find inside boxes. It also guides you through a quick inspection of your system.

Priority One: Safety

Always treat household current with the respect it deserves. You may be tempted to take shortcuts—say, by just flipping off a switch to a light you will replace. It's human nature to cut corners, but resist this temptation! Take the time to turn off power at the service panel and test to be sure power is off at several stages of the project.

In most cases, the basic steps for safety are as follows:

- Shut off power at the service panel.
- Test to verify that power is off.
- Take steps to ensure power will not be restored while you are working.
- Use tools and wear protective clothing to minimize harm in the unlikely event of a shock.

Double protection

The pros not only take the time and trouble to shut off power and test to verify that power is off, but they also use insulated electrician's tools and wear protective gear. The idea is to remove the possibility of shock, but also to act as though the power is still on, to ensure you will not be injured if shock occurs.

THE SERVICE ENTRANCE. Wires from the utility company to your home may pass through an overhead service head like this. Be sure to keep clear of these wires at all times. In particular, keep any metal ladders away.

Three Ways to Get a Shock

Household electricity either travels in a circuit from the service panel and back or it travels to the earth. The human body is mostly water, which makes it an excellent conductor of electricity. Shock occurs when power flows through your body on its way to complete a circuit, either back to the earth or back to the service panel.

1. If you touch both a hot (usually black or colored) and a neutral or ground (white, green, or bare copper) wire, electricity will travel through your body on its way back to the service panel. In this case, it doesn't matter whether you are wearing rubber-soled shoes or not.

2. If you touch only a hot wire, power can pass through your body and into the earth. This is much more likely to happen if you are kneeling or not wearing rubber-soled shoes and if the ground (or a concrete surface) is damp. Wearing rubber-soled shoes, standing on a rubber mat, or standing on a wood floor will greatly lessen—but not eliminate—the possibility of shock.

3. In a house, most metal housings, pipes, and appliances are connected to other metal objects that eventually lead to the ground. So if you touch a hot wire and also have contact with a metal object that is connected to the ground, you will get a shock.

THE SERVICE WIRES. In most homes there are three thick service wires entering the service panel. Shown here is an overhead service entrance. Shutting off the main breaker (or pulling the main fuse if you have a fuse box) will de-energize the wires on the house side, but you cannot turn off power to the service wires. Stay well clear of these wires.

What not to touch

Stay well away from the wires that bring electricity to your house. These include the wires that lead to an overhead service head or run underground to your home (see p. 14), those that lead to the electric meter, and the thick service wires that enter the service panel. You have no way of shutting off power to these wires (only the utility company can do that), and they carry plenty of juice. See pp. 142–143 for more information on working in a service panel.

An underground service entrance may emerge outside the home or in the basement. These wires should be well sealed with thick conduit. If the entrance is damaged or compromised in any way, call your utility company and stay away from this area.

Your wiring may not be correct

The photos and illustrations in this book show wiring that was done correctly. Unfortunately, many homes have wiring that was done incorrectly, either by an unqualified person or in a slipshod manner by a pro.

See pp. 33–37 to identify some of the more common wiring mistakes. If you see anything suspicious, or wiring that you do not understand and that does not correspond to the images in this book, call in a professional electrician for evaluation.

Shutting Off Power and Verifying That Power Is Off

Unless you are working with new wiring that is not connected to power, the first step is to shut off the power and then to make sure the power is off. Shutting off power and testing for power go hand in hand. Always do both, and test at several points, to ensure that you are working with de-energized wires and fixtures.

The steps here emphasize testing when working on a device (that is, a switch or a receptacle). The same approach is used when removing a light fixture; see pp. 62–63 for more specific instructions.

Of course, in all the testing cases, if the tester's light comes on, then power is present and you need to turn off a different breaker or remove a different fuse.

1 **SHUT OFF THE BREAKER OR REMOVE A FUSE.** So you can quickly make a first test for the presence of power, flip on a light switch or plug a tester into a receptacle. At the service panel, turn the appropriate breaker to the OFF position, or unscrew and remove a fuse.

2 **MAKE SURE POWER WILL STAY OFF.** If your service panel can be padlocked, do so. If not, tape a clearly written sign over it, to be sure nobody will restore power while you work.

3 **INITIAL TESTING.** Before you remove a cover plate or start to remove a light fixture, use a voltage detector to see if power is present. A tool like this is not as reliable as a voltage tester, but it is a good first step. On a receptacle, poke the prongs of a voltage tester into the slots to test for power. Be sure to insert the metal prongs fully, while keeping your fingers well away from the prongs.

A Brighter Tester

The little light on most voltage testers can be difficult to see, especially in a bright room. For a light you are certain to see, you can use a rubber light socket with a bulb. (Use a bulb that is crack resistant, such as one made for a garage-door opener.) Be sure to twist the stranded wires tightly before inserting them into the holes of a receptacle or connect them to the fixture wires using wire nuts. Do not use this method for testing after the cover plate is removed, because you are more likely to touch the bare wires.

4 **TEST WITH THE COVER PLATE OFF.** Remove the cover plate or the light fixture and use a voltage detector again to test for power.

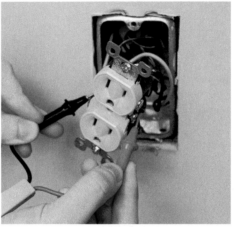

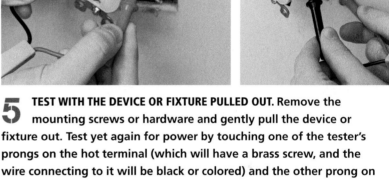

5 **TEST WITH THE DEVICE OR FIXTURE PULLED OUT.** Remove the mounting screws or hardware and gently pull the device or fixture out. Test yet again for power by touching one of the tester's prongs on the hot terminal (which will have a brass screw, and the wire connecting to it will be black or colored) and the other prong on the neutral terminal (with a silver screw and a white wire attached). If the electrical box is metal rather than plastic, also test by touching one prong to the hot terminal and the other to the box.

More Protective Measures

Shutting off power is the main way to protect yourself, but there are other measures you can take to keep yourself safe while you work.

The right clothes and tools

To be doubly protected, wear shoes with rubber soles. (Gym shoes are characteristic apparel among professional electricians.) Gloves are usually not worn, because electrical work calls for handling small objects. But if you can wear them comfortably, they do provide some insulation against shock. Safety goggles are generally recommended, in case of sparks. Also wear them when using power tools or when cutting holes in walls and ceilings.

Be sure to use tools specifically designed for electrical work. These include screwdrivers, lineman's pliers, and strippers with rubber-sleeved handles. If the rubber gets damaged so that you might touch a metal handle, replace the tool with a new one.

FLOOR SAFETY. A concrete floor, especially if it is damp, can conduct electricity efficiently. Wear rubber-soled shoes and place a rubber mat on the floor for an added safety measure.

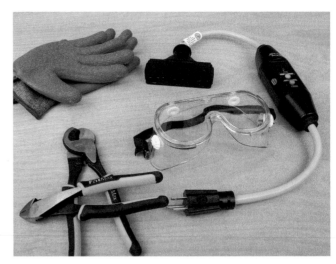

ELECTRICIAN'S GEAR. Electrician's tools have rubber-coated handles, making them even more shock-protective than plastic handles. Protective eyewear is a good idea for almost any construction work. Gloves may help in some situations. A GFCI-protected extension cord will ensure against shocks when working with power tools.

Saw Carefully

If you need to cut a hole in a ceiling or wall, first use a voltage detector to test for the presence of live wires behind the drywall or plaster in the area where you will cut. Cut with a handsaw rather than a power saw so you can feel any pipes or cables.

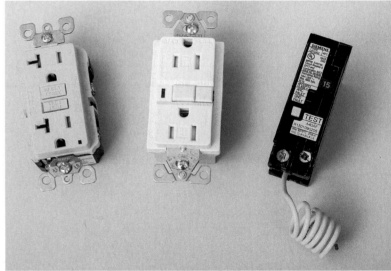

DEVICES THAT PROTECT. A number of protective receptacles and circuit breakers can make your home safer and can shut off power very quickly in case of a ground fault or crossed wires. These include GFCI receptacles (left), AFCI receptacles (center), and GFCI circuit breakers (right); see pp. 114–116 and pp. 142–143 for more information on these devices.

The Basics of Household Electricity

Electricity in a wiring system is often compared to water in a plumbing system. When electrical power is turned on, electrons flow through wires and pass through electrical users—light fixtures, as well as small and large appliances—energizing them and causing them to illuminate, heat up, power a fan, and so on. Of course, electrons travel much faster than water.

It travels in circuits, at least usually

All those wires you see in boxes and service panels actually work to cause power to travel in a very simple way. Power travels in a circuit, or circle. Hot wires (which are black or colored) carry power out from the service panel (see p. 18) to one or more outlets, and white wires carry power back to the panel, to complete the loop.

Power can travel in another way. If there is a clear path from a hot wire to the earth (or to a metal or other conductive material that leads to the earth), then power will travel in that path. This is called a ground fault—a situation that wiring systems strive to avoid.

Switches

The circular flow can be stopped or started by flipping a switch. When the switch is in the OFF position, the circuit is broken and the electrons cannot flow. When a switch is in the ON position, the circuit is completed and the electrons flow, energizing any outlets along the circuit's path. In the case of a receptacle and an appliance with no switch, the loop can be completed or broken by plugging in or unplugging a cord.

HOW A SWITCH WORKS

When a switch is turned off, the electrical pathway is broken and the power does not flow. When the switch is on, the circuit is completed and power flows through the outlet and back to the service panel.

A circuit breaker or fuse is a type of switch inside a service panel, which shuts off power for safety reasons (see pp. 18–22).

— black wire
— white wire

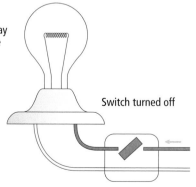
Switch turned off

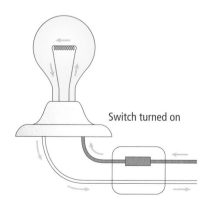
Switch turned on

Volts, watts, and current (amps)

Voltage refers to the electrical pressure exerted onto a system. It is much like the water pressure within pipes. Most household electrical circuits are supplied with (or "carry") between 115 and 125 volts. (Usually these are called 120-volt or 125-volt circuits.) Large appliances like electric water heaters or ranges carry 240 volts.

Even though most circuits carry 120 volts, different outlets use different amounts of power, or *current*. This is measured in amperes, usually shortened to *amps*. The thicker a wire, the more amps (current) it can carry. If a wire is too thin for the amps it carries, it will overheat dangerously.

The energy actually consumed by an electrical outlet is measured in *watts*. Household electrical consumption is often measured in kilowatt-hours, which is the use of one kilowatt (1,000 watts) of power sustained for one hour.

A basic calculation: watts = volts $\times$ amps. Or, amps = watts $\div$ amps. For more on this, see pp. 154–155.

Grounding and Polarization

Electrical systems have insulated wires, devices, and components; in addition, fixtures, tools, and appliances are well protected with double insulation. As long as electrical devices are installed and used correctly, power will travel safely through outlets in a circuit and you will not receive a shock. However, very occasionally something can go wrong: A receptacle may be damaged, a wire may come loose and touch the wrong metal surface, a lamp cord's insulation may be frayed causing wires to touch, and so on. If someone touches these damaged objects, a painful shock could result. In some cases, an electrical fire may be kindled when wires heat up. Grounding and polarization are two measures that significantly reduce the risk of these dangers. Nearly all homes built after World War II have receptacles, fixtures, and service panels that are protected with grounding and polarization.

TIP To quickly make sure that a receptacle is grounded and polarized, plug in a receptacle analyzer (see p. 33).

Polarization

You have probably noticed that most receptacles have one slot that is longer than the other. In addition, most plugs have one prong that is wider than the other, so they can be inserted in only one way. These plugs and receptacles are polarized.

The narrow slot of a polarized receptacle is connected to the hot (black or colored) wire, the one bringing power from the service panel; the wide slot is connected to the neutral (white) wire, which carries juice back to the panel. A lamp or small appliance is wired so that its switch connects or disconnects the hot wire; in a polarized situation,

UNGROUNDED, BUT POLARIZED. This receptacle has no hole to accept the grounding prong of a plug, so it is not grounded. One slot is longer than the other, so it is polarized.

turning off the appliance will shut off the path of the hot wire and no power will be present in the appliance. If polarization is not present, then the switch could turn off the neutral wire and power would still be present in the appliance. This is a safety hazard.

Very old homes have nonpolarized receptacles with equal-size slots. (These are almost always ungrounded as well, posing an added hazard.) If you have this situation, it's a good idea to unplug appliances rather than simply turning them off. Better yet, upgrade to a system that is grounded and polarized.

Grounding

Grounded receptacles have two slots and a hole (a.k.a. three holes). The grounding hole, into which the grounding prong is inserted, connects to either a grounding wire or to the metal sheathing of conduit or armored cable (see pp. 25–26). Almost all the time, the grounding wire or sheathing is unused. But if something goes wrong and a ground fault occurs—say, a receptacle's wire comes loose and touches something it shouldn't—the current is carried back to the service panel via the ground wire instead of the neutral wire. This can cause the power to flow harmlessly to the earth via the service panel's ground wire, but more often it causes a breaker to trip or a fuse to blow.

Many modern homes have ground wires that are green or bare copper, which attach to the ground/neutral bar in a service panel and to the grounding terminals of receptacles, switches, and fixtures. Or, if a home is wired with metal conduit through which wires pass, the conduit can act as the ground path. (Metal-clad flexible cable can also act as the ground, though only short lengths of it are allowed by code.)

Grounding and Bonding

To be completely accurate, the wires or sheathing commonly referred to as "grounding" are actually "bonding." That is, they bond metal parts back to the service panel, causing a breaker to trip or a fuse to blow in case of a short circuit. True "grounding" really refers to the grounding wire and other elements that connect the service panel—and the entire system—to the earth. However, it is common to refer to bonding as grounding (almost nobody calls a ground wire a "bond wire"), and we will do that in this book.

Grounding requirements have grown more stringent over the years. For instance, it used to be considered unnecessary to ground light fixtures. Then it became common practice to run a ground wire past a switch from the power source to the fixture. Nowadays it is required that you connect a ground wire to both the fixture and the switch.

GROUNDING WITH A GROUND WIRE

Here's an example of a modern way to ground a receptacle and light. The ground wire is connected to the receptacle, the switch, and the light. In earlier installations, the ground connection to the switch and/or the light may have been omitted.

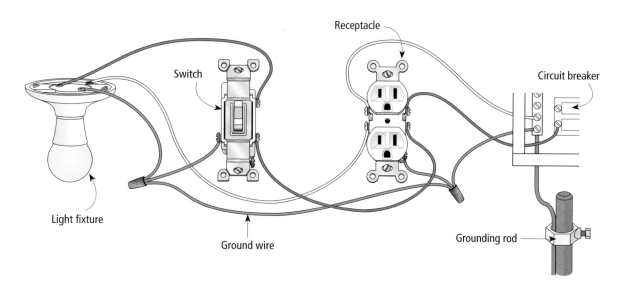

Switch

Receptacle

Circuit breaker

Light fixture

Ground wire

Grounding rod

When a ground fault or an overload occurs, the ground wire provides a path for the electricity to travel back to the service panel, rather than to the body of someone who is touching the object where the fault is occurring.

How Power Gets to Your Home

Your electrical utility company delivers power to its customers' homes via overhead or underground wires. Starting at the power plant (or perhaps a step-up transformer), the utility may begin by sending power through high-voltage power lines (the kind you can hear hum). Before power reaches your home, however, it will likely pass through a substation and several step-down transformers, so that the individual hot wires (which may travel individually or may be bundled in a cable) each carry about 120 volts. Wires of this voltage enter a house either through an overhead service head or an underground entrance.

The service entrance

The service entrance (sometimes called the service drop) is the place where wires enter your house. In most cases, the wires enter through a metal pipe. Before reaching the service panel, the wires pass through a meter, which measures the amount of electricity your home uses, for billing purposes.

NEIGHBORHOOD TRANSFORMER. A cylindrical step-down transformer like this is a common sight in areas with overhead power lines. Wires that emerge from it carry household current—between 115 and 125 volts.

UNDERGROUND SERVICE ENTRANCE

Wires that travel underground are usually encased in strong metal conduit. Underground service also uses transformers to step down the power to household level.

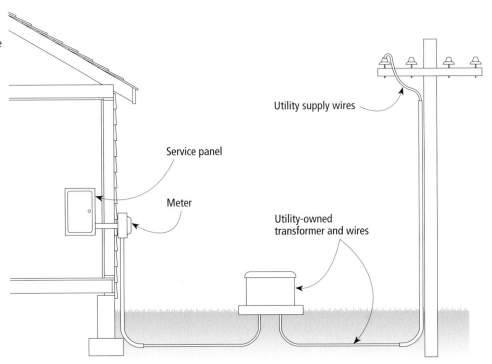

Service panel

Meter

Utility supply wires

Utility-owned transformer and wires

ENTRANCE WITH METER. An underground entrance may simply be visible as a pipe with wires running inside, or it may be a unit like this, which houses the wires and the meter. (Small conduit pipes that emerge from this unit do not hold the utility wires; they carry wires to outside electrical receptacles and other services.)

OVERHEAD SERVICE ENTRANCE. An overhead service entrance has a service head that is shaped and sealed to keep water out. Just before entering an overhead masthead, the service wires are connected with special utility splices, so the power company can easily disconnect them when needed to shut off power to the entire house. The wires attach to a strong metal cable and bracket near the service head.

UPDATED UTILITY SPLICES. Here an overhead entrance uses a newer and more secure type of utility splices.

FROM THE METER TO THE SERVICE PANEL

Whether the utility wires arrive underground or overhead, the meter can be connected to the service panel in various ways. Here are three examples.

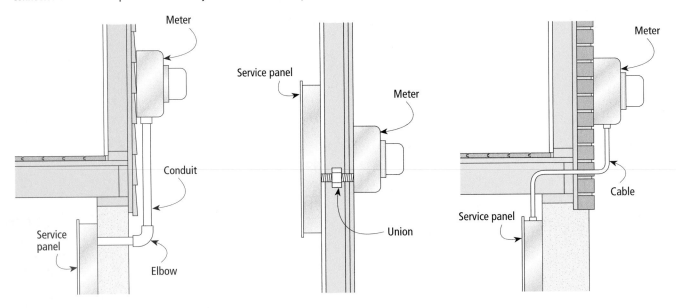

Meter

Service panel

Conduit

Service
panel

Elbow

Meter

Union

Meter

Cable

Service panel

Electric and Gas Entrances

If you have gas service entering your house, be sure it and the electrical service entrance are safely located. A gas meter will sometimes emit small puffs of natural gas, so the electrical service entrance should be a safe distance from the meter and should be shielded with a cover. Local codes vary widely on the required distance between the two utility entrances.

Service wire number and size

The vast majority of homes built after World War II have three service wires. One is neutral and the other two are hot, each carrying 120 volts. Most circuits use one of the hot wires plus the neutral to power 120-volt circuits.

Both hot wires can be combined to energize 240-volt circuits, which power high energy users like central air-conditioning, hot-water heaters, ranges, and dryers.

A very old home may have only two wires, one of which is hot. That means that it is not possible to have any 240-volt circuits. Such service is usually connected to a fuse box rather than a breaker panel and will severely limit your electrical use options, especially if you want to upgrade your home. Consider upgrading your service (see pp. 223–227).

The thickness, or "size," of the service wires matters as well. Wires of a certain size can carry enough power for 100-amp service. If you need to upgrade to 200-amp service—which is common in medium to large homes with modern conveniences—you may need to have the power company supply larger wires (see pp. 223–225).

Meter and Bill Reading

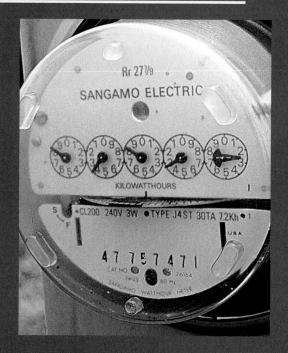

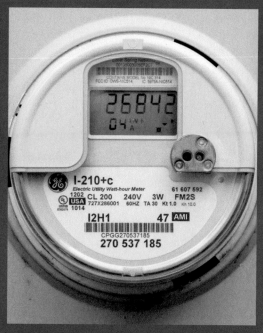

Your electric bill should tell you the number of kilowatt hours you have used in a month. Nowadays most utilities use automatic meter reading (AMR) so they don't have to visit and look at your meter. (Often the readings are taken using a radio device while driving past your home. Other methods include WiFi and satellite transmission.) Whereas in the past bills were often based on estimates and predictions of use, AMR gives real-time, accurate information. It can also supply additional helpful information, such as the times when you use the most electricity. Your bill should give you much of this information.

However, you may want to read your meter yourself, to double-check your bill or keep close track of your usage. Some areas still have older dial-type meters like the one shown above left, which has four or five small dials that rotate alternately clockwise and counterclockwise. Read the dials from left to right and record the numbers. If the pointer is between two numbers, record the lower number. If the pointer is between 0 and 9, record 9 and reduce the reading from the dial on its left by one. Ignore the dial on the far right. There is also

a wheel below the dials, which spins slowly or more quickly depending on how much power is being consumed at the moment. This can give you a very general idea of your current power usage.

If you have a digital or electronic meter (shown above right), you will simply see five or six numbers, one of which is in red. Record the first five numbers and ignore the sixth, if there is one. Some meters will display two rows of numbers, one of which shows usage during times when power costs the most (generally during the day) and usage during off-peak times (often at night). To calculate the number of kilowatt hours used during a specific period of time, subtract the recorded reading at the beginning of a period from the reading at the end. This will give you an idea of usage during certain times—say, when the air conditioner is running much of the time.

Many utilities offer a service where if you supply readings, they will give helpful advice on saving money on your electric bill.

The Service Panel

Command central for your home's electrical system is the service panel, a.k.a. the service entrance, the fuse box, or the breaker box. Get to know your service panel, but treat it with respect: Wear protective clothing when dealing with it, and do not touch the thick entrance wires that bring power into the box.

Your service panel may be in the basement or in a first-floor utility room if you have no basement. It is usually located on an outside wall, near the electric meter (though the meter may be on the outside and the panel on the inside). In areas with warm climates, it may be on the outside of the building. On the next few pages we show several types of meters, but yours may look different. Just be sure you understand where power enters, where the main disconnect is, which areas of your home each breaker or fuse controls, and how the hot, neutral, and ground wires (if any) are attached.

Breaker service panels

Most homes these days have service panels with circuit breakers. When a circuit overloads or there is a ground fault or short circuit, the breaker will "trip," shutting off power to the circuit. Power can be easily restored by flipping the breaker back on. However, such power outages indicate that you need to assess your system and either find the source of a short or take steps to ensure against overloading the circuit.

BREAKER SERVICE PANEL

A typical breaker service panel has two hot bus bars, to which the circuit breakers attach. Hot wires lead to the breakers. There are usually one or two neutral/ground bus bars, for the neutral and ground wires. Some older boxes have separate bus bars for the neutral and ground wires.

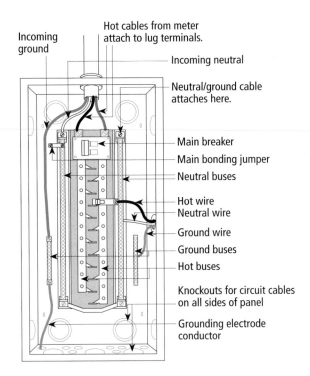

Incoming ground

Hot cables from meter attach to lug terminals.

Incoming neutral

Neutral/ground cable attaches here.

Main breaker

Main bonding jumper

Neutral buses

Hot wire
Neutral wire

Ground wire

Ground buses

Hot buses

Knockouts for circuit cables on all sides of panel

Grounding electrode conductor

Overloads, Ground Faults, and Short Circuits

Circuit breakers trip and fuses blow for three reasons: an overloaded circuit, a ground fault, or a short circuit.

■ An overloaded circuit usually occurs when too many outlets operating at the same time use more amperage than is safe for the capacity of the wiring. (A common example is a toaster, microwave, and coffee maker all plugged into receptacles that are on the same circuit and all running at the same time.) In this case, the breaker or fuse will shut down to keep the wires from overheating.

■ A ground fault commonly occurs when a hot wire touches something metal that it's not supposed to touch, causing power to travel along the path of the metal object, rather than back to the service panel via the neutral wire.

■ The term "short circuit" is often used very generally to refer to any of a number of electrical problems. To be more accurate, it means that the hot wire touches another wire in the circuit, providing electricity with a path of less resistance. Examples include when a lamp cord has damaged insulation, so the hot and neutral wires touch each other. An old or broken appliance can develop a short inside its circuitry.

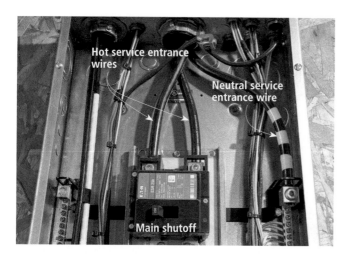

Hot service entrance wires

Neutral service entrance wire

Main shutoff

SERVICE WIRE CONNECTIONS. Two hot service entrance wires attach to the two hot bus bars. Just below that attachment is the main breaker, which can shut off power to everything below it—that is, the whole house. The neutral service entrance wire, which here is marked with three wrappings of white tape, attaches to one of the neutral bus bars. The other neutral bus bar, on the left, is connected to the one on the right with a metal strap.

The main shutoff and the hot bus bars

Unless you have a very old home with a small 40-amp or 60-amp fuse box, there will be three thick wires entering the service panel. Two attach to the hot bus bars, which run down the middle of the panel and to which the individual breakers attach. The hot bus bars are shaped so that they alternate: Two breakers stacked on top of each other will get their power from separate bus bars. Having a roughly equal number of 15- and 20-amp breakers on each bus bar keeps the panel in balance.

Also called the main disconnect, the main shutoff will disconnect power to the entire house when flipped off (or, in the case of a fuse box, pulled out).

Branch circuits

Individual breakers attach to the hot bus bars. For each branch circuit in the house, a hot wire attaches to one of the breakers or fuses. For each circuit, a neutral and a ground wire (unless the system uses conduit as the ground path) attach to the neutral bus bar, providing a circular pathway from the panel to the outlet and back to the panel. Shutting off the breaker or removing the fuse will turn off power to the circuit.

Large 240-volt circuit breakers have two electrical attachment points. Because the hot bus bars are arranged in an alternating pattern, each of the two attachments hooks to a different hot bus bar; the two 120-volt bars combine to provide 240 volts of power.

The service ground

Grounding the panel—and your whole system, as ground wires run from each branch circuit to the panel—is important to your home's safety. The ground bus bar (in some panels the neutral/ground bus bar) connects to a thick grounding wire, which runs to a metal grounding rod driven deep into the ground or to a cold-water pipe.

SERVICE GROUND. A system ground wire is thick, and may be bare or green insulated, like the one shown above left. It runs to a grounding rod that reaches 2 ft. or more into the ground (shown above right). Or it may run to a cold-water pipe, which in turn is attached to other pipes that run deep underground (shown below).

Jumper

JUMPER WIRE AROUND METER. If your ground wire connects to a pipe, look at the water meter, which has nonmetal parts that will interrupt the flow of electrons. There should be a jumper wire that attaches to the pipe on each side, to ensure an uninterrupted path for any wayward electricity.

SUBPANELS. Some homes have subpanels, which supply additional electrical service when the main panel is not large enough. There will be a breaker or fuse in the main panel that can shut off the entire subpanel.

THE STANDARD PANEL NOWADAYS. A 200-amp breaker panel provides plenty of power for most homes.

REMOVING THE COVER. To remove the cover from a service panel, remove the four or six screws holding it on and simply pull it away.

If Your System Is Ungrounded

Some old homes have electrical systems that are ungrounded. Such a system is lacking a very helpful safety measure but can be safe as long as it is kept in good working order. Local codes usually permit an ungrounded system that was built long ago to remain as long as it is sound and as long as you do not add new service to it. The receptacles should have only two slots and no grounding hole, so you don't get the wrong idea that things are grounded. Take special care to use appliances that are double-insulated and in good working order, and inspect lamp and extension cords often for any damage to the insulation. To make a single receptacle safer, replace the receptacle with a GFCI (see pp. 114–116).

A LOOK INSIDE. This service panel has extremely well-organized and neatly routed wires, which have been wrapped with ties. There are seven open spaces for any added future circuits.

Inspecting a breaker panel

You can find the total amperage for a breaker service panel written on the main shutoff, or somewhere on the panel cover. A newer or recently remodeled home may have a 200-amp panel. This is plenty of power for medium to large homes with big users like central air-conditioning, an electric dryer and range, and a water heater. (A very large home with lots of goodies may opt for 320 amps.) A medium-size home can usually get by just fine with 100-amp service, especially if it has gas rather than electric appliances. See pp. 154–155 and p. 224 to calculate your needs.

Inside, the wires should be at least fairly well organized around the perimeter of the panel, so there is no chance they will cross over the breakers or get trapped when you replace the cover. It's important that the breakers are all the correct size for the wires inserted into them (see p. 37).

Different breakers shut off and turn on in different ways, so get to know how your system operates before the lights go off. Some have a toggle that flips over and a red tab that pokes out when it blows. To restore power, simply flip the toggle back to the ON position. Others have a toggle that moves slightly; to restore power, flip the toggle all the way off, then back on. Still others have a button that you push to make the lights come back on.

240 AND 120/240 BREAKERS. Thick breakers like these 40-amp and 30-amp double breakers hook onto both bus bars to provide double the power.

Fuse panels

Many older homes have fuse service panels. These are rarely larger than 100 amps, and many are 60 or even only 40 amps (40-amp panels are often ungrounded). Though they may look old, fuse panels are safe. However, they have limitations: Most supply only eight circuits, so there is little room for upgrading a home in any significant way. Some have a single 240-volt circuit, but some do not even have that. If you have a fuse box and want to upgrade your home, it's usually a good idea to replace it with a 100-amp or 200-amp breaker panel.

Fuses are actually very effective at sensing overloads and short circuits and shutting off the power before any damage is done. (In fact, some say they are more reliable than circuit breakers.) Shut off power to a circuit by unscrewing its fuse.

If a circuit has overloaded, the little metal tab inside the fuse (visible through glass) will be broken. You can screw in a new fuse—and take care not to use too many outlets in the future. If there has been a short circuit or a ground fault, the glass will be black and cloudy. In that case, you need to look for the source of the problem—perhaps frayed wires or faulty wiring.

FUSE PANEL.
This fuse panel supplies 60 amps of total service, divided into eight circuits—there is no room for any more.

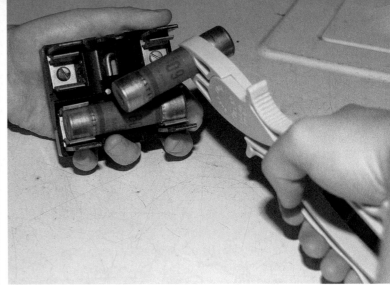

THE MAIN DISCONNECT. Some fuse panels have a 240-volt circuit, but this one does not; the main fuse block at the top is the main disconnect. To shut off power to the house—or if all power has been lost and you need to check the main fuses—pull out the main fuse block (shown above left). If power to the house was lost, check the fuses inside the fuse block. Remove the fuses (shown above right) and test as shown on p. 45.

Don't Overload a Circuit

You may have heard stories of old-time guys who put a penny or a nickel in a fuse opening to keep it from blowing. That's a really, *really* bad idea: Fuses are there to tell you when the circuit is overloaded or when you have a ground fault or short circuit (see p. 18), and eliminating a fuse can lead to electrical fire, shock, or even worse.

Here's another bad idea: replacing a fuse with one of higher amperage (for example, putting a 30-amp fuse where there should be a 20-amp fuse) in order to stop all that annoying fuse blowing. Again, fuses have important safety features that keep wiring from overheating, and misusing them to increase your home's amperage can lead to dangerously hot wires.

To make sure nobody can put a wrong-size fuse into an opening, buy S-type fuses with inserts. Once an insert is screwed into the panel, it will receive only a fuse of the correct amperage.

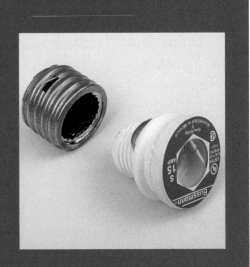

TIP You'll see the lights go out after you've only partially unscrewed a fuse. For safety, don't stop there. Take it all the way out before working on the circuit to be sure power will not flicker on.

BE PREPARED. Keep plenty of fuses on hand so you don't need to run out to the store when the lights go out.

Indexing a Service Panel

Whether you have a breaker box or a fuse panel, it's a great idea to have it indexed: An index is a simple chart that indicates which outlets are controlled by which breakers or fuses.

You might expect that creating an index would be laborious, but with a teamwork approach it really doesn't take much time. One person should be next to the service panel with a pad of paper and a pencil [A]. The other person roams the house, and the two communicate with cell phones. To start, turn on all the lights in the house and check that appliances have indicator lights on if possible. For empty receptacles, plug lights into as many as possible.

Then shut off one of the circuits and have the roamer check outlets to see which lights, receptacles, and appliances shut off. Once those are recorded, move on to the next circuit, until all outlets have been accounted for.

A two-part circuit finder can be of help. Plug one part (the transmitter) into a receptacle [B], then point the other part (the receiver) at the circuit breakers [C]. It will light up when it finds the corresponding breaker.

You can list the outlets on the little tabs next to each breaker [D]. Or you may find it easier to type or write up a list and attach it to the inside of the panel door.

Types of Cable and Wire

Though we won't get into running cable and new wiring until Chapter 6, you should be aware of the various types of wire that run inside your walls, floors, and ceilings. You can see them poking through in receptacle and switch boxes, in junction boxes, and in the service panel.

Individual wires are encased in plastic insulation to keep them safe, except at the ends, where the insulation is stripped to join the wires to terminals or other wires (see pp. 46–51 for stripping and joining methods). The exception is when bare copper wire is used as ground wire.

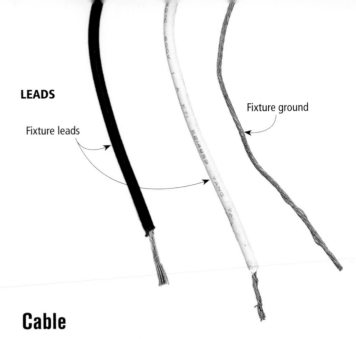

LEADS

Fixture ground

Fixture leads

Individual wires

Wire is sized according to thickness; the lower the American Wire Gauge (AWG) number, the thicker the wire. The numbers are printed on the wire insulation. The most common sizes in household wiring are 14 gauge and 12 gauge, also referred to as #14 and #12. For higher amperages, thicker wires are called for (14-gauge wire is thick enough to carry 15 amps; 12-gauge wire can carry 20 amps). Much household wiring is done with solid-core wires; stranded wires, which are more flexible, are used when running wiring in conduit. Very thick wires—8 gauge and larger—are usually stranded and are used for high-amperage wiring, such as to supply large appliances.

White-insulated wire is used for neutral lines. Black and red are the most common colors for hot wires. Ground wires may be bare copper or green insulated.

The thin wires that attach to light fixtures are referred to as "leads." These are typically 16 gauge or 18 gauge and are usually stranded, though some fixtures use solid-core leads.

Cable

Cable consists of several individual wires encased in flexible sheathing. Though the printing on the sheathing may not tell you, cables are referred to by the gauge and number of wires they hold. For instance "14-2" cable has two 14-gauge wires (plus the ground wire); "12-3" cable has three 12-gauge wires (plus the ground wire).

NM cable

The most common cable is nonmetallic sheathed, called type NM (or sometimes Romex, which is a brand name). Standard NM cable is approved for use in most parts of the country. Because it could be easily pierced by a nail or screw, safe practices require that when running NM cable through framing it should never be closer than 1¼ in. to the wall surface, and in many cases, it should be protected with a nailing plate (see p. 200). It should not be installed in areas where it could get wet. Most NM cable sold today is called NM-B (though it may not say that on the cable's sheathing) and is rated safe to 194°F. Most cable sold before 1984 was rated to only 149°F.

TIP Professional electricians often use the term "wire" to refer to either individual wires or cables that encapsulate several wires. They may also speak of "conductors" for both wires and cable. This is a book for homeowners, so we will distinguish between cables and individual wires, and will usually avoid the term "conductor."

Large-appliance cable, which usually contains thick stranded wires, typically has black sheathing. Underground-feed cable (UF) has gray sheathing that is molded to the individual wires so moisture cannot enter. It is used for outdoor wiring and for places that may get wet.

WIRES

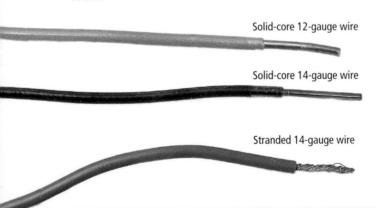

Solid-core 12-gauge wire

Solid-core 14-gauge wire

Stranded 14-gauge wire

CABLES

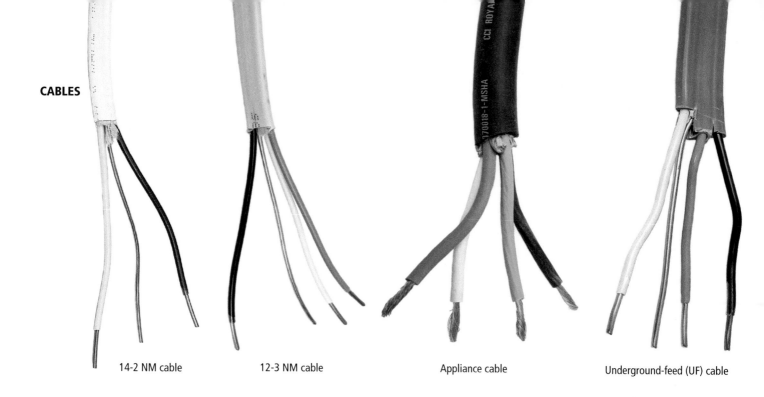

14-2 NM cable   12-3 NM cable   Appliance cable   Underground-feed (UF) cable

NM cable sold today has color-coded sheathing. The colors tell you the size, but not the number, of the wires:

- White for 14-gauge wires (for 15-amp circuits)
- Yellow for 12-gauge wires (for 20-amp circuits)
- Orange for 10-gauge wires (for 30-amp circuits)
- Black for 6-gauge and 8-gauge wires (for 45-amp and 60-amp circuits)
- Gray for underground-feed wire of various wire sizes

Metal-clad cable

Also called armored cable or "flex," metal-clad (MC) cable has a flexible coiled metal sheathing. This protects the wires better than NM sheathing, but it will not reliably turn away a driven nail or screw. Older BX cable has no ground wire; the metal sheathing was used as the ground path. It has a thin aluminum "bonding wire" that acts as a sort of backup ground. Newer MC cable has a green-insulated grounding wire, required by modern codes.

Even in areas where MC or NM cable is allowed, you may choose instead to install metal conduit in places where the wiring is exposed, such as in basements and utility rooms.

Both BX and MC cables should have red plastic bushings inserted in between the metal sheathing and the wires to protect the wires from the cut ends of the sheathing. You should be able to see the bushings when you open electrical boxes. If there is no bushing, insert one to make sure the wire insulation will not get nicked.

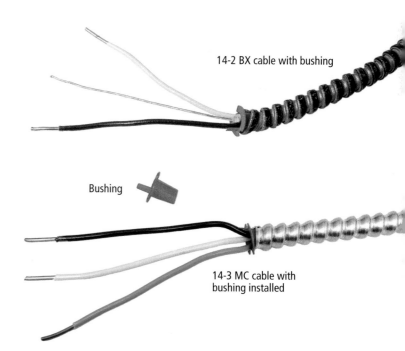

14-2 BX cable with bushing

Bushing

14-3 MC cable with bushing installed

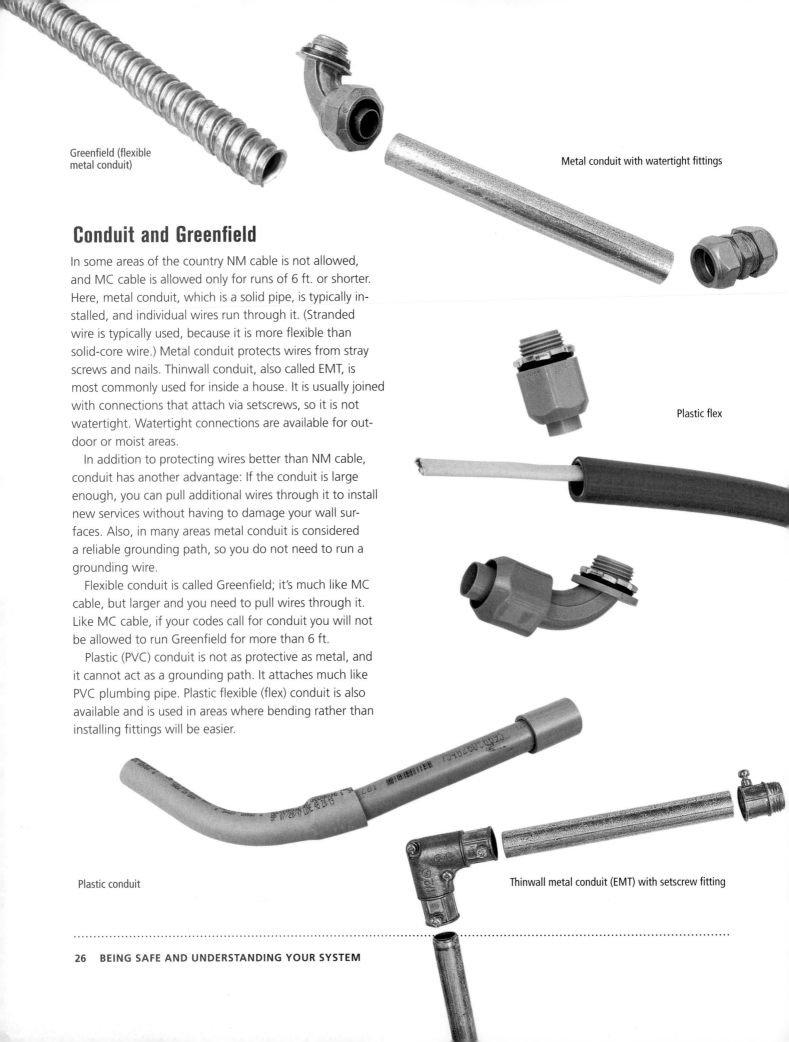

Greenfield (flexible metal conduit)

Metal conduit with watertight fittings

Conduit and Greenfield

In some areas of the country NM cable is not allowed, and MC cable is allowed only for runs of 6 ft. or shorter. Here, metal conduit, which is a solid pipe, is typically installed, and individual wires run through it. (Stranded wire is typically used, because it is more flexible than solid-core wire.) Metal conduit protects wires from stray screws and nails. Thinwall conduit, also called EMT, is most commonly used for inside a house. It is usually joined with connections that attach via setscrews, so it is not watertight. Watertight connections are available for outdoor or moist areas.

In addition to protecting wires better than NM cable, conduit has another advantage: If the conduit is large enough, you can pull additional wires through it to install new services without having to damage your wall surfaces. Also, in many areas metal conduit is considered a reliable grounding path, so you do not need to run a grounding wire.

Flexible conduit is called Greenfield; it's much like MC cable, but larger and you need to pull wires through it. Like MC cable, if your codes call for conduit you will not be allowed to run Greenfield for more than 6 ft.

Plastic (PVC) conduit is not as protective as metal, and it cannot act as a grounding path. It attaches much like PVC plumbing pipe. Plastic flexible (flex) conduit is also available and is used in areas where bending rather than installing fittings will be easier.

Plastic flex

Plastic conduit

Thinwall metal conduit (EMT) with setscrew fitting

Switches

Wall switches and receptacles are called "devices." In a typical home, most devices are either single-pole switches or duplex receptacles, but there are plenty of special devices for special situations.

Basic switches

The basic operation of a switch is simple: In the OFF position, the electrical circuit is broken (or interrupted), so power cannot travel in a circle from and to the service panel. In the ON position, the circuit is completed, so power can flow through the circuit.

A single-pole switch has two terminals to which the hot wire attaches and the switch toggles on and off. The words ON and OFF are often visible on the toggle. A rocker switch operates in the same way, but with a more modern look.

Two three-way switches are used to control a fixture (or group of fixtures) from two different locations—for instance, from the top and bottom of a stairway or from far sides of a room that has two entries. Three-ways have three terminals (plus the ground) and can be hooked up in various ways (see pp. 211–212 for wiring methods). Three four-way switches can control a fixture from three locations, but this is less common. (See p. 213 for wiring.)

15-amp standard   20-amp commercial   Rocker

SINGLE-POLE SWITCHES. Single-pole switches have two terminals (plus the ground). The feed wire attaches to one terminal and the wire carrying power to the fixture attaches to the other terminal.

THREE-WAY SWITCH. A three-way switch has three terminals (plus the ground). Its toggle is not marked ON and OFF because either position could be up or down.

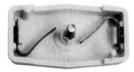

SWITCH INNARDS. The inner workings of a basic switch are clearly visible if you open up a simple cord switch like this one. (Of course, be sure to unplug the cord or shut off power before doing this.) Here, the switch is shown in the OFF position, and you can see a gap in the hot wire's path. Turn the switch to ON, and a piece of metal bridges the gap.

TIP Many older switches did not have grounding terminals because it was not thought necessary to ground them. Modern switches have grounding terminals, and if your wiring includes ground wires they should attach to these terminals. Ungrounded switches are not actually dangerous—they just lack the extra measure of protection that grounding supplies.

Dimmers

If you want to control the level of light in a fixture, you can usually replace a regular switch with a dimmer. An older style has a rotary knob (center) that turns to adjust the illumination and shuts off either by continuing to turn or by pushing the knob. Newer styles like the one at right not only look sleeker but also have a separate toggle so it can remember the lighting level you last used. The dimmer switch on the left has a toggle that operates like a standard switch and a small sliding switch to its right, which sets and remembers the light level. (See pp. 106–108 for installing dimmers.)

Specialty switches

You can buy specialty switches that sense motion when someone enters a room. Others can turn on and off when things get dark or light, turn on or off with a timer, or perform other duties to make your life more comfortable. (See pp. 107–109 for installing these switches.)

Receptacles

Often called "outlets" or "plugs," electrical receptacles are found throughout a home. Codes typically call for receptacles to be placed no farther apart than 6 ft. in living areas, and more specific codes call for closer spacing in bathrooms and kitchens. The 120-volt duplex receptacle, which has slots and holes for two plugs, is the most common type.

Basic receptacles

Receptacles are easy to replace (see pp. 112–114), so go ahead and replace any in your home that are cracked, covered with ugly paint, or simply not to your liking. The screw holes in electrical boxes have been standardized since the beginning of home wiring, so no matter how old your home is, you should be able to replace old receptacles with new. However, be sure you have the proper wiring. For instance, if you have a very old ungrounded system, do not install grounded receptacles. Install a

15-amp receptacle where wires are 14 gauge and are protected with a 15-amp circuit breaker or fuse; install a 20-amp receptacle when the wires are 12 gauge and the circuit breaker or fuse is 20 amp. A 20-amp receptacle is easily identified: Its neutral (longer) slot has a horizontal leg that makes it look like a sideways T. Amperage ratings are printed on the receptacles, but you can also tell by the slot shapes.

TIP Some people prefer receptacle grounding holes to be on top, and others prefer the holes on the bottom. Electricians sometimes have recondite reasons for their preferences, but it really doesn't matter. Position all the holes in a room the same way, for a neater appearance.

Inexpensive receptacles are fine for most normal purposes. But if you will often plug and unplug, or if a receptacle is in a place where it may get bumped (for instance, by a vacuum cleaner), pay more for a receptacle labeled "commercial" or "spec rated."

20-amp receptacle

Ungrounded receptacle

15-amp receptacle

RECEPTACLE WITH USB OUTLETS. A receptacle that includes USB outlets can help minimize the modern problem of cord tangle.

GFCIs and AFCIs

A ground-fault circuit interrupter, or GFCI (often referred to as a GFI), provides an extra measure of protection and shuts off in milliseconds if there is danger of shock. GFCIs are generally required in bathrooms, basements, garages, and other areas that can become damp. Properly installed, one GFCI on a circuit can provide protection for other standard receptacles on the same circuit. See pp. 114–116 for installing a GFCI and/or AFCI. Outdoors, a GFCI with a weatherproof cover is usually required.

Arc-fault circuit interrupter (AFCI) protection is nowadays required for living areas to minimize the danger of electrical fires due to damaged cords (see p. 154 for more info). The usual solution is to install AFCI circuit breakers, but you can instead install AFCI receptacles. For a bit more money, you can even install a dual-function AFCI/GFCI receptacle to protect against problems created by both wetness and damaged cords.

GFCI receptacle   AFCI receptacle

240-Volt Receptacles

Some heavy-duty appliances use 240 volts. The receptacles for them have specially arranged slots and holes to ensure that only the correct plug can be inserted into them. Be sure that the wires and the circuit breaker are correctly sized (for installation, see pp. 222–223). Most of these receptacles are available as floor- or wall-mounted units. Here are some common types.

4-wire dryer receptacle

Older 3-wire dryer receptacle

Electric range receptacle

20-amp receptacle for large air conditioners

- A dryer receptacle supplies both 240 volts for the heating element and 120 volts for the timer. The newer one shown at right uses four wires; some older types used only three wires. It is rated at 30 amps, so the wires should be 10 gauge and the circuit breaker should be 30 amps.

- A receptacle for an electric range (or oven or cooktop) supplies 240 volts for the heating elements and 120 volts for the light and clock. The one shown here is rated at 50 amps, so the wires should be 8 gauge and thecircuit breaker should be 50 amps.

- A receptacle for a large air conditioner supplies 240 volts (see p. 222). (Many smaller models can be plugged into a standard 120-volt receptacle, either 20 amps or 15 amps; be sure to read the rating.) This one is rated at 20 amps, so the wires should be 12 gauge and the circuit breaker should be 20 amps.

Some Common Wiring Setups

If you open up an electrical box, all may not be instantly clear to you. Here are some of the most common wiring configurations you may encounter. As in much of this book, we will show both illustrations, which make things more easily understood, and photos, which give more of a real-world sense. Many more setups can be found elsewhere in the second half of this book.

➟ **Before removing a cover, be sure to shut off power at the service panel. Test several times to verify that power is off, as shown on pp. 8–9. For double protection, use electrician's tools and work as if the wires were hot.**

Plastic and metal boxes

Depending on where you live and when your wiring was installed, you may have either plastic or metal electrical boxes. (In some areas of the country metal boxes are becoming more common as codes get stricter, but there are plenty of plastic installations in other areas.) Both box types are safe, but metal boxes allow for more secure grounding methods, and plastic boxes are more easily damaged than metal ones. (In particular, the threads on the mounting holes can become stripped, making it difficult to firmly attach devices.)

Where the box is exposed—for instance, on a concrete basement wall or in a garage with unfinished walls—metal boxes should be used. When installing a ceiling fan, be sure to install a strong "fan-rated" metal box, as shown on pp. 84–88.

If your system uses metal conduit as the grounding path instead of a grounding wire, then the boxes must be metal as well. But sometimes metal boxes are also used with NM cable. Metal boxes use strong cable connectors (which may be integrated or may be separate pieces), which hold the cable firmly. Most plastic boxes have feeble little flaps that sort of hold the cable, which means that the cable must be stapled to a nearby framing member.

TIP Most codes do not allow more than one wire to be connected to a switch or receptacle terminal. If you need to connect two wires to a terminal, first splice the two wires to a short wire called a pigtail, then fasten the pigtail to the terminal.

Grounding Methods

If you have plastic boxes in your home, grounding is done by simply connecting the ground wire to the grounding terminal on the device. In the case of a mid-run receptacle [A], a pigtail attached to a pass-through grounding nut is used. In a metal box, you may see any of a number of methods. The example [B] uses a pass-through grounding nut, which has a hole in its end so one wire can pass through. For extra grounding protection, a ground pigtail is attached to a grounding screw inside the box [C]. The one shown uses a standard wire nut. Note that if you have metal conduit, there may be no ground wire, because the metal conduit acts as the ground path [D]. Sometimes the ground wire is green insulated rather than bare copper. One example is seen on p. 32, with ground wires that are mid-stripped.

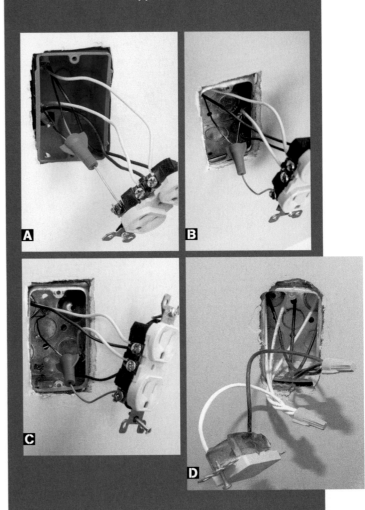

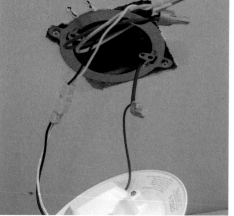

GROUNDING SWITCHES AND FIXTURES.
Contemporary codes call for grounding both switches and fixtures. A switch has a grounding terminal, and a fixture typically has a grounding lead, which attaches to the ground wire with a wire nut. In older installations, the switch and/or fixture may not be grounded.

MID-RUN AND END-RUN RECEPTACLES

There are usually multiple receptacles on a receptacle circuit. Most are in the middle of the run, meaning that the wiring continues on to other receptacles. In a mid-run receptacle, two cables enter the box. Usually two black or colored hot wires connect to the two brass terminals, and two neutral wires connect to the silver terminals. However, some electricians prefer to use pigtails and connect to only one brass and one silver terminal, as shown below left. At an end-run receptacle (below right), only one cable enters the box, and the wires are connected to one terminal on each side.

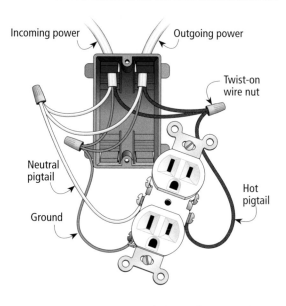

Incoming power · Outgoing power · Twist-on wire nut · Neutral pigtail · Ground · Hot pigtail

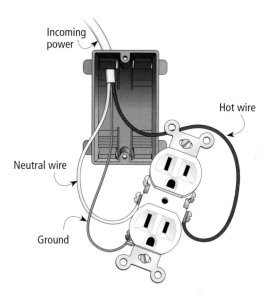

Incoming power · Hot wire · Neutral wire · Ground

Switch Wiring Methods

In older installations it was common to run power to the fixture box first, and then run wires to the switch box in a configuration called "end-line" or "switch-loop" wiring. With this method, only one cable enters the box, coming from the fixture. The white wire should be marked with black tape or paint to show that it is actually hot. Modern homes usually have "through wiring," with power running first into the switch box, and then out to the fixture. Here, two cables enter the box. The neutral wires are spliced together, and the hot wires attach to each of the switch's terminals.

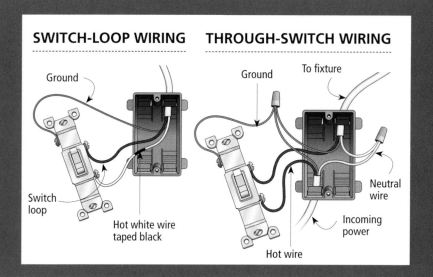

SWITCH-LOOP WIRING

Ground · Switch loop · Hot white wire taped black

THROUGH-SWITCH WIRING

Ground · To fixture · Neutral wire · Incoming power · Hot wire

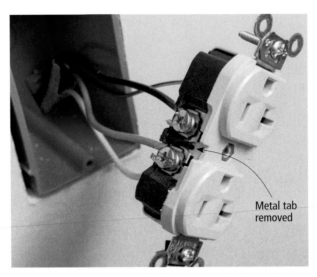

Metal tab removed

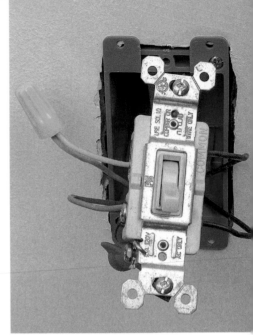

MID-STRIPPED WIRES.
Some electricians strip off about an inch of insulation on wires that would run through a box (for example, for mid-run receptacles) and connect the bare wire to the terminal, rather than cutting the wire and connecting to two terminals or to a pigtail. This method has fallen out of favor and is against most codes, but it is safe, as long as the terminal connection is tight and secure.

SPLIT RECEPTACLES. On a duplex receptacle there is a metal tab that joins the two hot (brass) terminals. If the tab has been removed and different hot wires connect to each, the receptacle is "split": Different power sources control each of the two outlets. A split receptacle is also called a "half-hot." Kitchen countertop or workroom receptacles may have this arrangement, so that each of the outlets is on a different circuit, letting you plug in two high-energy users without overloading a single circuit. A receptacle can also be split so that one outlet is controlled by a wall switch while the other is always hot.

THREE-WAY SWITCHES. A pair of three-way switches controls a single light or group of lights from two locations. You can spot a three-way because it has three terminals; the wiring methods vary, depending on where power enters (see pp. 211–212 for various wiring methods).

SWITCH AND RECEPTACLE SHARE A BOX. If a switch and receptacle share a box and are on the same circuit, as is common in a bathroom, here's one typical wiring method: Two two-wire cables enter the box. The black wires from each cable attach to the terminals on each device, and a short black pigtail runs from one device to the other. In this arrangement, the receptacle is always hot. A different wiring method would be used to "switch" the receptacle, so that it's controlled by a switch.

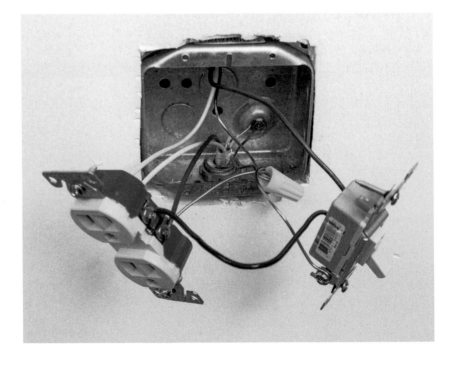

Inspecting Your System

You cannot, of course, perform a complete inspection of your total electrical system, but there are a good number of problems and potential dangers that you can spot by looking carefully. Some of these issues are visible with a surface inspection, but most call for removing cover plates, the service panel cover, or a light fixture.

▶ **Be sure to shut off power at the service panel. Test several times to verify that power is off, as shown on pp 8–9. For double protection, use electrician's tools and work as if the wires were hot.**

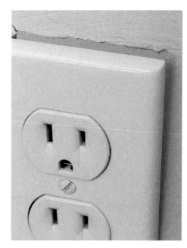

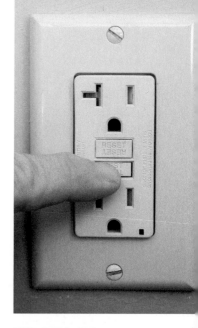

LOOSE BOX. If a cover plate can be easily pulled out from the wall even though it's firmly screwed in, the box is loose. You may be able to drive a screw sideways through the box and into an adjacent wall stud. Or you can replace the box with a remodel box that fastens to drywall (see pp. 188–189).

TEST GFCIS. GFCI receptacles sometimes fail to shut off when they should. It's recommended every month or so that you push the "test" button. If power does not shut off, you need to replace the receptacle.

RECEPTACLE ANALYZER. This is probably the most important—and the simplest—test that a homeowner can perform on an electrical system. With power ON, plug in a receptacle analyzer and look at the little lights. They should tell you whether the receptacle is properly grounded and polarized, and should indicate whether the wires are all on the correct terminals. The analyzer shown here can test a GFCI or standard receptacle. If a problem is indicated, ▶ shut off power, remove the receptacle, and see that the wires are firmly connected to the correct terminals, as shown on pp. 50–51. Also look for damaged wires.

NON-GFCI RECEPTACLE IN A WET AREA. Wherever a receptacle is near a sink or in an area that could get damp, it should be GFCI protected. This can be achieved with a GFCI receptacle or a GFCI circuit breaker.

MISSING CABLE CONNECTOR. Cable that enters a metal box (the type most likely to be visible) must be held firmly in place with a strong cable connector, also called a cable clamp. If the box is plastic, cable must be stapled near the box and then pass through the box's flap-type clamp. Unclamped cable can be damaged due to slight vibrations, and the opening can allow dust into the box, which can cause wires to overheat. These cables should be removed and run through approved clamps, then reconnected inside the box.

OUTSIDE CONNECTIONS. Check that exterior pipes and boxes are in sound condition. Minor rust is usually not a problem, but it's a good idea to brush on some metal primer and/or cover a worn spot with exterior caulking. Of course, a really bad situation like the one shown above right needs to be replaced by a professional electrician. If there are problems with pipes that carry the large service wires, do not try to solve them yourself; instead contact your utility company.

Knob-and-Tube Wiring

An old home may have knob-and-tube wiring like this. Individual hot and neutral wires run through knobs and tubes (which are inserted through framing members). This system may work for a long time, but it has serious drawbacks: It cannot be grounded; wire insulation is exposed to air so it becomes brittle over time, which can lead to exposed wires; and, of course, the wires are easily damaged, especially during remodeling. We strongly encourage you to replace this type of wiring with modern wiring.

At the very least, take steps to prevent accidental damage to or contact with knob-and-tube wiring. And do not cover the wires with insulation because that could cause them to heat up dangerously.

DAMAGED CORDS. A cord for a lamp, portable fan, or small appliance may look unprepossessing, but it actually carries serious electrical current. If the bare wire is exposed it can deliver a shock or cause a fire. Cords may be damaged, for instance, if they are old and brittle, or if they get caught in a closing door or vacuum. To replace damaged cord, see pp. 132–137.

TOO MANY PLUGS IN A RECEPTACLE. You can buy multi-outlet units that allow you to plug a plethora of devices into a single receptacle, but this can be dangerous if the devices are running at the same time. The overloaded receptacle can heat up dangerously. At the very least, buy a power strip that has its own overload shutoff. Or consider a unit like the one shown above right, which has one side that can swivel. Better yet, install additional receptacles where needed.

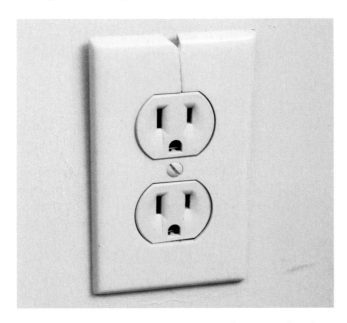

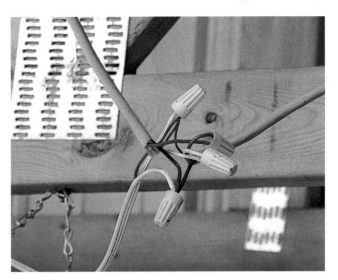

DAMAGED OR TOO-SMALL COVER PLATE. If a cover plate is cracked, or if it is too small to completely cover the hole in the wall, replace it. If the wall surface is uneven so that the plate can crack when tightened into place, either repair the wall or try a flexible vinyl cover plate (see p. 126). If part of the wall hole is exposed, either patch the wall or buy an oversize cover plate.

EXPOSED SPLICES. All electrical splices and terminal connections must be made inside an approved electrical box, where bare wire ends will be protected against damage and fires. An unboxed splice like the one shown here is not only dangerous, but it also indicates that some of the electrical work done in this house was performed by a rank amateur; there are likely other serious wiring problems as well. Call in a pro for evaluation of the whole system.

RECESSED BOX. If wood paneling or another surface was installed after the wiring was installed, the box may not be flush with the final wall surface. Especially if wood paneling is exposed, this can pose a fire hazard. In this situation, you can install a box extender.

TWO WIRES ON A TERMINAL. It is against code and unsafe to connect two wires to a single terminal because they could come loose. If you see two wires on a terminal and there is no other available terminal, remove them, splice them to a pigtail (p. 53), and connect the pigtail to the terminal.

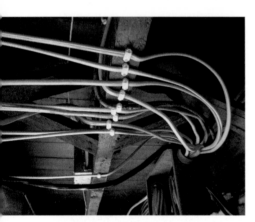

CABLES EXPOSED TO DAMAGE. Local codes may allow exposed NM or armored cable in a basement, crawlspace, or garage, or they may demand that solid metal or plastic conduit be used instead. If cable is exposed, it must be securely stapled and positioned where it is out of harm's way. An arrangement like this, with cable running in mid-air between joists, is asking for problems.

MISSING BOX PLUG. If a knockout plug is missing, debris can easily blow into a box and may create a fire or overheating hazard. To solve the problem, you can usually simply tap in a "goof plug" to fill the hole.

DAMAGED INSULATION. If wire insulation is nicked or cracked so that bare wire is visible, take steps to protect the wire. If possible, wrap the wire with three or more tight windings of electrician's tape, or use heat-shrink wire wrap, as shown on p. 129.

TOO MUCH INSULATION STRIPPED. If too much insulation has been stripped, bare wire can be exposed. Protect it with several windings of electrician's tape. Or better yet, remove the wire, cut off the bare portion, re-strip, and reconnect (see pp. 46–47 and pp. 50–51). (Do not just cut off part of the stripped wire and re-bend it; that could weaken the wire and cause it to break.)

RED BUSHING FOR ARMORED CABLE. If armored cable is used, check to be sure that there is a red plastic bushing pushed firmly into place to protect where the wires enter the box. If not, slip a bushing carefully around all the wires and push it down until only the top is visible.

MYSTERY BOX. An older home may have a large box like this with a tangle of many wires. This was once a fuse box but was bypassed when a new circuit breaker box was installed. As long as all the wire splices are firm and secure, it's best to just keep the door closed.

THE RIGHT SIZE WIRES AND BREAKERS. In a service panel, see that all 15-amp breakers or fuses have 14-gauge wires attached, all 20-amp breakers have 12-gauge wires, all 30-amp breakers have 10-gauge wires, and so on. If a too-large breaker or fuse is used, the wires can heat up dangerously before the protection kicks in. (It's OK if the wires are thicker than needed, but that rarely happens.)

TIP In general, do not hesitate to ask a professional electrician to evaluate your system if there is anything you don't understand that looks like it might be dangerous. In particular, if lights flicker when turned on and replacing the switch does not solve the problem, call for a consultation.

CHAPTER TWO

Tools and Techniques for Basic Replacements and Repairs

WITH THE INFORMATION IN THIS CHAPTER, you'll be able to tackle the most common DIY household electrical projects, as shown in Chapters 3 and 4: installing lights, fans, switches, and receptacles using existing circuits and wiring. These projects do not require running new electrical cable or installing new circuits.

Many readers of this book will perform only these installations and may consult later chapters—which call for running new electrical lines—mostly to learn about how a hired professional will work in their home. But learning these methods can also be a first step toward the more serious work shown in the second half of the book.

Basic Tools

The projects in the first half of this book can be accomplished with a modest set of tools. Do yourself a favor and buy tools made especially for electrical work—for instance, pliers and screwdrivers with rubber grips—instead of using all-purpose tools. The extra cost will be minimal, and you will work more safely. The rest of this chapter will provide information about how to use all the tools shown on these four pages.

Testers

If you buy nothing else, get a *receptacle analyzer*. Just plug it in and it will tell you if your receptacle is grounded and polarized. If you have GFCI receptacles in your home, buy one that also tests those. To test for the presence of power, you'll need two types of testers on hand:

A *voltage detector* senses the presence of electrical power even when it cannot touch bare wires. It can sense power inside fixtures, inside boxes, and through walls, without actually contacting the wires. Voltage detectors are not as reliable as *voltage testers*, so use them only as a first step in the testing process.

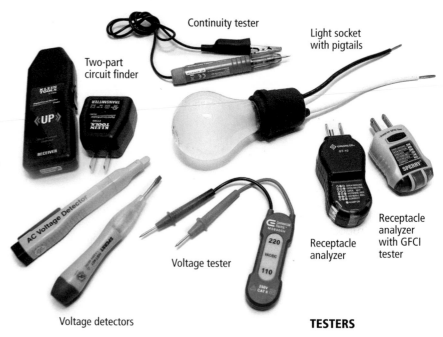

Continuity tester

Two-part circuit finder

Light socket with pigtails

Voltage detectors

Voltage tester

Receptacle analyzer

Receptacle analyzer with GFCI tester

TESTERS

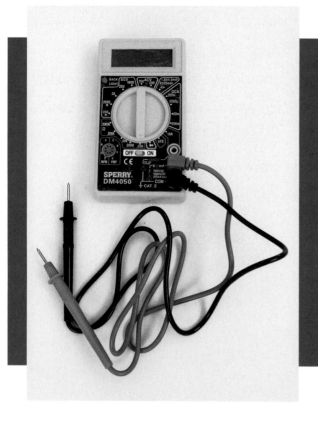

The Multitester Option

If you have a bent toward gadgetry, you might be inclined to buy a *multitester*, also known as a *multimeter*, which can handle a number of testing tasks. It may take an hour or more to master the tool, but once you do, you'll have a number of testing options at your fingertips. You can test for voltage at various levels (including low voltage and 240-volt units). You can also test for continuity. If you are a hobbyist, you'll be able to test for DC (direct current) power, including batteries. Older multitesters had a dial with a needle; newer ones tend to be digital and are easier to learn.

To test for the presence of power, an inexpensive small neon voltage tester will do the job. However, its light is dim, so in some situations it can be difficult to see. Most of your tests will be for 120 volts, but many testers also test for 240 or other voltages. For a very bright testing light, use a light socket with pigtails (see p. 9); just be sure to keep your fingers well away from the bare wires.

A *continuity tester* does not test for voltage. Instead, it lets you know if the wiring inside a device or fixture is damaged, so that power cannot flow through it continuously. A *two-part circuit finder* enables you to quickly determine which circuit in your service panel controls a particular receptacle.

Screwdrivers

Choose screwdrivers that are made for electrical work, with rubber—not just plastic—handles. Screwdrivers with 6-in.- or 7-in.-long shanks are used most often. You may occasionally need a *short-shank,* or *stubby,* screwdriver. Drivers with #2 *Phillips* and *slot* (or *straight)* heads take care of most tasks, but #1 heads are sometimes needed.

A *rotary screwdriver* has a shank that is loosely attached to the handle, so it can be spun around quickly, making short work of driving mounting and cover-plate screws. A *multi-screwdriver* typically contains #1 and #2 Phillips and slot tips, and the shafts can be used to drive hex-head screws as well.

Pliers and cutters

A pair of *lineman's pliers* is possibly the most-used electrician's tool. It grabs in front rather than on the side, making it ideal for twisting wires together when splicing. It also cuts on the side, so you can quickly twist, then snip off the end of a splice. *Long-nose pliers* also perform fine work and are handy for twisting stripped wire ends into loops. They also have a cutting feature.

Side cutters (also called diagonal cutters, side-cutting pliers, or dikes) cut in tight spots, and they can nip wires off more precisely than lineman's pliers. Many electricians use side cutters to strip wire insulation; this takes a bit of practice.

Slot screwdriver

Stubby screwdriver

Rotary screw-driver

Phillips screw-drivers

Multi-screwdriver

SCREWDRIVERS

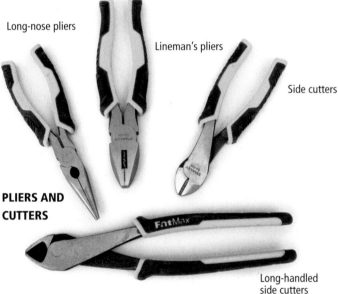

Long-nose pliers

Lineman's pliers

Side cutters

PLIERS AND CUTTERS

Long-handled side cutters

Strippers

A pair of *combination wire strippers* has a series of holes for stripping wires of various gauges. As long as you put the wire in the correct hole, it will remove insulation without nicking the bare wire. Combination strippers also can cut wires, and their front end can be used to grab wires and twist, like long-nose pliers. Once you have adjusted a pair of *one-hole strippers* to a particular size, you can strip wires of that size more easily, because you don't have to search for the correct hole. Some people prefer to use a *multipurpose tool,* which has its stripping holes in the middle rather than at the end.

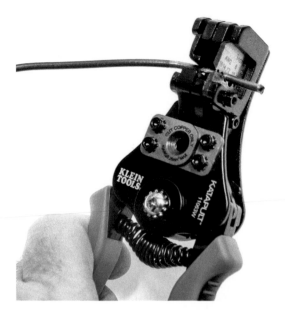

AUTOMATIC STRIPPERS. This tool is well worth its price if you have a lot of stripping to do. Insert the wire into the correct slot and at the desired location for the length of the strip, and squeeze the handles. The insulation will be instantly and neatly removed.

Multipurpose tool

One-hole strippers

Combination strippers

STRIPPERS

Electrician's Tape

Though it is usually called *electrical tape,* the correct term is *electrician's tape.* Spend a little more for professional-grade tape, which will stay more reliably stuck than the homeowner stuff—with one caveat: If you just pull on it to cut it, you will end up with a curly end that is difficult to work with. Instead, cut with a knife or use a cutting dispenser.

Tool belt

Keep your electrician's tools in a separate tool belt or container so you won't be tempted to use tools lacking insulation when you do wiring work. It's also best to spare your wiring tools from serving double-duty as construction tools.

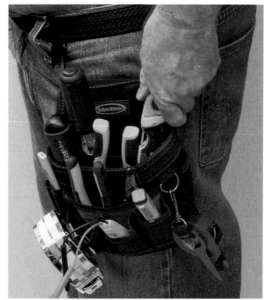

ELECTRICIAN'S TOOL BELT. An electrician's tool belt is smaller than a carpenter's belt and keeps the tools you need in easy reach.

GENERAL TOOLS. (from left to right), combination square, flashlight (headlight), utility knife, jab saw, pencil, hammer, fiberglass ladder.

General tools

When you need to use carpentry and other tools, be sure they are safe for electrical work. Use a *fiberglass* or *wood ladder* when working on the ceiling. The ladder should be labeled "nonconductive." Have a *flashlight*—a headlamp leaves your hands free—on hand for when you need to work in a dark place. Use *hammers* and other tools with rubber grips that keep your fingers away from the metal parts. A *jab saw* with a rubber handle is the safest tool to use when you need to cut into wall surfaces. And a *utility knife, pencil,* and *combination square* often come in handy.

Safe Power Tools

Some heavy-duty power tools have plugs with grounding prongs. If you use them, be sure to plug into a grounded receptacle. Most hand power tools have only two prongs, but nearly all modern power tools are double-insulated, making them as safe as grounded tools. Avoid using older two-prong tools, which may not be double insulated.

TIP Keep tools dry. If one gets wet, wipe it with a dry cloth as soon as possible and leave it where it can quickly dry out. See that the rubber insulation and other safety features of your tools are in good shape. If rubber insulation gets nicked or otherwise damaged, replace the tool.

Testing

Testers may show you whether power is present or whether a fixture or appliance is internally damaged. In addition to the tests shown here, see p. 33 for testing a receptacle with a receptacle analyzer.

TESTING FOR POWER IN RECEPTACLES. Be sure to test for power in several ways and at several times, as shown on pp. 8–9. To test for power on a 240-volt receptacle (above left), use a multitester that can handle 240 volts. Wear protective clothing and take care to hold the prongs of a tester well back from the metal ends. Insert one probe into a side (hot) slot and one into a top or bottom (neutral or ground) slot. The tester should read 120 volts. Try this with several combinations of side plus top/bottom slots. Then insert the probes into the two side (hot) slots. The tester should read 240 volts. If you get any other readings, shut off power to the circuit before removing the cover and inspecting the receptacle (see pp. 8–9). A single two-prong neon tester (above right) can tell you whether or not a receptacle is live.

TESTING A JUNCTION BOX. Use a voltage detector to check for power both on the outside of a junction box and on the inside after the cover is removed. Carefully check all the wires, because there may be two or more circuits in the box and some wires may be shut off while others are still live.

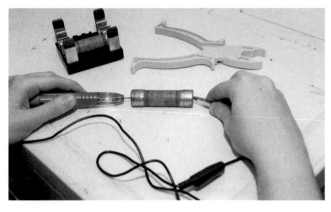

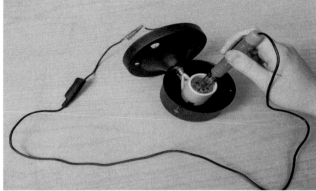

TESTING FOR CONTINUITY. A continuity tester has a battery-powered light that comes on if there is a continuous wiring path through a device or fixture. If a part or a wire is broken inside, the light will not come on. Use a continuity tester to check if a block fuse has blown (above left). Or clip one end to a fixture's lead wire and touch the probe to the inside tab of the socket (above right). If the light does not come on, the fixture needs to be rewired. You can also use a continuity tester to test a switch or receptacle. Or use a multimeter to test for continuity (right).

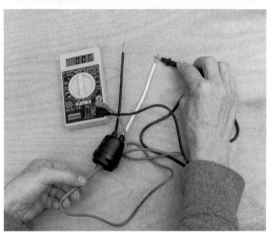

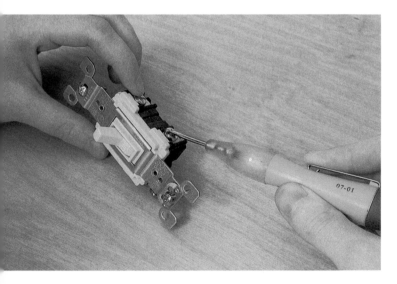

VOLTAGE-AND-CONTINUITY TESTER. This type of tester actually uses your body as part of the circuit. It's safe, because only a tiny amount of power passes through your body. To test a receptacle, touch the screwdriver-like probe to one terminal, touch the other terminal with your finger, and press down on the clip on the tester; the light should come on. To test a receptacle for power, insert the probe into the hot (narrower) slot only and press the clip. The light will glow if power is present.

WALL SCANNER. A scanner like this senses the presence of wood studs, metal studs, or live power inside a wall. Follow the instructions for adjusting the tool, considering the thickness of your wall material (which may be ½-in. drywall or thicker lath and plaster). As with a voltage detector, remember that this is a good but not perfect testing device. Even if it indicates no power in the wall, work carefully and periodically retest as the job proceeds.

Stripping and Joining Wire

When replacing a ceiling fixture, receptacle, or switch, or when making repairs, you'll need to strip and join wires. There are three basic operations: stripping wire ends, splicing wires together, and joining wires to terminals. Using good tools, you can gain proficiency at these operations with a small amount of practice. Once you've mastered these operations, work carefully and develop solid work habits to ensure that every splice or terminal connection you make is consistently firm, so none will come loose.

Stripping wire ends

Use the correct tools to strip insulation from wire ends. If you use a knife, you're likely to nick—and weaken—the bare wire. Tools made for stripping will take off the insulation without damaging the metal—and do it more quickly and easily than using a knife.

TIP Metal wire weakens when it gets bent and may break if it is bent several times. For that reason, when detaching and reattaching wires to other wires or to terminals, it's a good idea to cut them behind the bent parts, then strip again before reattaching.

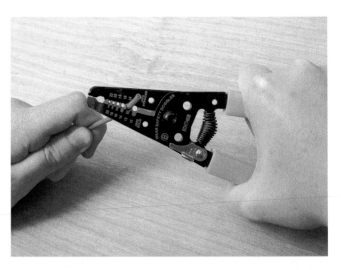

2 **INSERT, SQUEEZE, AND SPIN.** Insert the wire into the appropriate hole. (Note that some strippers, like this one, have different holes for solid and stranded wire.) Squeeze the handles of the stripper and rotate the tool around the wire about a quarter turn in each direction.

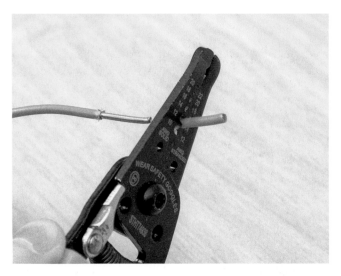

3 **REMOVE THE INSULATION.** Slide the insulation off the wire. Check that the copper is not nicked. If it is, make sure you are using the correct hole in the stripper tool. Then cut off the bare wire and strip again.

1 **MEASURE.** Strip off 1 in. of insulation if you're connecting to a terminal. Strip ¾ in. if you're splicing to other wires. In the example shown, the distance across the stripping tool just above the printed numbers is exactly ¾ in. You can likely find other parts of your strippers to use as quick guides for length.

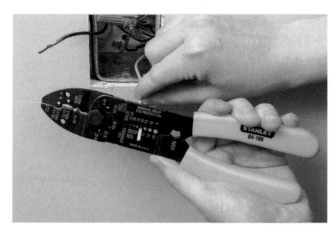

MULTIPURPOSE TOOL. A tool like this has stripping holes near the middle rather than at the end. It is more difficult to use in tight spots, but it may make it easier to find the correct wire hole.

ONE-HOLE STRIPPER. To use this tool, test on a scrap length of wire until you find the exact point where the tool removes the insulation easily without biting into the metal. Tighten the adjustment screw, then test again. Once the tool is set for the wire gauge you will be stripping, you will not have to squint to find the correct hole each time. You may want to adjust two of these tools—one for 12-gauge and one for 14-gauge wires.

Automatic Strippers

Once adjusted correctly, this tool will not only strip insulation easily but also eliminate the need to measure for the length of insulation to be stripped. On this model, experiment with the adjustment screw [A] until the tool strips easily but without nicking the wire. Then adjust for the length you want to strip [B]. Now you simply insert the wire into the strippers and squeeze to achieve the perfect wire strip [C].

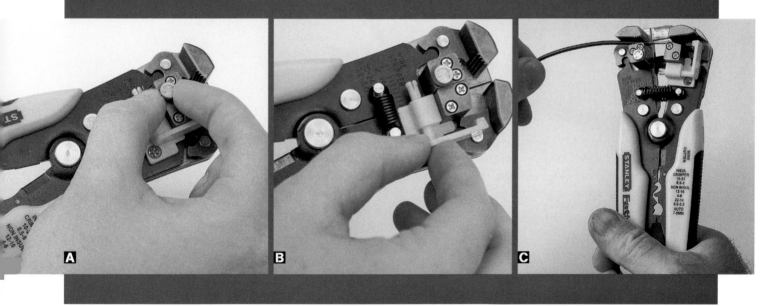

Splicing wires

When splicing two or more wires, the joint should be firm and secure. The recommended method is to first twist them together, then cover and add strength with a wire nut.

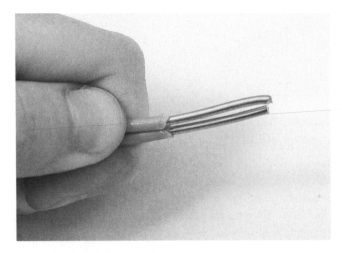

1 **STRIP AND HOLD TOGETHER.** Strip about ¾ in. of insulation from the wires and hold them together closely. Grasp both wires tightly.

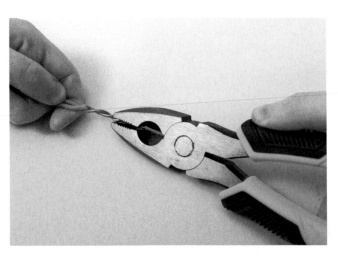

2 **GRAB AND TWIST.** Using lineman's pliers, grab the tips of both wires at once and twist clockwise. Make three or four turns and see that both wires twist; do not just wrap one wire around the other.

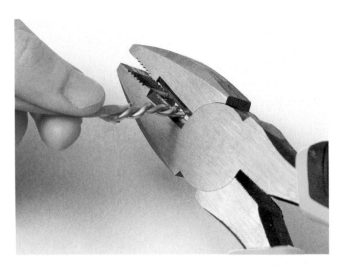

3 **SNIP.** Cut the tip of the wires at a slight angle, so it is easy to slip on a wire nut. Lineman's pliers work fine for this, but you may prefer to use side cutters.

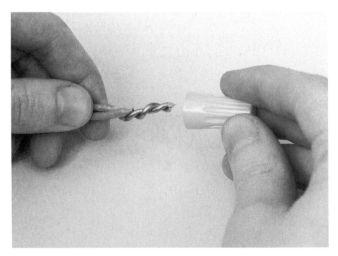

4 **ADD A WIRE NUT.** Twist a wire nut on counter-clockwise, to cover the stripped wires and consolidate the splice. If some bare wires show, remove the nut, snip the bare wires a bit shorter, and reinstall the nut. Tug on the wire nut to check that it is firmly on.

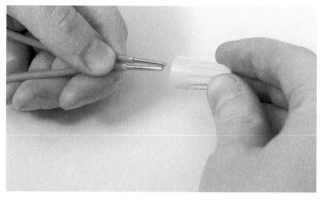
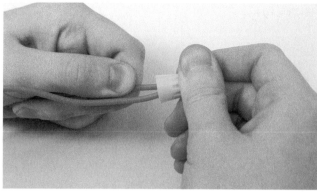

WIRE-NUT-ONLY METHOD. Some electricians find that simply twisting on a wire nut, without any twisting of the wires beforehand, produces a strong connection. Be sure to use a wire nut that has metal threads inside. Hold the stripped wires tightly together and twist on the nut. Test the splice by tugging firmly on each wire; you should feel no looseness whatsoever.

Splicing Stranded to Solid

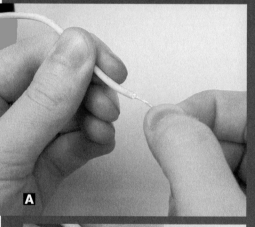

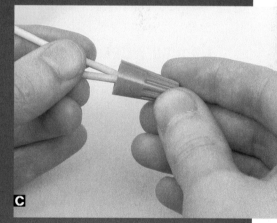

To splice a stranded fixture lead to a solid wire (as usually happens when installing a light fixture), strip off about 1 in. of insulation from the stranded wire and ¾ in. from the solid wire. Twist the stranded wire together, so there are no loose strands [A]. Wrap the stranded wire around the solid wire, so that the stranded wire protrudes just slightly beyond the solid wire [B]. Firmly twist on a wire nut, and then pull on the stranded wire to make sure it is solidly attached [C].

Though it's not usually required and many electricians do not bother, it's a good idea to tightly wrap three or four windings of electrician's tape around the bottom of the wire nut, lapping onto the wires [D]. The tape provides an extra measure of protection.

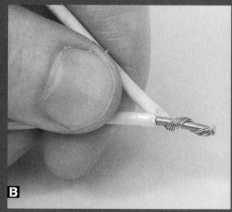

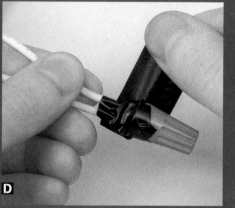

Splicing Three Wires

To splice three or four wires together (Chapter 8 shows instances where this is needed), hold them tightly parallel, but with the center wire crossed over one of the outer wires [A]. Twist clockwise with lineman's pliers. Work to make all the wires—including the center one—twist, rather than just wrapping the two outside wires around the center one [B]. Cap with a large (probably red) wire nut and tug on the wires to be sure they are all tightly joined [C].

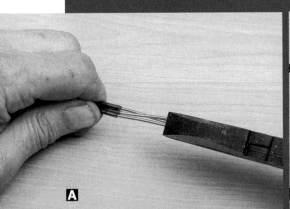

A

B

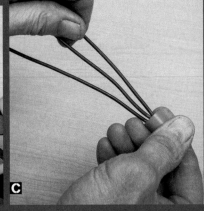

C

Joining wires to terminals

Most receptacles and switches have screw-down terminal screws. Stripped wire ends must be bent into loops that wrap snugly around the screw shafts so the screw heads can screw down to hold the wire tightly and securely. You can learn to do this with a bit of practice, but if you find it difficult, you may choose to buy more expensive devices that have hold-down connections so you don't have to make the loops.

The devices will probably come with their screws tightened down, so you need to loosen them first. On a receptacle, be sure to attach hot wires (black or red) to the brass terminals and neutral wires (white) to the silver terminals.

1 STRIP AND LOOP. Following the instructions on pp. 46–47, strip off 1 in. of insulation. Then form a loop that will wrap around the terminal screw's shaft. A pair of long-nose pliers works well for this. Make the loop incomplete at this point, so you can easily slip it into place.

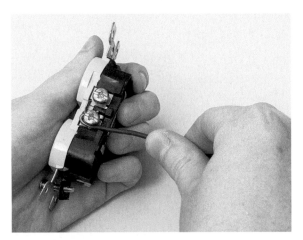

2 SLIP IN THE WIRE. Slip the loop under the terminal screw's head, positioned so the loop runs clockwise around the screw. It should fit easily, yet be closed enough so you can tighten it without trouble (next step). If the loop is too tight or too wide, take it out and use pliers to re-form it.

Using Strippers for the Whole Operation

Strippers have small plier-like ends that can be used to twist wires into loops and to tighten them down around the screw shaft (step 3). Long-nose pliers are a bit easier to use, but using strippers for everything can save you time. Use whichever tool you are most comfortable with.

3 TIGHTEN THE LOOP. Use long-nose pliers or the tip of your strippers to tighten the loop end around the screw shaft. It should feel nice and snug, and the wire should be completely under the screw head along about half the loop.

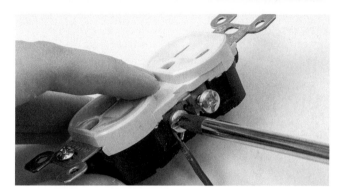

4 TIGHTEN THE SCREW. Turn the screw with a good deal of force. Tug on the wire to test that the connection is very firm. Again, about half of the loop should be hidden under the screw head. If not, loosen the screw and repeat step 3.

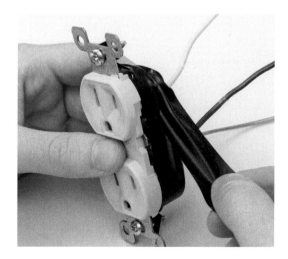

5 WRAP WITH TAPE. Local codes may not require you to do this, but it's good practice to wrap two or more windings of electrician's tape around the sides of the terminal, so the metal parts are covered.

NO LOOP TIGHTENING REQUIRED. This type of receptacle is shaped so as to capture a partial loop. It's a bit more expensive, but eliminates the need for step 3. Be sure to pull on the wire as you tighten the screw so the bare wire is fully captured under the screw head.

Push-In Terminals

Most inexpensive devices have holes in the back into which you can simply insert stripped wire, eliminating looping and attaching to screws (below). These most often work, but "most often" is not good enough with electrical work. They are generally not considered secure enough and should not be used. Other, more expensive devices have a much better system: Insert the stripped and un-looped wire, then tighten a screw to securely hold the wire (far right). Devices like this can be worth the extra cost, especially if you have trouble looping and tightening.

Wire Nuts and Pigtails

Always use wire nuts, also called wire connectors, when you splice two or more wires together. (In the old days, two types of electrician's tape were often used for this, but that has been out of code for a long time.)

THE RIGHT SIZE FOR THE JOB. Have a collection of wire nuts on hand so you can use the right size nut for the number and size of the wires being spliced. See the chart at right to find the right nut for the job.

COMMON WIRE NUTS AND THE WIRES THEY CAN HOLD

Blue	Up to two 16-gauge leads
Orange	Up to two 14-gauge wires, or a 14-gauge wire and a fixture lead
Yellow	Min. two 14-gauge wires, max. three 12-gauge wires
Red	Min. two 12-gauge wires or three 14-gauge wires, max. four 12-gauge wires

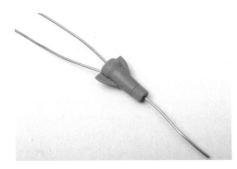

PASS-THROUGH GROUNDING WIRE NUT. A grounding nut like this saves you from making a pigtail, because one of the wires passes through a hole in the end. It can hold up to four 12-gauge grounding wires, with one of them passing through.

NUTS WITH EARS. Wire nuts with this shape make it possible to twist with extra torque, which can be helpful when splicing a number of thick wires. However, the ears add bulk and may contribute to overcrowding a box.

METAL INNARDS ARE BEST. When selecting small wire nuts for joining leads and other narrow-gauge wires, make sure they have metal threads inside. All-plastic nuts just don't grab as well.

WATERTIGHT WIRE NUTS. When working outdoors or in spaces that could get damp, use waterproof wire nuts like these.

Pigtails

Some wiring setups call for pigtails, also called jumper wires. A pigtail is a short length of wire—6 in. to 8 in. long—that is stripped on each end; one end is spliced to other wires with a wire nut, and the other end connects to a terminal. The most common reason to use a pigtail is when only one wire can be safely connected to a terminal.

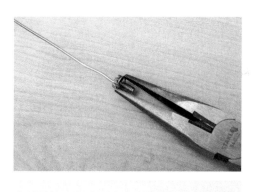

PREP THE ENDS. Strip insulation at each end. Where you will join to a screw-down terminal, form a loop, as shown on p. 50.

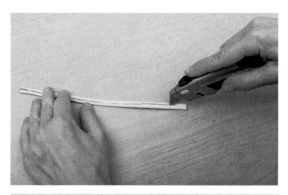

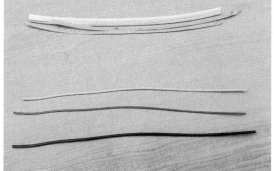

CUT LENGTHS OF WIRE. To get lengths of wire for a pigtail, cut a cable 6 in. to 8 in. long. Slice down the center of the cable, taking care not to damage any wire insulation. Separate out the individual wires.

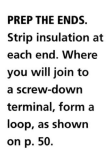

GROUNDING PIGTAILS. Use bare copper or green-insulated wire for grounding pigtails. If one end will join to a screw driven into a hole in a metal box, form a loop and bend it into a sort of lariat, as shown at top left. Bend the loop around a grounding screw. You can also purchase ready-made grounding pigtails (bottom left). One end has a loop connector for joining with a grounding screw, and the other end has an open connector for joining to a terminal.

Installing Lights and Fans

IF YOU WANT TO REPLACE a light or fan, you may be tempted to start with this chapter. But before jumping into a wiring project, we urge you to read through Chapters 1 and 2, which show how to work safely with electricity, give a basic understanding of electrical systems, and present tutorials on the basic wiring techniques you'll need to have under your belt before tackling an installation. This chapter shows how to replace fixtures or install low-voltage systems. If you need to install fixtures where none now exist, look to the second half of this book to learn about running new electrical cable or installing new circuits.

Replacement projects start with an existing ceiling or wall fixture that is controlled with a switch. Fortunately, electrical hardware has not changed much over the decades, so you can usually install a new light, fan, or track system onto an existing box with little trouble. However, if your ceiling box is very old and it's not clear how to install a new fixture onto it, see pp. 128–131 for tips on securing new to old.

Choosing Light Fixtures

Chances are, most of your house's rooms have a single light fixture in the center of the ceiling; there may be occasional wall sconces as well, especially in bathrooms. The following pages show options for replacing those lights. (For planning and installing new lights in new locations, see the second half of this book.) Although installing most of these fixtures is not difficult—indeed, replacing a light is an ideal do-it-yourself project—you can achieve a surprising number of style and illumination changes if you choose the right fixtures.

In addition to choosing a style and color that suits your tastes and coordinates with the room, also consider the way a fixture delivers illumination. Some produce diffused, or ambient, light throughout the room, whereas others offer more focused brightness. Your choice of fixture may depend on the tasks performed in the room, as well as whether there are also floor or table lamps and bright windows. Track lights can give you the most flexibility.

Choose lights that are a size that suits the room and that produce enough illumination. Before installing a light, have a helper hold it up in place and see how it looks; you may end up taking it back and getting a smaller or larger fixture.

Incandescent fixtures limit the total bulb wattage, and it's easy to screw in too much wattage, risking dangerous overheating. Fortunately, today's LED bulbs need far less wattage than incandescents to produce the same amount of brightness, so this is no longer a big concern. Also consider installing dimmer switches (see pp. 106–108), which allow you to turn the illumination up or down.

Also think about how easy it will be to keep the fixture clean. Flush lights that hug the ceiling may not make a flashy fashion statement, but lights that hang down need to be washed much more often.

TIP At a home center you will find a good selection of light fixtures on display. But there are thousands more options out there. To gain access to a wider range of choices, check online or ask in the lighting section of your home center if you can look through catalogs; usually, the salesperson can order most anything for you. To see a broad range of options firsthand, visit a lighting store, where you'll likely find the latest styles, as well as a salesperson who will help you choose lighting that coordinates with your home's style.

Flush ceiling fixtures

These are often the most economical choice, and they produce a nice ambient light throughout the room that you can supplement with other lights. Flush lights usually draw little attention to themselves, but there are stunning and stylish exceptions.

SIMPLY CLASSIC. This versatile minimalist-style ceiling fixture is made from pressed glass with a frosted finish that conceals the bulbs within, making its ambient light less glaring and more pleasant.

A LITTLE LOW. Some flush lights are almost pendants. This fixture with a cloth shade hangs down a few inches, so it makes a halo effect on the ceiling as it spreads gentle illumination throughout the room.

Pendants

Lights that hang down add decorative features to a room. Some types produce diffuse light, but most pendants direct light at a limited area. If a pendant will hang over a table or a sitting counter, it usually should be about 30 in. above the surface, and the fixture itself should be a good deal narrower than the surface, so people don't bump their heads. The fixture should light up the table area without shining in people's eyes. Many track systems have pendant lamp options (see p. 59).

LONG WORK LIGHT. This unusual pendant, nearly as long as the desk it shines on, hangs from a pair of thin, nearly invisible cords. A dimmable LED strip light inside the canopy produces even, non-glare light on the work surface below.

GLOWING BUBBLES. This dimmable LED chandelier features a grouping of delicate glass globes in the popular socket and cord pendant style. Installing a fixture like this is not much more trouble than installing a simple flush light.

PRETTY BOXES. As with many chandeliers, much of the installation work is not wiring—which is as simple as almost any fixture—but assembling the housing and decorative elements. This one features a cage within a cage, with seeded glass dispersing light from three LED filament bulbs.

PENDANTS OR CHANDELIER? This one-of-a-kind overhead light includes a number of pendants grouped to give the appearance of a chandelier. The cut-crystal lamps are draped with chain mail to create a unique lighting centerpiece.

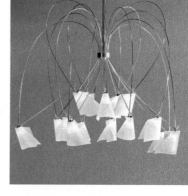

FLUTTERING POINTS OF LIGHT. This whimsical chandelier has 15 arms curving out from a central core, each tipped with a frosted lamp and white paper. Low-voltage lamps make it possible to fit the wiring inside the slender arms.

Chandeliers

A chandelier is pretty much a pendant fixture with a number of separate lights. Older styles often had curved arms, flowery decorations, and/or lots of glass parts that were a cleaning headache. Newer chandeliers come in a wide range of styles, and some need only a quick vacuuming or dusting once in a while.

SUMMER SPARKLER. With 24 gracefully arched rods, each tipped with a bright dot of light, this chandelier is reminiscent of a summertime sparkler. The 12-volt, 10-watt lamps are dimmable with a low-voltage dimmer.

LIGHTING THAT WORKS. This type of attractive minimalist sconce, UL listed for damp locations, also has a built-in night light that can be operated by a second wall switch. For makeup and other grooming tasks, lights on either side of the mirror are preferable to overhead lights.

MAGICAL MIRRORED LIGHT. This small, round mirror, surrounded by a cove of diffused white light, provides shadow-free task and ambient light. The mirrored light is available for use with halogen, fluorescent, or LED bulbs.

Bathroom lighting

Lights for a bathroom mirror or medicine cabinet may take the form of a strip above or sconces on each side. To plan for bathroom lighting, or if you want to change the location of the lights, see pp. 162–163. But you can improve the lighting and make a serious fashion statement by simply replacing the fixtures, as shown later in this chapter.

Sconces

If you are fortunate enough to have existing wall lights, a.k.a. sconces, you have the opportunity to make some stunning design statements for a small outlay of money and labor. When the wiring has already been run, installing sconces is usually a simple matter. If possible, buy a fixture with a canopy that will cover up the hole in the wall. Otherwise, you may need to do some wall patching.

READING LIGHTS. The base of this pendant fixture has the capacity to accommodate a variety of different pendant lights, on a short cord of course. It features a two-way touch dimmer and works with halogen or xenon pendants.

SIMPLE BUT EFFECTIVE. This carriage-style light, tightly sealed to make it suitable for damp locations, has a cylinder glass shade with a metal wall plate and classy hand-welded metal details.

Track lighting

Track lighting comes in a dizzying assortment of types and styles. Some are completely preassembled, others have preformed tracks that allow you to choose and position various types of lamps, and others can be shaped to any configuration you choose.

SPOTLIGHT FOR ART. This simple and sleek straight rail has three matching lamps (but can accommodate a variety of different lights). The low-voltage directional LED bulbs light up a favorite work of art to create a focal point and add warmth to the room's color scheme.

RAIL FIXTURE WITH TWO TYPES OF LAMP. This system, made by Tech Lighting, supplies a wide range of lamp options, which can be easily adjusted. For instance, non-pendant lamps available in almost any color or style can be rotated 360 degrees and pivoted to fine-tune the beam. Pendants have cable that can be cut to the desired height. Often rails like this can be bent to your desired shape (see p. 74). Here the canopy attaches to a ceiling box in the center of the rail, but it could be located anywhere along its length.

RECTANGULAR. This track system is about 12 in. narrower and shorter than the table below, so lights do not shine directly at eyes. Pendant lamps can be moved along the rail as desired.

TRACK SCONCE. A track light strip can be attached to a sconce box in the wall. Here the lamps, which pivot at the head, shine on artwork, but they could be directed upward and outward to provide general ambient light for the room.

Light Bulbs

At a home center or hardware store you'll find a wide assortment of bulbs and tubes to choose among. Nowadays, LEDs are the bulbs of choice for most situations, but there are times when other bulbs are used as well. In particular, LEDs can be difficult to find for base sizes other than medium.

Incandescents

Incandescent bulbs were standard for many years. Most inexpensive incandescents produce a warm, slightly yellow illumination that most people feel comfortable with. Frosted bulbs produce more diffused light, with less glare. However, they produce more heat and use far more electricity than CFLs and LEDs, so nowadays it is usual to replace a burned-out incandescent with an LED bulb. In fact, it may be difficult if not impossible to find standard-size incandescent bulbs in your area. However, incandescent may be the only option for some base sizes (especially candelabra or intermediate), as well as for decorative bulb shapes.

Compact fluorescents

Compact fluorescent bulbs, commonly called CFLs, produce more light for less energy costs. They were popular for a while but are now fading out because of the superiority of LEDs. Most CFLs produce a cold, slightly greenish light that many people find distasteful. Although they were advertised as long-lived, in fact they are notorious for burning out in fairly short order. Most have a spiral shape, but some are shaped like standard bulbs.

Halogens

Halogen bulbs are often small, and they fit into special low-voltage fixtures and lamps. Some screw in as usual, but some have two pins that poke into the socket. They save in energy costs and last a good long time. However, they can get very hot.

LED bulbs

Light-emitting diode (LED) bulbs are stingy with energy costs, comfortably warm in color, and very long lasting. As of this writing they are somewhat expensive but are coming down in price every year and are well worth the cost in the long run. Many LEDs are sized to replace old screw-in incandescents. You can also replace fluorescent tubes with LED tubes, and a number of special LED fixtures, including strip lights, are coming onto the market. LEDs

Standard incandescent with medium base

Candelabra base

Decorative bulbs with medium bases

Compact fluorescent (CFL)

can be found in Christmas lights, low-voltage landscaping lights, and lights with decorative shapes. Because LEDs last so long, many fixtures now come with LED bulbs permanently installed; it's expected that in many cases you will never need to replace the bulbs.

Frosted LEDs

Filament LEDs

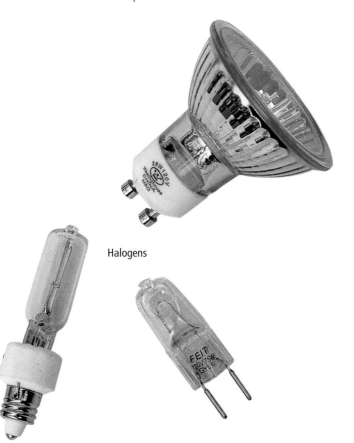

Halogens

REPLACING AN INCANDESCENT WITH AN LED

Incandescent bulbs are rated by wattage, but the actual light they produce is measured in lumens. When replacing an incandescent with an LED, use the following chart to determine how much wattage to buy in order to achieve the same level of light. This chart shows clearly how much energy is saved by switching to LEDs.

LUMENS	INCANDESCENT WATTS	LED WATTS
450	40	10
800	60	15
1,100	75	19
1,600	100	25
2,600	150	38
3,000	200	50

TIP Most fixtures and lamps use bulbs with "medium" or "standard" size bases. Some chandeliers and other decorative fixtures call for "candelabra" size bases, whereas some desk lamps and other small lamps use "intermediate" bases. A large floor lamp may need a three-level bulb with a large "mogul" base. If you are in doubt, bring the bulb you want to replace to the store with you and compare bases.

Kelvin and Full Spectrum Ratings

The higher a bulb's Kelvin (K) rating, the colder—or bluer—its color. Lower ratings mean warmer—more yellow—color. Natural light on a sunny day is about 5,000K; light on a cloudy day is about 8,000K. Lights labeled "full spectrum" or "grow lights" are generally around 5,000K. Some people prefer sunny, colder light in task areas like a kitchen and warmer, cloudy-like light in living areas.

Replacing Light Fixtures

Changing out an old dingy or cheap-looking overhead light fixture for a new stylish model is one of the quickest and easiest ways to brighten up a room. Unless you have very old wiring with a pancake box, the hardware for attaching a new light—either a strap or a center stud—will be easy to attach to your ceiling box.

However, consider the size of the new light's canopy—the part that snugs up to the ceiling. If the new canopy is smaller than the existing one, you may need to touch up paint or even patch the ceiling. If your new canopy does not cover ceiling imperfections, a medallion may be the best solution.

Fixture Mounting Hardware

Here are the three most common types of mounting hardware. A circular strap has plenty of threaded holes and open slots, so it is adaptable to almost any fixture. A straight strap has fewer hole and slot possibilities but still works in most situations. If your new fixture mounts via a center stud, it needs not only the threaded stud but also a strap or other device with a threaded hole, as well as a nut and washer to hold the canopy in place.

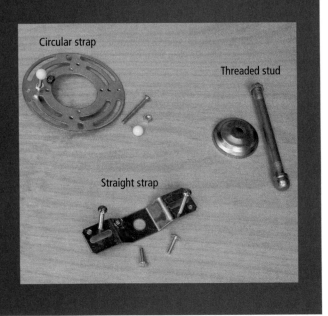

Circular strap

Threaded stud

Straight strap

TIP If you have an old fixture box that does not easily accept a strap or center stud, see pp. 130–131 for ways to use adaptive hardware.

Removing an old fixture

To take down the existing ceiling fixture, first shut off the power and test that power is off; see the safety tip below. Then remove the globe (the part that covers the bulbs), which is often held onto the canopy with several small setscrews.

▸ **Be sure to shut off power at the service panel. Test several times to verify that power is off, as shown on pp. 8–9. For double protection, use electrician's tools and work as if the wires were hot.**

TIP Simply turning off the wall switch will probably de-energize the light and its ceiling box, but "probably" is not a safe standard. Especially in older homes, juice may still be present in the box after the switch is off. Most commonly, this happens when there is switch-loop wiring, when another circuit runs through the ceiling box, or when the light is neutral switched (see p. 92). See pp. 44–45 for basic safety procedures.

1 PREP FOR CANOPY REMOVAL. After shutting off power and testing for power, check the condition of the ceiling around the fixture. You may want to patch, smooth, and paint blemished areas. If the canopy was painted, or perhaps caulked, run a knife around the canopy's perimeter so you won't tear the drywall paper when you remove the canopy.

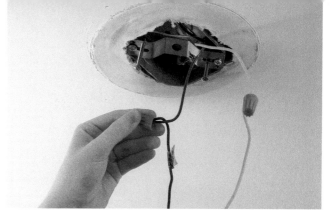

2 REMOVE THE CANOPY. Most often, the canopy is held in place with two mounting screws. Loosen them so they come down ¼ in. or so, and then twist the canopy so you can pull it out. You may need to completely remove the screws. If the light is a pendant, you may need to support the light temporarily.

4 REMOVE THE OLD FIXTURE. Unscrew the wire nuts holding the fixture's leads to the house wires. If the fixture has a ground wire connected to the box, also loosen the grounding screw and pull the ground lead out.

Installing a Flush Light Fixture

A flush light is the most common type of ceiling-mounted fixture and is also easy to install. There are many different types of canopies and globes, so read the manufacturer's literature for specific mounting instructions. You may be able to reuse the existing strap hardware in the box, as long as the mounting screws or strap holes line up with the new light. However, most fixtures come with their own mounting hardware, and it's usually simpler to use that.

TIP If you have old wiring, inspect the insulation for any gaps or cracks, and repair as shown on p. 129.

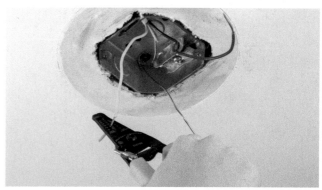

3 TEST AGAIN. Gently pull the canopy down. Test again for power using a voltage detector. Touch the detector on the wires, the wire nuts, and in the box.

TIP Most ceiling light canopies are lightweight, so they easily hang by the wires. If yours is heavy, support it with blocks of some sort set on top of your ladder. Or suspend it from the box with a wire.

1 PREPARE THE HOUSE WIRES. After removing the old fixture, remove the strap or other mounting hardware and inspect the box. Determine how you will attach the fixture's ground lead, as well as the house ground wire (see p. 13 and pp. 52–53 for various possibilities). If the wires are long enough, snip off the bare ends and restrip ¾ in. of insulation. (Old bare wires that have been bent and rebent may break off during installation.)

2 **ASSEMBLE THE STRAP.** Prepare the strap as needed. See that the mounting screws will line up with the screw holes in the canopy. Some newer fixtures have the arrangement shown, where there are no metal nuts in the canopy for extra safety (see step 7 below). Here, you estimate how far down the mounting screw needs to extend and use a nut to tighten the screw in that position. (You may need to adjust the position later.)

3 **ATTACH THE STRAP.** Thread the house wires through the center of a circular strap as shown, or move them so they come through either side of a straight strap. Attach the strap firmly to the box with 8-32 screws. (Short screws of this size will be provided; if the box is recessed and you need longer screws, you can buy them at a hardware store.)

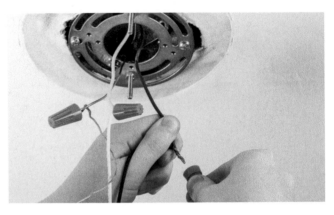

4 **CONNECT THE GROUND.** Hook up the fixture's ground; see p. 13 and pp. 52–53 for various options, and be sure to comply with local codes. In this situation, we spliced the ground lead to a pigtail that is attached to a grounding screw in the box. You could also attach the lead to the grounding lead on the strap. In the case of a plastic box, splice the fixture's ground lead to the house's ground wire.

5 **WIRE THE LIGHT.** Splice the fixture's white and black leads to the house's white (neutral) and black or colored (hot) wires. See p. 49 for instructions on making these connections nice and firm. If the box is controlled by a pair of three-way switches, see pp. 211–212 for wiring.

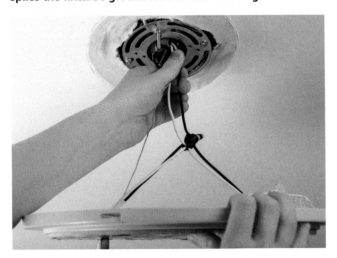

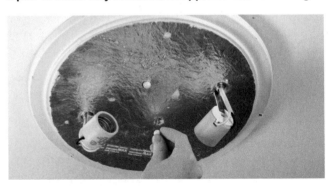

6 **PUSH THE WIRES UP.** Carefully fold the wires and wire nuts up into the box. All house wires should end up inside the box; only fixture leads can be below the strap.

7 **ATTACH THE CANOPY.** Push the canopy up so that the mounting screws poke through the holes in the canopy. Screw on the mounting nuts (which in this case are round and plastic) and tighten until the canopy is snug against the ceiling. With this type of hardware, the nuts may poke down too far or not far enough, in which case you need to adjust their position.

8 **ADD THE GLOBE.** Install the globe. This type gets pushed up and then turned to hold it into position. Other globes attach with three small horizontal setscrews.

Straight-Strap Attachment

In this setup, a straight strap with two mounting screws is attached to the box [A]. Push the canopy up and tighten the mounting screws to secure the canopy to the ceiling [B], and then attach the globe via a center stud [C].

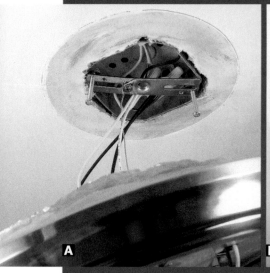

A

B

C

Installing a Pendant Light

Most modern pendants have solid downrods through which the wires travel. An older style uses a chain, through which you thread decorative cord.

A lightweight pendant like the one shown here can be installed onto a standard ceiling box. However, if you're installing a heavy chandelier, it's a good idea either to install a heavy-duty fan-rated box or to attach the mounting hardware to a nearby ceiling joist (see p. 85). At the least, drive an extra screw or two to make the box nice and strong. Test the box's strength by pulling on its hardware.

If possible, buy a pendant with a canopy at least as wide as the fixture you will replace. If it is smaller, you may need to patch and paint the ceiling, or to cover any imperfections with a medallion.

▶ **Be sure to shut off power at the service panel. Test several times to verify that power is off, as shown on pp. 8–9. For double protection, use electrician's tools and work as if the wires were hot.**

Remove the existing light fixture, as shown on pp. 62–63.

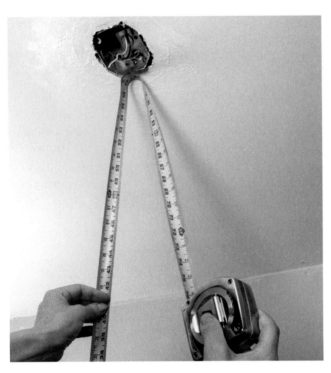

1 DETERMINE THE HEIGHT. As a general rule, if you have 8-ft.-high ceilings, a pendant is typically placed 28 in. to 34 in. above a countertop or table and 65 in. to 68 in. above a floor. If your ceiling is taller, raise the light about 3 in. for each additional foot of ceiling height. But to find the most comfortable height, have a helper hold the pendant in place while you sit at a table or walk under it. Make sure the light will not glare into people's eyes.

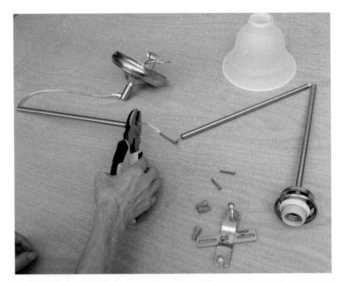

2 PREPARE THE RODS AND CORD. If your fixture has multiple rods, you remove one of them to raise the light. Or you can cut a rod for more precision. Assemble the rod(s) and canopy, leaving yourself 6 in. to 8 in. of cord at the canopy.

3 **INSTALL THE STRAP.** The fixture probably comes with its own strap. A swivel strap like the one shown here allows you to position the mounting nuts where you want them.

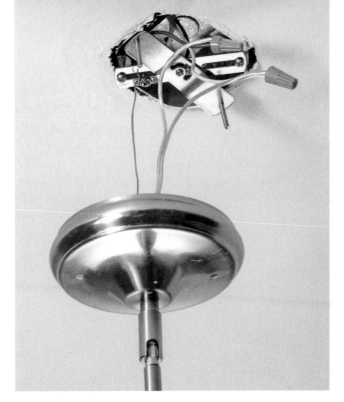

4 **WIRE THE PENDANT.** If the pendant is light, it can easily hang by wires. If it has some heft, place it on top of a ladder, or have a helper hold it as you work. Attach the ground wire. Splice the neutral (white) lead to the house's white wire and the hot (black or colored) wire to the house's hot wire. If the box is controlled by a pair of three-way switches, see pp. 211–212 for wiring.

5 **FOLD UP WIRES AND FASTEN THE CANOPY.** Carefully fold the wires and wire nuts up above the strap and into the box, and then attach the canopy.

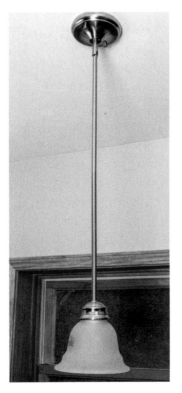

6 **FINISH.** Attach any additional hardware and screw in a bulb. Restore power and test the light.

Chain-Type Chandelier

If your pendant is a chandelier that hangs by a chain, use pliers to open and remove chain links [A] to adjust its height [B]. Thread cord through the chains [C] and attach to the ceiling box. Wire the fixture, then slide up the canopy and attach it [D].

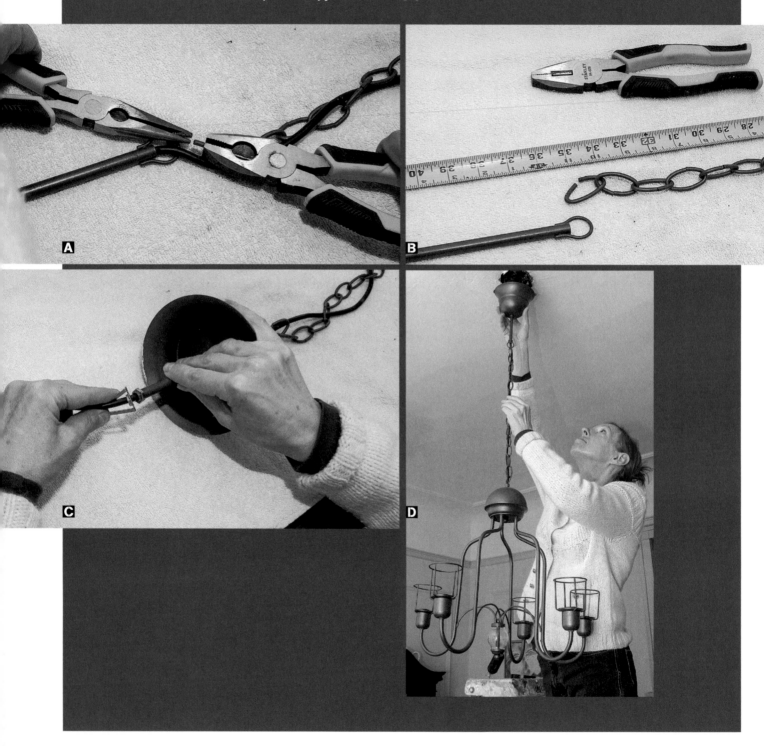

LED Upgrade to a Recessed Canister Light

Here's a project that usually doesn't require any tools. (Though a pair of long-nose pliers may come in handy if the fastening system is difficult to attach.) In fact, you don't even have to shut off power at the service panel; just turn off the light switch, because you won't expose an electrical box or any house wires. It's actually very much like changing a light bulb, with a little extra work attaching the light trim.

Once installed, you'll have brighter light and lower energy costs. LED upgrade kits are sold at home centers and elsewhere in several sizes. Measure your canister light's opening and choose one to fit. The one shown here will work for a 4-in. or 5-in. opening.

1 REMOVE THE OLD TRIM. ➡ **Shut off the light switch.** Remove the fixture's light bulb. Then remove the trim. Some trims, like the one shown, are simple rings that attach to the inside of the canister with spring clips. Others are more substantial, but the fastening system will be clear and easy to disassemble.

2 SCREW IN THE KIT. The kit assembles easily, with a simple clip wire attachment. At its end is a socket just like the base of a light bulb. Screw it into the fixture, just as you would a bulb.

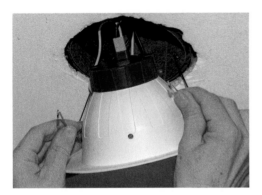

3 ATTACH THE KIT. The kit has a pair of two-headed clips; each clip head slips into a slot inside the canister. Insert one head from each clip into a slot. Start moving the kit up into the hole and insert the other two heads into the other slots. This may be a bit awkward, and you may find that a pair of long-nose pliers helps.

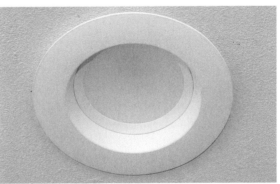

4 PUSH THE TRIM UP. Press up until the kit's trim is pleasingly snug against the ceiling. If it won't slide all the way up, pull it back out and make sure all four clip heads are in slots. You may need to bend one or more of the clip wires to get a firmer fitting.

Installing Track Lighting

Track lighting offers plenty in the way of options and versatility. You can choose:

- the direction the track(s) will run
- the style and illumination pattern of individual lamps (which may include two or more different heads or pendants on a single track)
- where along the track each lamp will be located
- which way the lamps will point

There are a number of different track lighting types. A traditional track system, as shown on the following pages, connects to a ceiling box anywhere along its length and needs to be attached at several points to the ceiling. It can be connected to additional tracks to form almost any shape you want. Some self-contained types come with the canopy preattached, making installation easier but giving fewer layout options. Rail lamps are another type and are shown on p. 77.

➠ **Be sure to shut off power at the service panel. Test several times to verify that power is off, as shown on pp. 8–9. For double protection, use electrician's tools and work as if the wires were hot.**

TIP In most situations, it works well to position track(s) in the center of a room or about 16 in. away from walls (or from wall cabinets) so you can aim the lamps at walls or around the room for ambient lighting.

Cutting Tracks

You can cut tracks to a desired length with a hacksaw or a reciprocating saw equipped with a metal-cutting blade. Hold the track very firmly as you cut and use a square as a guide. After cutting, remove the end cap from the cut portion and install it onto the end of the cut piece.

1 WIRE THE CONNECTOR. With the power off, remove the old ceiling fixture. (To run cable and install a new box, see Chapter 7.) Wire the twist-on connector as you would a light fixture: Connect the ground; in this case, the ground wire attaches to the mounting plate. Splice the black lead to the house's hot (black or colored) wire, and splice the neutral (white) lead to the neutral house wire. If the box is controlled by a pair of three-way switches, see pp. 211–212 for wiring.

2 ATTACH THE MOUNTING PLATE. Fold the wires up into the box. Check to be sure that they will not get in the way of the canopy (step 9). Position the mounting plate so it is facing the right way; the track will fit between two setscrews. Drive screws to firmly attach the plate.

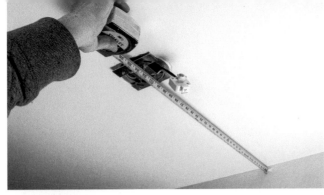

3 **MEASURE AND MARK FOR THE TRACK.** You probably want the track to be parallel with a nearby wall or row of cabinets. Measure from the wall to one side of the channel where the track will attach (step 6). Mark several spots the same distance from the wall. Also mark where you want the track to end.

4 **ATTACH THE TRACK TO THE MOUNTING PLATE.** If the mounting plate is firmly attached, it will hold a track temporarily. Back off one or both of the small setscrews, slip the track into the plate where you want it to go, and tighten one or both of the setscrews.

Attach to Joists for Heavy Lights

If any of the lamps will be heavy, it's a good idea to attach the track to ceiling joists where possible. (Note that this works only when the track will run across joists; if the track runs parallel to joists, use multiple toggles or plastic anchors.) Use a stud finder to locate the centers of joists. Drill holes in the track and then drive screws that are 1¼ in. or longer.

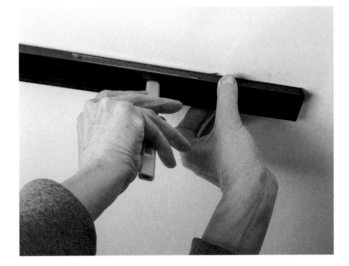

5 **MARK FOR SCREW LOCATIONS.** Hold the track against one of the layout lines you made in step 3 and draw marks where you will drive screws through holes in the track.

TIP If your box's mounting screws face in the wrong direction, you may need to use a swivel strap (p. 67) in order to get the mounting plate attached in the desired direction.

6 **ATTACH THE TRACK.** Here we show installing toggle bolts; for plastic anchors, see p. 76. Move the track over a few inches and drill holes through the marks you made in the previous step. The bit should be large enough to accommodate the toggles. Slip a bolt up through each hole in the track and screw on the toggle nuts. Push the nuts through the holes far enough that the toggle bolts open above the drywall, and then tighten the screws.

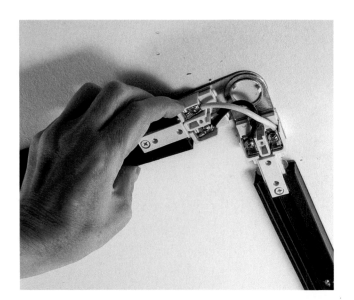 

7 **ATTACH ADDITIONAL TRACKS.** Use track connectors to join two tracks together. Here we show a right-angle connector, but you can also buy straight connectors or connectors that can be adjusted to various angles. Remove the end caps from both tracks and slip the connector into both tracks. You may have to push hard.

8 **ATTACH THE TWIST-LOCK CONNECTOR.** At the mounting plate, insert and twist the electrical connector so it is parallel with the track. This will supply power to the entire track.

9 PATCH THE CEILING IF NEEDED. The canopy may not completely cover the electrical box (step 10). If it doesn't, apply joint compound or caulk to cover. Paint the ceiling before installing the canopy.

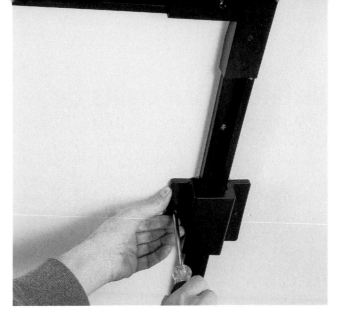

10 ATTACH CANOPY AND COVERS. Position the canopy over the mounting plate and drive little screws to attach it to the plate. You may need to work carefully in order to insert the screws into the little holes. Drive one partially, then drive the other, and then finish driving. Also install covers for any track connectors.

11 ADD THE LAMPS. The individual lamps mount via twist-on connectors, and the lights can be pointed in almost any direction. Restore power and test. Experiment with different light positions until the room is lit just the way you want it.

A Plug-In Option

A connector like the one shown here allows you to simply plug the track light's track into a wall receptacle. To control the lights, you can install pull-chain switches onto each one individually. Or install a cord switch at an easy-to-reach place on the cord.

Installing Rail Lights

Like track lights, rail lights (also called monorail fixtures) have almost limitless options for lamp style, spacing, and direction of their beams. Rail lights also allow you to choose the shape of the rail, which is essentially a track that you can bend into almost any shape. This bendability calls for some special techniques when planning the layout. After planning the layout, installation starts by wiring and attaching a canopy, which has a transformer inside to step down to low voltage.

The steps shown in the photo sequence here call for using a plumb bob to locate positions for the standoffs that hold the rail in place. You could instead:

• Lay out the rail on the floor as shown in step 2, and then measure from both walls to determine standoff locations. Use a framing square to make sure you are measuring at 90 degrees from the walls.

• Draw a scale layout on graph paper, and then use that as a guide to measure from the walls.

⟹ **Be sure to shut off power at the service panel. Test several times to verify that power is off, as shown on pp. 8–9. For double protection, use electrician's tools and work as if the wires were hot.**

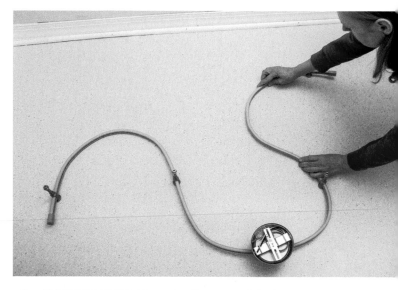

2 **MAKE THE SHAPE.** Place the fixture upside down on the floor or on a table directly beneath the place where the light will go. Bend it into the shape you want and position the standoffs in a pleasing pattern. Take time to bend the rail into graceful curves.

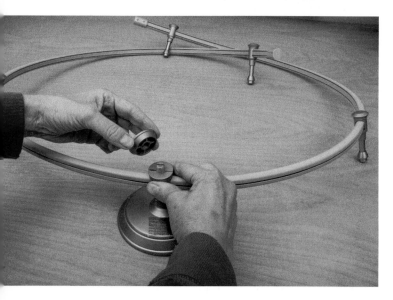

1 **ASSEMBLE THE PARTS.** Follow the manufacturer's instructions for attaching the canopy and standoffs to the rail. Once assembled, the standoffs can be slid along the track, but the canopy must be disassembled and reassembled to position it.

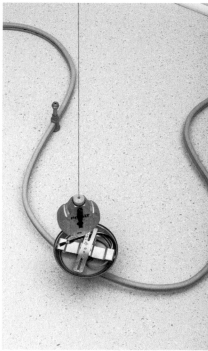

3 **LOCATE THE CANOPY.** Hang the clip of a plumb bob (a chalkline works fine) from the center of the ceiling box. Adjust the string length so that the bob hangs just above the canopy, and move the canopy so it is directly below the ceiling box.

4 **LOCATE THE STANDOFFS.** Use the plumb bob (above right) to mark the positions of the standoffs. Hold the clip against the ceiling and move it until it is directly above a standoff, then mark the location on the ceiling.

TIP Don't worry about getting the canopy and standoff locations perfectly precise. Usually the track can be easily bent. As long as the locations are within an inch or two of perfect, the fixture will look fine.

5 **WIRE AND ATTACH THE CANOPY/TRANSFORMER.** Install a swivel strap so the wires can be easily moved up into the box after attaching. Wire the fixture as you would any ceiling light: Connect the grounds (see p. 13 and pp. 52–53), then splice the hot (black) lead to the hot (black or colored) house wire and the neutral (white) lead to the neutral house wire (see p. 64). Tighten the screw to hold the swivel in the correct position, and then fold the wires up into the box. Attach the canopy to the strap.

6 ATTACH THE STANDOFFS. If a standoff location happens to be just under a joist, you can simply drive a screw to attach a standoff base. This is a rare occurrence, however. Either use toggle bolts, as shown in step 6 on p. 72, or plastic anchors, as shown below. Drive a screw to attach the base, and then screw on the standoff itself.

Attaching with Plastic Anchors

Plastic anchors are not as strong as toggle bolts and certainly not as strong as screws driven into joists or studs, but they work just fine for lightweight fixtures. Drill a hole through the drywall or plaster that is slightly smaller than the anchor's shaft. Tap the anchor into the hole, and you're ready to drive a screw, as shown in step 6.

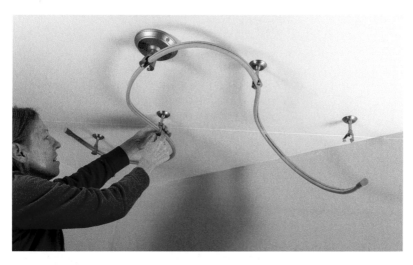

7 **ATTACH AND SHAPE THE RAIL.** If the rail is long, you may need a helper for this. Slip the rail into the jaws of a standoff, then close the jaws and screw on the cap that holds the jaws closed. Screw the cap on only partway, so you can slide the rail as needed. Once the rail is in all the standoffs and the canopy, make final adjustments until you are happy with the shape.

8 **ATTACH THE CANOPY/TRANSFORMER.** The canopy's attachment needs to be squeezed tighter than the standoffs, because it has metal barbs that poke into the rail and provide the electrical connection. You may need to use a clamp to hold the jaws tight before screwing on the cap.

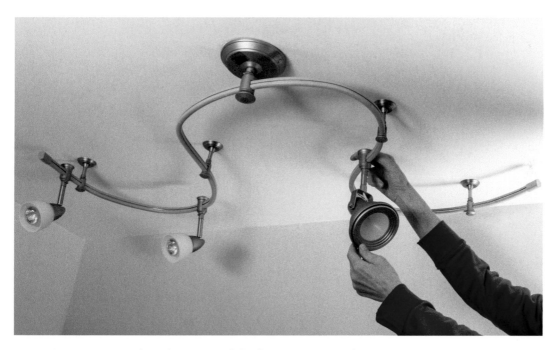

9 **ADD THE LAMPS.** These lamps attach in the same way as the canopy. Clamp their jaws onto the rail so their barbs create an electrical connection. If you want to move a lamp, disassemble it first; it cannot be slid. Restore power and test. Swivel the lamps to suit your needs.

Installing a Bathroom Strip Light

These pages show how to install a strip light above a bathroom vanity or mirror. If you need to replace sconces (individual wall lights) on each side of a vanity or mirror, see p. 80. If you want to move light locations—from an above-mounted strip to a pair of sconces, or vice versa—see Chapter 7 for installing new boxes and running new cable.

The electrical box for a wall light is usually round or octagonal, or it may be a rectangular switch box. In any case, attaching new strap hardware will rarely pose problems. Newer LED bath fixtures usually have integrated bulbs that do not need changing. They will last virtually forever and will daintily sip electricity when in use.

In an older home the existing light may not be grounded; current codes call for grounding, and it's a good idea to add this safety measure. See p. 131 for how to ground with a metal box and p. 80 for a ground in a plastic box.

TIP If your wall has been painted around an existing fixture, you'll save time and trouble if the new fixture's wall plate will cover the unpainted area. If not, you may need to patch the wall, then apply primer and paint. This is best done before installing the new fixture; it's hard to paint precisely around a wall plate.

▥▶ **Be sure to shut off power at the service panel. Test several times to verify that power is off, as shown on pp. 8–9. For double protection, use electrician's tools and work as if the wires were hot.**

1 REMOVE THE OLD FIXTURE. Older fixtures typically have multiple light sockets with metal trims that slide to hold the wall plate against the wall. Unscrew the bulbs, slide out the trims, and remove the wall plate. Use both a voltage tester and a voltage detector to be sure power is off in the box as you work. Remove wire nuts, pull out the fixture leads, and replace the wire nuts onto the house wires. Remove any screws holding the back plate to the wall, and gently remove it, taking care to thread wires through the hole without dislodging the nuts.

There May Be More Than One Circuit

Especially in older bathrooms, the box for the light fixture may also contain wiring for a receptacle, vent fan, or other user. Be sure to test multiple times to be sure all the power has been shut off.

2 **MOUNT THE NEW BACK PLATE.** You may need to replace the box's strap to accommodate the new back plate. Thread wires through the back plate's center hole, making sure not to trap wires against the wall or the side of the box. Drive screws to attach the back plate to the box's strap, checking for level as you work. Attach the back plate to the wall with screws driven into wall studs. If you cannot hit a stud, use plastic wall anchors.

TIP In the example shown, the slots for the mounting screws are a bit too wide for the screw heads. If that is your situation, use washers, as shown in step 2.

3 **WIRE THE FIXTURE.** Place the fixture on a stable surface while you work. Splice the house's ground wire to the fixture's ground lead, or attach the ground wire to a grounding screw on the fixture. Splice the neutral and hot leads to the neutral and hot house wires (see p. 64).

4 **MOUNT AND TEST.** Slip the fixture's front plate over the back plate so the slots slide under the mounting screws. Tighten the mounting screws. Restore power and test the fixture.

Installing a Sconce Light

A wall, or sconce, light is installed in much the same way as a ceiling light. The wiring is the same, but it usually attaches via a swivel strap, which is easily adjustable so you can make the fixture nice and plumb.

If your existing wall box is controlled by a switch, simply install a standard fixture. If the wall box is not controlled by a switch—that is, if the old fixture is controlled by a pull chain—then either buy a fixture with a pull-chain switch or install one yourself as shown on p. 139.

▶ **Be sure to shut off power at the service panel. Test several times to verify that power is off, as shown on pp. 8–9. For double protection, use electrician's tools and work as if the wires were hot.**

2 **WIRE THE SCONCE.** Connect the ground lead to the house's ground wire (see p. 13 and pp. 52–53). In this setup, the ground is also connected to the strap. Splice the hot lead to the hot house wire and the neutral lead to the neutral house wire.

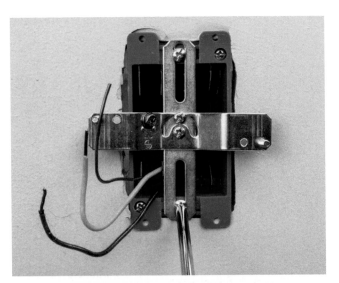

1 **INSTALL AND ADJUST A SWIVEL STRAP.** Remove the existing fixture and install a swivel strap. Loosen the setscrew on the horizontal bar, adjust it so it is level, and tighten the setscrew.

3 **MOUNT THE FIXTURE.** Slip the fixture into place, threading the mounting screws through the holes. Tighten the decorative nuts. Install the globe or shade, restore power, and test.

INSTALL HARDWARE. Remove the existing porch light. If the new light will not attach to the existing strap hardware, install the new strap that comes with the light. (In this case, the light mounts via a center stud.) Measure the canopy and scrape away any protrusions around the box that will keep the canopy from resting tight against the house.

WIRE THE FIXTURE. Thread the fixture's leads through the rubber gasket that came with the light, and make sure that you will be able to sandwich the gasket snugly between the house (or box) and the fixture's canopy (next step). Connect the ground wire (see p. 13 and pp. 52–53). Splice the black lead to the house's hot (black or colored) wire and the neutral (white) lead to the neutral house wire.

Installing an Outdoor Motion Detector Light

Motion detector outdoor or "porch" lights come on at night when motion is sensed, making them a serious deterrent against intruders. They also offer helpful no-switch-needed illumination when you bring in the groceries or take out the garbage when it's dark outside. They also can be turned on permanently for social gatherings. (In most cases, this is done by flipping the wall switch off and on several times.)

For this installation, you start with an outdoor light that is controlled by an indoor switch. If you don't have that, see Chapters 7 and 8 for instructions.

⟫ **Be sure to shut off power at the service panel. Test several times to verify that power is off, as shown on pp. 8–9. For double protection, use electrician's tools and work as if the wires were hot.**

ATTACH THE LIGHT. Work carefully so the rubber gasket will seal all rainwater out of the electrical box. Push wires and leads into the box as much as possible. Hold the gasket in place as you position the light, and then start to drive the mounting nut or screws. Check that the gasket is entirely inside the canopy and that it is not bent out of shape, and then finish fastening the light.

4 **MAKE ADJUSTMENTS.** Screw in LED light bulbs. On each lamp, loosen a nut, point the lamp in the desired direction, and tighten the nut to hold it in position. Point the motion sensor so it can sense movement. Adjust the light as discussed at right.

Solar Motion Detector Light

A unit like this needs no wiring. Position the solar panel where it will receive light during the day, position the motion detector light where you want it, and let nature take its course. The LED light will produce pretty decent illumination when it senses motion.

Adjusting the Sensor and Lamps

The sensors on these lights are quite sophisticated, so you can adjust how dark it needs to be for the light to operate, how long the light stays on when it senses motion, and how bright the light will shine.

Adjust the length of time you want the lights to stay on. Other adjustments are a matter of experimentation. At night, have a helper walk around and adjust the sensitivity; you want the light to come on when people approach the house, but not when they walk on a nearby sidewalk or when a branch moves slightly with the wind. Also adjust the brightness. Point the lamps so they help guide you as you approach the house but do not annoy the neighbors.

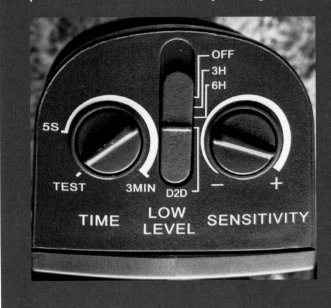

Choosing Fans

A ceiling fan not only adds a nice decorative touch but also helps keep a room cool in summer and can help move warm air around in the winter. Ceiling fans come in a wide range of styles. If you don't see a style you love at your home center, ask to look at a catalog; they should be able to order a fan from among hundreds of options. Because a ceiling fan is usually placed in the center of a room, it usually has a light. But if your room is already well lit, you may prefer the look of an unlighted fixture. For more tips on choosing fans, see p. 89.

SIMPLE AND ELEGANT. A modest fixture like this suits almost any décor. The globe looks a bit like an oversize light bulb, adding just a smidgen of whimsy.

READY FOR TAKEOFF. With three extra-long blades rather than the usual four, this model evokes an airplane propeller. The minimalist light and the stainless-steel housing make for a Deco look.

RED AND TWISTY. A colorful fan like this goes well with the colorful furnishings below. The twisted shape of the blades makes it fun to look at, too.

PORCH FANS. As long as the area is protected from rain, outdoor fan/lights can make a porch comfortable during hot days and nights. If you expect moisture, buy a unit that is made for outdoor use.

Installing a Fan-Rated Box

Most ceiling electrical boxes cannot be trusted to hold anything heavier than flush ceiling fixtures and modest pendants. If overloaded, they can come loose, and the fixture may even come crashing down. Whether you are installing a ceiling fan or a large chandelier, the box should be strong enough—and should be strongly attached enough—to suspend a weighty load. Even if a ceiling fan is not particularly heavy, it will vibrate, so the box needs to be good and strong.

In this section we show how to replace an existing box without running new cable. If you need a new box with new cable, see Chapters 7 and 8. (If you will do that, you may choose to run three-wire cable so you can install separate wall switches for the fan and the light.)

A variety of fan-rated boxes are available at home centers. Some attach to the side of a joist, others directly to the underside of a joist, and others have braces so they can be positioned between joists. The following pages show how to install most types.

TIP If your ceiling box feels firm, you may think it is strong enough to support a fan. However, the threads that you screw the hardware into are probably not strong enough. A real fan-rated box has very strong threads and bolts.

⟹ **Be sure to shut off power at the service panel. Test several times to verify that power is off, as shown on pp. 8–9. For double protection, use electrician's tools and work as if the wires were hot.**

Removing an existing box

A plastic ceiling box is likely attached to the side of a joist with two nails, with a flange through which fasteners are driven (see p. 175), or with a bracket. Here, we show how to remove one of those. However, in an old home there may be a "pancake" ceiling box that attaches to the plaster lath or to an old gas pipe. In those cases, the plaster or drywall around the box should be cut out.

TIP The cable that runs to the box will probably be stapled to the side of a joist. You don't want to cut through the cable or damage the sheathing, so cut and tap gently. Here, we show a surgical method, but if you are not sure you will not cut through the cable, first cut out a section of drywall, which you may need to patch later.

1 **FIND THE ATTACHMENT. Use a wall sensor to learn how the existing box is attached. Often, as in this case, it is attached to the side of a joist. You may be able to peek with a flashlight to learn more about the attachment.**

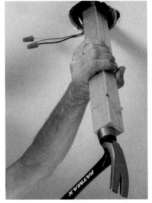

2 **DETACH THE BOX. Tapping with a hammer and a 2×2 may loosen the box and perhaps even detach it from the joist. You can also cut with a reciprocating saw or jigsaw equipped with a metal-cutting blade.**

3 **PULL OUT THE BOX. You may need to first push the box up, then tilt it and pull it down with pliers.**

Installing a side-mounted box

This type of fan-rated box mounts to the side of a joist. Installing it requires cutting the ceiling hole larger, so if the fan's canopy does not cover the entire hole, you will have to use a medallion or make a small patch in the ceiling.

1 **TRACE AND CUT THE DRYWALL. Slip the box into the hole and press it against the side of the joist. (You may have to slightly enlarge the hole first.) Trace its outline, and then cut with a jab saw. Finish the cut with a utility knife. Hold the box in place to make sure it will fit.**

2 **PREP THE BOX. Use a hammer and screwdriver to remove a knockout plug in the side of the box. The box comes with a plastic cable connector, which slips into the resulting hole.**

3 **RUN CABLE INTO THE BOX. Slide the plastic cable connector onto the cable an inch or so above where the bare wires emerge. Thread the wires through the box's hole, and then snap the clamp into the hole.**

4 **ATTACH THE BOX. The box comes with a long, heavy-duty screw. Drive it up into the joist to anchor the box firmly. If you encounter a knot in the joist so the screw is difficult to drive, remove the screw, drill a pilot hole, and drive the screw.**

Installing a box with a standard brace

This type of brace is made for situations where the framing is exposed. Installing one where the ceiling is finished is not difficult, though it will take some time to refinish the ceiling when you are done. It is a good option when you are not sure where the cable runs in the ceiling, or if there are any other obstructions, like ducts or pipes. It also allows you to adjust the location of the box; you can safely disconnect the cable from any staples to move it.

1 **MARK FOR THE HOLE.** Use a wall scanner to determine the location of joists. Start by poking a jab saw near where you think a joist is and saw until you hit the joist. Use a square to mark one side, as well as two parallel lines about 15 in. long.

2 **CUT THE RECTANGLE.** Cut along the parallel lines. Cut carefully; if you feel you are hitting an obstruction, stop and cut out a locator hole so you can avoid damaging any utility lines. Stop cutting when you hit the other joist. Then cut along the joists to finish making the hole. Keep the cutout piece for replacing (step 6).

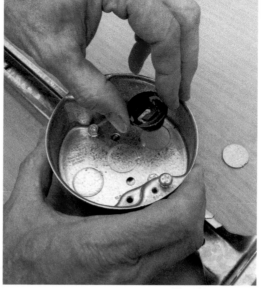

3 **ATTACH AND PREP THE BOX.** Adjust the brace so it is slightly shorter than the opening between joists. Drive screws to attach the box to the brace at the desired location (above left). Remove a knockout plug and insert a cable connector (above right). (Here we show a plastic cable connector, but you could use a metal one instead; see p. 180).

4 **RUN CABLE INTO THE BOX.** If needed, disconnect any staples holding the cable in place. Slip the cable through the connector so about ¾ in. of sheathing is showing in the box.

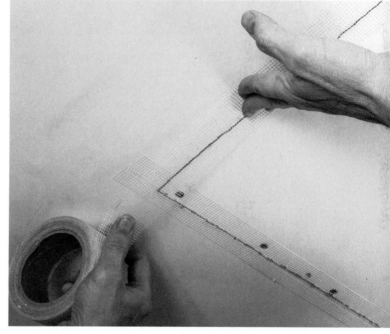

5 **ATTACH THE BAR AND ADD BLOCKING.** At each end, drive screws to attach the bar to a joist at the desired location. The brackets at the ends of the bar have a flange that automatically positions the box so it comes flush with the ½-in. ceiling drywall. Provide fastening surfaces for the patch by attaching scrap pieces of plywood or 1×2 along the bottoms of the joists.

6 **REPLACE THE PATCH AND FINISH.** You may be able to use the cutout from step 2 as the ceiling patch, though you will have to fill in the old hole and cut a new one if you have repositioned the box. Drive drywall screws to attach the patch. Cover the joints with mesh drywall tape and cover the tape with joint compound. Allow to dry, scrape, apply a second and third coat, and sand smooth. Prime and paint.

Installing an old-work brace and box

This brace and box is designed to fit back into the existing hole, so you don't have to cut out the ceiling and patch it afterward. It's a good solution when the hole is not next to a joist.

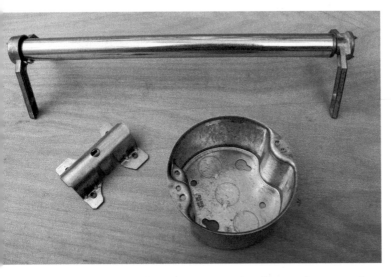

1 **ADJUST THE BAR.** Measure the distance between the joists. Adjust the bar so it is an inch or so shorter than the span between joists.

2 **INSERT THE BAR.** Slip the bar into the opening. Position it so it runs perpendicular to the joists and its feet rest on top of the ceiling drywall.

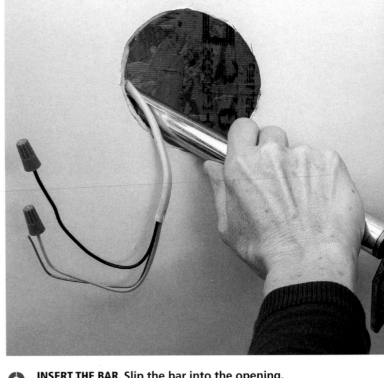

3 **TIGHTEN THE BAR.** Keeping the bar centered over the hole, turn the bar by hand until it snugs against the two joists. Then use pliers to tighten it very firmly.

4 **RUN CABLE AND ATTACH THE BOX.** Run cable into the box using a plastic cable connector, as shown in steps 3 and 4 on p. 87. Slip the attaching hardware over the bar and drive four screws to attach the box.

Installing a Ceiling Fan

Adding a ceiling fan is a popular project, because it both spruces up and adds comfort to a room for a fairly modest price and usually less than a day of labor.

Many ceiling fans come with a light fixture—which may be a single globe or several separate lights—included in the box. Another option is to buy a fixture without a light, and then choose among a variety of separate light kits that mount onto the fan. This gives you extra design options. Of course, you can also choose to install a fan with no light.

It's very important that the fan be mounted onto a fan-rated electrical box that is securely fastened to ceiling joists. See pp. 84–88 for different ways to accomplish this.

Choose a fan that's the right size for the room. A fan that's too large can feel windy, whereas one that's too small does little good.

FAN SIZES

BLADE LENGTH	MAX ROOM SIZE (SQ. FT.)
30 in. to 36 in.	100
42 in. to 48 in.	175
52 in. to 56 in.	350
60 in. or larger	400

"Ceiling Hugger" Fans

If you have a low ceiling or worry about hanging fan blades, you may choose a ceiling-hugger fan, which does not have a downrod. Be aware, however, that it will not move air as effectively as a fan that hangs lower. As a general rule, fan blades should hang at least 10 in. below the ceiling in order to create an effective breeze or updraft.

Switch options

When it comes to controlling both a fan and a light, there are three basic options:

- **Use the pull chains.** Most existing ceiling fixtures are controlled by a wall switch, with two-wire cable running from the switch to the ceiling box. If you hook up the ceiling fan in the simplest way, you can then operate the fan and the light using the pull-chain switches that come with the fixture. Be aware, however, that these pull-chain switches often fail after a few years, especially if they are used often. Replacing them is not difficult (see p. 139), but can be a bit annoying. And the pull chains can be difficult to reach, especially if the fan is over a table or a bed.

- **Two switches on the wall.** If you have three-wire cable running from the wall switch, you can install two separate wall switches, one for the fan and one for the light. This is the most elegant solution, but most ceiling fixtures have only two-wire cable running into them. If you want to replace your two-wire cable with three-wire, or run a second two-wire cable, see Chapters 7 and 8 for instructions. You may need to install a larger switch box for the two switches or buy a dual-control switch that fits into a single-gang box.

- **Remote control.** Also consider installing a remote-control sending unit inside the fan's canopy, which communicates with a remote-control switch that you can carry around or mount on a wall. This works with standard two-wire cable and a standard wall switch. You still use the wall switch to turn the entire unit on or off, and the remote to control the fan and light separately. See p. 92 for more on wiring options.

➡ **Be sure to shut off power and test to verify that power is off before wiring.**

ALL THOSE PARTS. Ceiling fans have a good number of small and large parts; this photo does not even include the light and its globe. Work systematically, and keep the parts well organized on a table.

1 **MOUNT THE BRACKET.** Thread the house wires through the mounting bracket, making sure not to trap them between the bracket and the box or wall. Drive screws to attach the bracket firmly to a strongly attached fan-rated box (see pp. 84–88).

OPTION: ATTACH BRACKET DIRECTLY TO THE JOIST. If your box is not fan rated, you may be able to attach the fan's bracket directly to an adjacent ceiling joist. Be sure the wiring will be mostly inside the box and entirely inside the fixture's canopy. You may need to patch the ceiling or install a medallion to cover up the ceiling box.

2 **ASSEMBLE AND ATTACH THE DOWNROD.** Following the manufacturer's instructions, thread the wires through the downrod and attach the downrod.

EXTEND THE FAN DOWNWARD. Fan manufacturers sell downrods of various lengths, so you can choose how far down the fan will extend. The 12-in. downrod shown here will bring the fan blades about 13 in. below the ceiling.

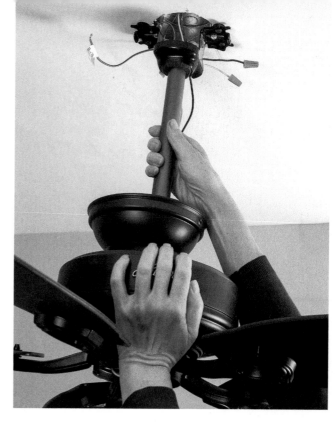

3 **ASSEMBLE THE FAN BLADES.** You can do this before or after mounting the fan on the ceiling. This model comes with the five fan brackets already attached to the motor, and the blades attach by simply pushing them down onto the rubber fittings. With other models, you may have to drive screws to attach the brackets as well as the blades.

4 **HANG THE FAN ON THE BRACKET.** Because they are heavy, ceiling fans are made so you can hang them by the bracket while wiring. Make sure the canopy is in position so you can slide it up to the ceiling after wiring. With this model, you slip the top of the downrod directly into the bracket; others hang temporarily by a hook on the bracket.

5 **WIRE THE FAN FOR PULL-CHAIN CONTROL.** Connect the fan's leads to the house wires. First connect the ground (see p. 13 and pp. 52–53). The fan will have a black lead, a colored lead, and a white lead. In this case, the black lead goes to the light and the colored lead goes to the fan. Here, we show the simplest wiring, where there are two house wires—black and white—coming from the wall switch. Splice the black and blue leads to the black house wire and splice the two neutrals (whites). Now both the fan and the light will be controlled by the switch; use pull chains to control each separately. For other options, see p. 92.

If You Have Three-Wire Cable

If three wires run first to the wall switch and then to the ceiling box, they can be connected to two wall switches, one for the fan and one for the light. At the ceiling box, splice the ground (see p. 13 and pp. 52–53). Splice the fan lead (often blue) to the black house wire and the light lead (usually black) to the colored (usually red) house wire.

If you have switch-loop wiring with power first entering the ceiling box (below) and three-wire cable running to the switch box, connect the grounds at the ceiling box. Splice the black house wire to the white wire running to the switch, and mark the white wire black. Splice the white house wire to the fan's white lead. Splice the black wire that leads to the switch to the colored (often blue) fan lead. Splice the red wire that leads to the switch to the black light lead.

Wire the switches as shown in the drawing. If the switches are already wired, chances are they are already wired correctly. After you restore power, flip the switches on and off to be sure.

TWO-SWITCH WIRING FOR A CEILING FAN

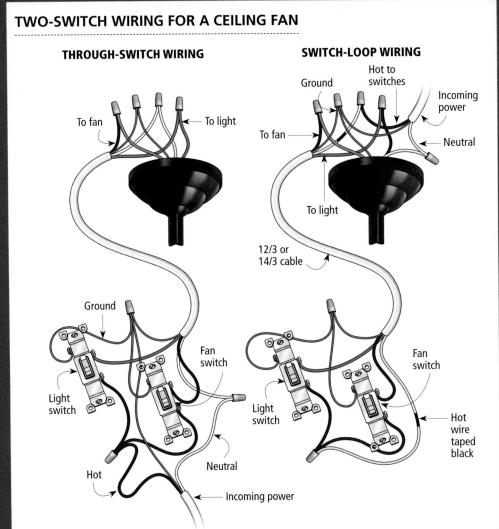

THROUGH-SWITCH WIRING

To fan / To light

Ground

Fan switch

Light switch

Hot

Neutral

Incoming power

SWITCH-LOOP WIRING

Ground / Hot to switches / Incoming power

To fan / Neutral

To light

12/3 or 14/3 cable

Fan switch

Light switch

Hot wire taped black

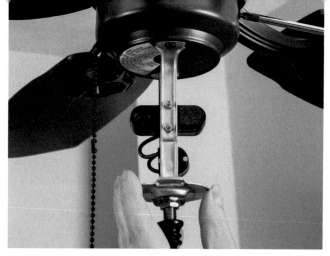

6 **ATTACH THE CANOPY.** Fold the wires and leads into the ceiling box as much as possible and carefully slide the canopy up so you do not trap any wires. Drive screws to mount the canopy to the ceiling bracket.

7 **ADD A LIGHT.** If you want a light, use one made for your fan model. Install the light to the bottom of the motor. Remove the bottom plate, splice the wires, and attach the light to the fan.

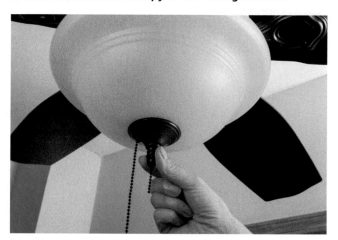

8 **FINISH.** Install the finishing touches, following the manufacturer's directions. Here a single globe covers both light bulbs; one pull chain hangs along the side of the globe, and the other is threaded through a hole in its center. Restore power and test.

WIRE FOR A REMOTE CONTROL. Without much trouble and for a modest cost you can install a remote-control receiver unit inside the fan's canopy. It will communicate with a remote-control switch that controls both the fan and the light. Wire the receiver following the manufacturer's directions. Connect the grounds. Splice the three white wires together. Splice the other wires so the fan and the light buttons on the remote will control the fan and the light. Carefully wrap wires either up into the ceiling box or near the receiver.

Using Up and Down Settings

Even if you have a remote control, you will probably need to use the reversing switch on the body of the fan when you want to change the direction of the fan's spin. It is most common to have the fan turn counterclockwise to push air down; this creates a breeze that you can feel. However, consider reversing the fan to turn clockwise, so it pulls air up. This helps gently circulate warm heated air during the winter. Or, if you have opened a window on a summer night, it can draw cooler outside air into the room.

TIP If the fan wobbles when running, first inspect the fan brackets and blades to see that they are correctly and firmly connected. If that does not solve the problem, use a fan balancing kit, which is usually provided with the fan. Follow instructions to experiment as you attach a small weight to one or another of the blades, then test, until you achieve stability at even the fastest fan speed.

Low-Voltage Landscaping Lights

Low-voltage (LV) lights are an easy way to make your backyard or front lawn a more inviting place and to discourage intruders as well. LV landscaping systems, which often come in kits that contain all you need, connect to a standard electrical receptacle but also have a transformer that ramps down the power so that a very low level goes to the lights. Because you simply plug into a receptacle, there is no need to shut off power at the service panel.

Older landscaping lights delivered only a small amount of illumination, but today's LED lights are nice and bright. If they are too bright for your taste, you may be able to position them behind plantings to mute the glow.

If you need to install a GFCI-protected outdoor receptacle, see pp. 114–116 and pp. 185–186. As an alternative, drill a hole through your siding and run the cord into the house to plug the unit in there.

1 **ASSEMBLE THE LIGHTS.** Most outdoor LV lights assemble quickly with no tools. Push a stake into the bottom of the shaft, making sure not to trap the cord with the electrical connector. Then add the globe and top cap to the other end of the shaft.

2 **ROUTE THE CORD.** Run the cable from the receptacle you will plug into (step 7) to the area where you want the lights. If the cable must run through a lawn, use a shovel or garden trowel to slice a very thin trench about 4 in. deep and run the cable through it. Along a flower bed, as shown, simply lay the cord on the ground.

3 **ARRANGE AND STAKE THE LIGHTS.** Position the lights in a pattern that pleases you and poke their stakes into the ground. If the ground is very hard, you may need to use a shovel or trowel to make a slot in the dirt or lawn and insert the stake into the slot.

4 **MAKE THE CONNECTIONS.** Most electrical connectors have barbs that poke into the cord to make the electrical connections. Hold the two pieces of a connector aligned so they poke into each of the cord's wires and push them together until they snap. The connection should feel firm. Though it's not required, you can wrap the connection tightly with electrician's tape for added protection.

5 **BURY THE CORDS.** Pull the cord fairly taut so it doesn't want to bunch upward, and push it down into the soil or under the lawn.

7 **PLUG IN.** Plug the transformer/controller into an electrical receptacle and position the sensor so it is not in a dark place during the day. This unit simply turns lights on at night, whereas others have controllers with timers and other features.

6 **COVER UP.** If you ran the cord through a trench in the lawn, push the lawn back into place and press down to smooth it out. In a garden bed, cover with soil, mulch, and other material to make the lines invisible.

Switches and Receptacles

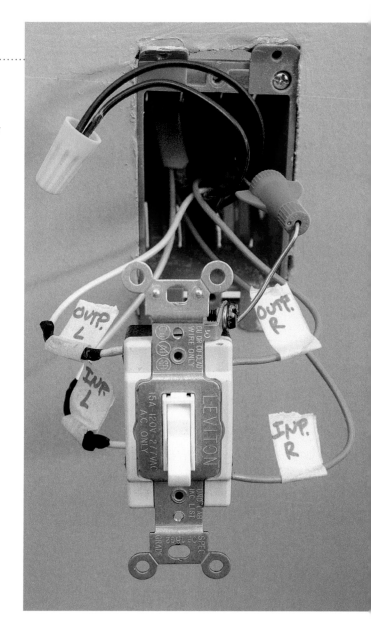

ELECTRICAL DEVICES—switches and receptacles—can last a very long time, but they do sometimes fail and need replacing. More often, people find they would like to upgrade their devices. You can make your home a bit more adaptable to your needs by replacing a standard on–off toggle switch with a dimmer so you can adjust the brightness. You can install a switch that turns on when it senses motion or turns on and off at certain times of the day, and there are many other possibilities.

Standard receptacles are often replaced with units that have additional safety features—most often GFCI or AFCI protection. Some are tamper-resistant, making it nearly impossible for a youngster to accidentally get electrocuted.

You can also change the style and color of your switches and receptacles for a sleeker or flashier look. All the projects in this chapter are replacements that can be accomplished using the tools and skills described in Chapter 2. To install switches and receptacles in new locations, you'll need to run cable and install boxes, as shown in Chapters 7 and beyond. The exceptions are the easy switches shown on pp. 98–99, which can simply be plugged into receptacles or screwed into lamp sockets.

Easy Switches

The switching devices shown on these pages mostly require no tools (or skills, really) to install—just plugging or screwing into receptacles or lamp sockets. And they often give you the option to dim or time the lights.

The brightness of lights in your home has an effect on mood, and it's nice to be able to easily control the light level to make your home feel comfortable. Most of the dimmer products shown here are battery operated and need no hardwiring. Their range will be affected by battery life. The dimmer unit also works as a remote control that can be attached to a wall or cabinet. In some cases you can also use your phone as a remote by downloading an app. The remote function makes it easy, for instance, to dial up or down dining room lights without having to leave the table or to control a bedroom light without leaving bed.

You may also be able to use your phone app as a timer for lights. There are many creative possibilities with timers. Some people like to use them to wake up in the morning (rather than an alarm) or to have their coffee waiting. Others use them to automatically adjust the thermostat at night. Some people like to have the lights on when they come home from work, and fish owners may use a timer to be sure the aquarium light goes off at night.

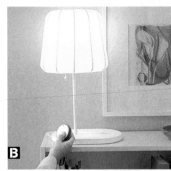

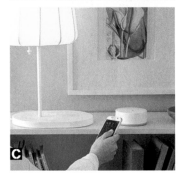

TWO DIMMER OPTIONS. To install this dimmer, just plug the special bulb, which contains a sending unit, into a lamp. Now you can control the lamp with a dimmer [A]. The dimmer can be handheld [B] or can be mounted onto the wall. By downloading an app, you can also use your phone to control the light level [C]. On this unit, the range for a remote or phone is about 30 ft., as long as walls do not interfere. You may be able to control several lights with a single dimmer, turning them all on or off or dimming them at the same time.

MOUNTED REMOTE. A remote control like this can be mounted on a wall or under a cabinet. This simple remote can dim lights to two levels and can control several lights at once within a distance of about 18 ft. (It works best when the batteries are fully charged.)

MOTION SENSOR. A motion sensor switch like this can be mounted anywhere in a room to turn the light on when someone enters or when there is movement in the room. The sensor can also be used to control several lights at once.

The light(s) stay on for an adjustable length of time, often from 1 to 10 minutes. The product shown is battery operated and does not require a hardwired installation. Its range is up to 15 ft. at a 120-degree angle.

The most common use for motion detector lights is on the exterior of a home (see pp. 81–82), but they can also be useful inside a home. The front entrance or just inside the garage may be the most popular place, and if your hands are full you'll be happy you don't need to set things down to turn on a light. There are, of course, numerous possibilities. Some people use them in the hall so that it's easy to find the bathroom at night. Others use them along stairs so the light comes on just before needing to ascend or descend. Other possibilities are in a closet or at various spots in the basement, like the utility room or stairs.

OPEN DOOR, LIGHT COMES ON. This battery-operated light strip (using rechargeable batteries) can be attached wherever needed. The round motion sensor turns the light on and off when you open and close a door.

LOOKS LIKE THE REAL THING. This one looks much like a regular wall switch, but there are no wires. Install a battery into the switch and attach it to a convenient spot on a nearby wall with two screws. (You will probably need to use plastic anchors, as shown on p. 76.) Plug the receiving unit into a receptacle, and plug the lamp into the receiving unit. Now it will seem like you have a standard wired light with switch.

SCREW-IN DIMMER TIMER/ SENSOR CONTROL. This works with a lamp that is near a window that gets good sunlight. Turn the light off. Unscrew the bulb, screw the timer/sensor control into the socket, and screw the bulb in. Rotate the control so the photo sensor is facing a source of sunlight. Turn the lamp back on and program the control.

You can make the light stay on for a set number of hours. Or press "Random," which will turn the lights on and off at unpredictable times, thereby discouraging intruders.

Dimmer with Remote and App Control

This ensemble offers three ways to control one or two lamps that you plug into a wall receptacle: by a wall-mounted switch, using a small remote-control switch, and using your cell phone. With the phone app you can control the lamps from anywhere in the world. To install this unit you will need to follow steps in Chapters 2 and 4 for splicing wires and installing a wall switch.

The sending unit connects to the modem via a cable, and the switch is wired in a normal way. Once everything is connected and you have downloaded the app, you can control the fixture either with a sophisticated wall switch or remotely on your cell phone.

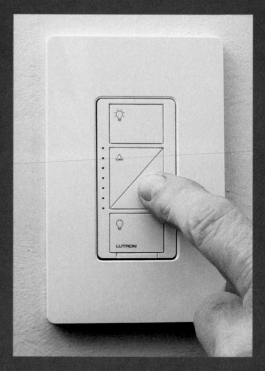

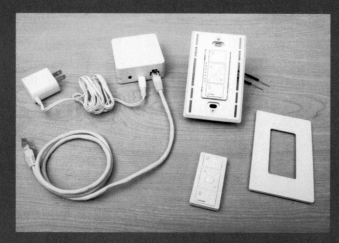

ALL THE COMPONENTS. This unit comes with all the parts needed for dimming and turning on and off a light in your home.

LOTS OF CONTROL. Once installed, you can control the light with a wall switch that either toggles on and off or dims up or down.

PLUG IN. The controlling module plugs into a wall receptacle and into an Internet router.

CONTROL VIA MOBILE PHONE. The light can also be controlled with your cell phone using a free app.

Replacing a Single-Pole Switch

A single-pole switch, which controls a light or other fixture from a single location, is the most common type of switch. If a switch does not turn the light on and off and power is present, or if the toggle feels loose, replace it. You can also test the switch, as shown below. If a switch is one of a pair of switches that controls a fixture from different locations and if it has three terminals (plus the ground), then it is a three-way switch (see pp. 104–105 for replacing).

Depending on whether you have through-switch or switch-loop wiring, you may find two cables (four wires plus the grounds) or one cable (two wires plus the ground) entering a box. See p. 92 for more information. If there are four wires, the two neutral (white) wires are spliced together and the two black or colored hot wires connect to the terminals. If there are two wires, the white neutral should be marked black with tape or paint and both connect to the switch terminals.

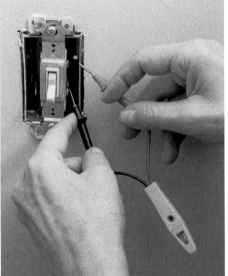

1 TEST FOR POWER. Remove the cover plate and test for the presence of power. If you have a metal box, touch a tester's probes not only to each terminal and the ground but also to each terminal and to the box (left). (If you have metal conduit with no ground wire, the box is part of the ground path.) In a plastic box (far left), touch probes to the ground wire and to each of the switch terminals (or the wires leading to the terminals).

➠ **Be sure to shut off power at the service panel. Test several times to verify that power is off, as shown on pp. 8–9. For double protection, use electrician's tools and work as if the wires were hot.**

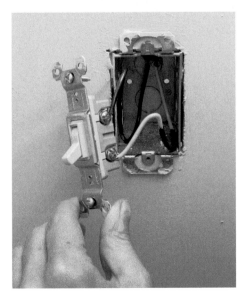

2 REMOVE SWITCH AND INSPECT WIRING. Unscrew the mounting screws holding the switch to the box and gently pull the switch out. See that the wiring is in sound condition. If insulation is nicked, cracked, or otherwise damaged, see p. 129 to repair it. Also see if the wires are long enough so you can cut and restrip them.

TIP Touching the tester probes to the two switch terminals is not a good test. If you touch the probes to just the two switch terminals, the tester will light up only if power is traveling through the switch. If the light fixture has a burned-out bulb or is not working, you could get a negative result even if power is present.

Testing Switches

With a continuity tester (or multimeter, as shown on p. 45) you can test to see if a switch is damaged. On a single-pole switch (top), clip to one terminal and touch the probe to the other terminal. If the light glows with the switch's toggle in the ON position and does not glow in the OFF position, the switch is OK. If not, replace it.

To test a three-way switch (bottom), clip to the common terminal, which is darker colored and marked with a "C" or the word "common." Touch the probe to one of the other (non-ground) terminals. The tester's light should glow with the toggle in one position, but not in the other position. Test the other terminal in the same way. If either test fails, replace the switch.

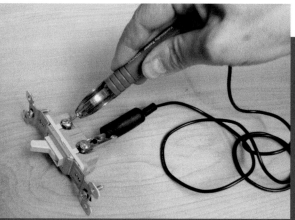

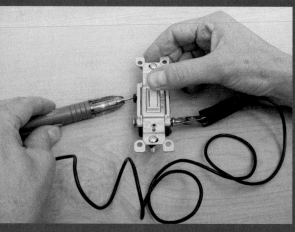

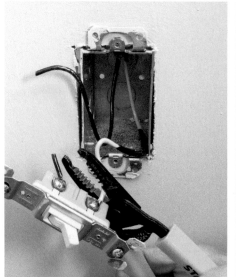

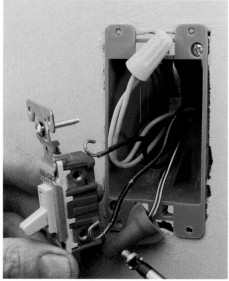

3 **CUT WIRES, OR BACK OUT SCREWS.** Wire ends that get bent, straightened, and bent again may break, so be judicious about bending. If there is plenty of wire length, make cuts near the switch (left). If wire length is minimal, back the terminal screws all the way out to minimize twisting when you reattach the wires to the new switch (right).

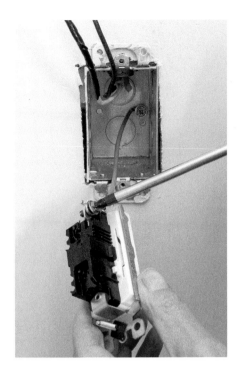

5 **CONNECT GROUNDS.** See p. 13 and pp. 52–53 for recommended and required grounding methods. If the existing ground wiring is in sound shape and correct, you can use it. If not, make modifications, which usually involve adding pigtails (see p. 53). In this example, a system with metal conduit has no ground wire. You can update the arrangement by adding a grounding pigtail, which attaches to a hole in the box via a grounding screw.

4 **CLEAN OUT ANY DEBRIS.** Dust and debris can pose a slight fire hazard or cause the box to overheat. Take a few seconds to wipe or vacuum out any schmutz.

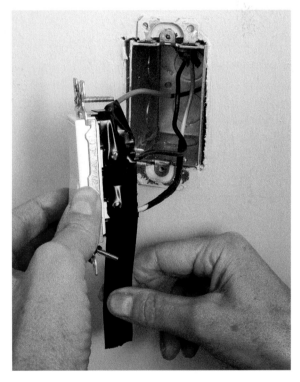

6 **WIRE THE NEW SWITCH.** See pp. 46–47 for stripping wires and attaching to terminals. The switch shown above has push-in terminals. For other switches, follow the steps on pp. 50–51 for bending wire ends and attaching to standard terminals.

7 **WRAP WITH TAPE.** Many electricians skip this step, but it does provide extra protection because it covers all live metal inside the box. Tightly wrap electrician's tape around the switch body to cover the terminals, taking care to avoid trapping the mounting screws.

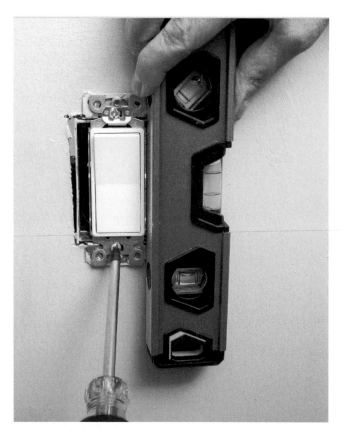

8 **MOUNT THE SWITCH. Fold the wires back into the box.**
Drive the mounting screws to attach the switch to
the box. If you are not sure that the box is plumb, use
a level to check as you drive the screws. Add the cover
plate. If the plate does not lie flat against the wall, or if it
does not completely cover the opening, see pp. 126–127
for possible fixes.

Replacing Three-Way and Four-Way Switches

If a fixture (or group of fixtures) is controlled by two switches in two different locations, the switches are three-ways. These can be wired in several different ways (see pp. 211–212), but replacing one is pretty simple. Just make sure the correct wire goes to the common terminal.

⫸ **Be sure to shut off power at the service panel. Test several times to verify that power is off, as shown on pp. 8–9. For double protection, use electrician's tools and work as if the wires were hot.**

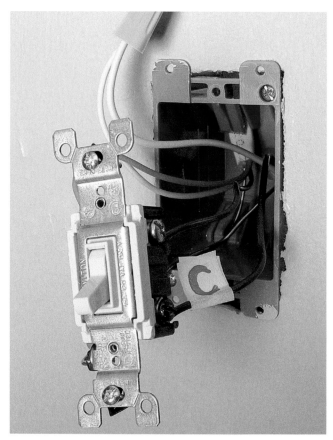

1 **MARK THE COMMON WIRE. The common terminal is**
a different color—usually darker—than the others
and is likely marked with a "C" or the word "common." To
make sure you don't get confused, clearly label the wire
for the common terminal with a piece of tape.

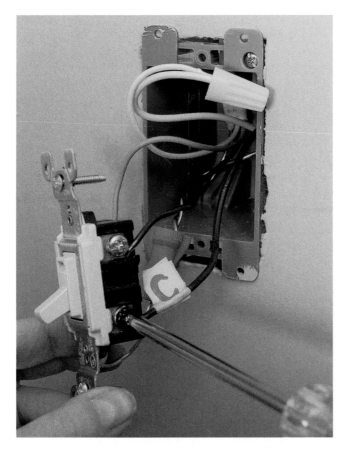

2 WIRE THE NEW SWITCH. Follow the instructions on pp. 101–103 for removing the old switch and replacing the new one. When you wire the ground, upgrade the wiring if needed (see pp. 52–53). Connect the common wire to the common terminal. The other two wires can be wired to either of the other two terminals.

Replacing a Four-Way Switch

If three or more switches control a single fixture (or group of fixtures), one of them will be a four-way switch. (The others will be three-ways.) See p. 213 for typical wiring. To replace a four-way, it's safest to mark each of its four wires so you can replace them in the same configuration.

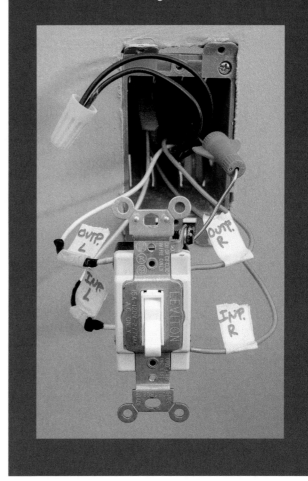

Wiring Dimmers and Other Specialty Switches

You can usually replace a standard single-pole switch with a dimmer, timer, motion sensor, or other special-duty switch with little difficulty, using the methods shown on pp. 101–104. However, there are some differences:

- These switches are often bulky, so if your electrical box is small and crammed with wires, you may have to work extra hard to carefully arrange and stuff in the wires. In extreme cases you may choose to use a box extender.
- Some specialty switches require a separate neutral wire in the box. This means that they will work if you have through-switch wiring but not if you have switch-loop wiring (see the drawings on p. 92).

- Some specialty switches have standard terminals, but others have leads—short lengths of stranded wire—instead. That means that you will splice house wires to leads rather than connecting to terminals.

⮕ **For all the switch replacements on the following pages, be sure to shut off power at the service panel. Test several times to verify that power is off, as shown on pp. 8–9. For double protection, use electrician's tools and work as if the wires were hot.**

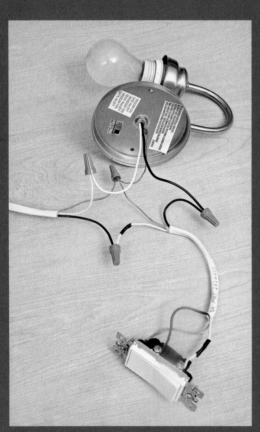

Some Switches Need a Neutral

As explained on p. 92, if a switch box has switch-loop wiring (photo left), there are only two wires (plus the ground): a black wire and a white wire that should be marked black. If there is through-switch wiring (photo right), the box will have four wires (plus the grounds).

Some specialty switches, such as dimmers and manual timers, have only two leads or terminals (plus the ground). They can be installed with either type of wiring. Others, such as a pilot-light switch or electronic timer, have three leads or terminals (plus the ground). They need a separate neutral connection, and so can be installed only with through-switch wiring.

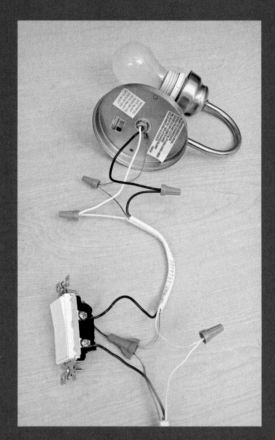

Installing a dimmer

To install a dimmer switch, follow the general instructions for replacing a two-way switch on pp. 101–104.

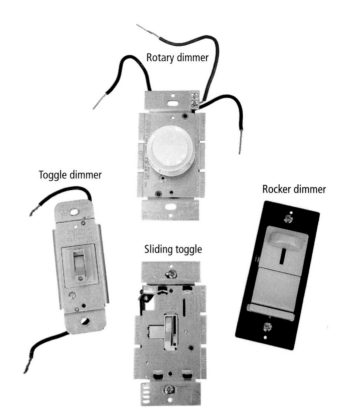

Rotary dimmer

Toggle dimmer

Rocker dimmer

Sliding toggle

DIMMER OPTIONS. An inexpensive rotary dimmer (top) works fine, but you may opt for other types. A toggle dimmer (left) looks like a regular toggle switch but raises the light level as you raise the toggle. The switch at bottom has a toggle that turns on and off, plus a small sliding toggle that sets the light level, so you get the "remembered" brightness when you flip on the switch. The switch at right has a rocker toggle and a sliding brightness control.

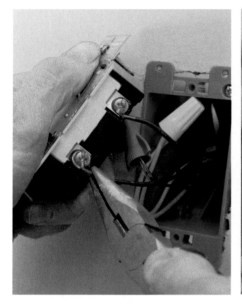

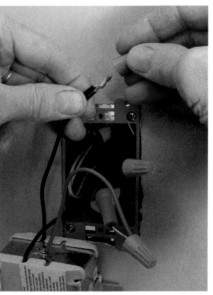

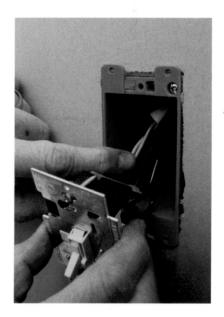

1 CONNECT TO TERMINALS OR LEADS. Shut off power and test that power is off. Disconnect the old switch, clipping and restripping the wires if they are long enough or backing off screws and carefully removing wires if they are short. Connect the grounds (p. 52). Either connect to terminals or splice leads, depending on the switch.

2 PUSH THE WIRES INTO THE BOX. Because a dimmer is bulkier than a standard switch, carefully arrange the wires and then press them firmly into the box.

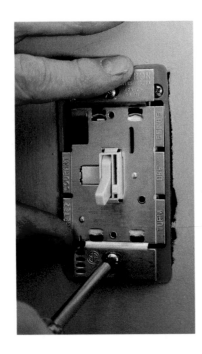

3 **MOUNT THE SWITCH. You** will probably finish pushing the wires back when you drive the mounting screws to attach the switch to the box. Drive screws firmly all the way, so the switch is nearly flush with the wall surface.

INSTALLING A THREE-WAY DIMMER. Before removing the existing three-way switch, mark the wire that goes to the common—usually darker-colored—terminal (see p. 104). Connect the grounds and splice the neutrals together. Connect the remaining wires to the traveler terminals.

Single-location three-way dimmer

If two switches each control a single fixture or group of fixtures, you have a three-way setup. When making a replacement with existing wiring you can probably install only one three-way dimmer; the other must remain a regular on–off toggle.

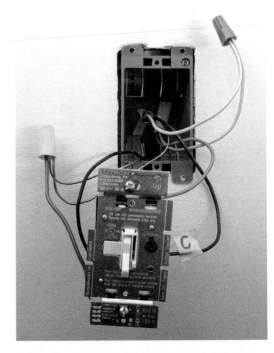

Dimmer Pairs

You can, for a hefty price, buy a pair of three-way dimmers that work together. One switch has a sending unit and one is a receiver, so it is essentially a remote-control arrangement. Wiring depends on the arrangement of cables, as shown on pp. 211–212.

Manual timers

Wire a manual timer as you would a standard two-pole switch. Simply connect the two black (if there are two cables entering the box) or the black and white-marked black (if there is only one cable) to the switch's terminals, or splice to the switch's leads.

Electronic timers

An electronic timer can turn a light on and off at preset times and days of your choosing. Wiring is very straightforward once you've identified the feed wire (see the sidebar below).

MANUAL TIMERS. These devices are a good option when you want to be sure that a light or fan will not be left on for hours. The user turns the dial, which turns on the fixture until the mechanical dial runs down.

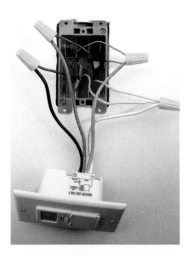

1 WIRE THE SWITCH. Splice the black switch lead to the feed wire, the red lead to the load wire, white to white, and green to the ground.

2 PROGRAM. Follow instructions for programming. The model shown here can have up to seven presets, which repeat weekly. Some models have rechargeable batteries, so they remember your presets even if there is a power outage.

Identifying the Feed Wire

When installing switches that need a neutral wire, you need to know which of the hot (black or colored) wires is the feed wire—the wire that brings power into the box. (The other hot wirecarries power from the switch to the fixture.)

➧ Turn off power at the service panel and test to verify that power is off. Remove the wires from the old receptacle. Spread them apart, so there is no danger of them touching each other or a metal box—and no danger of you touching their bare ends as you work. Make sure nobody comes close to the box as you work. Restore power, then work very carefully: Touch the probe of a voltage detector to each hot wire. The tester will glow to identify the feed wire. Shut off power again, and mark the feed wire with a piece of tape.

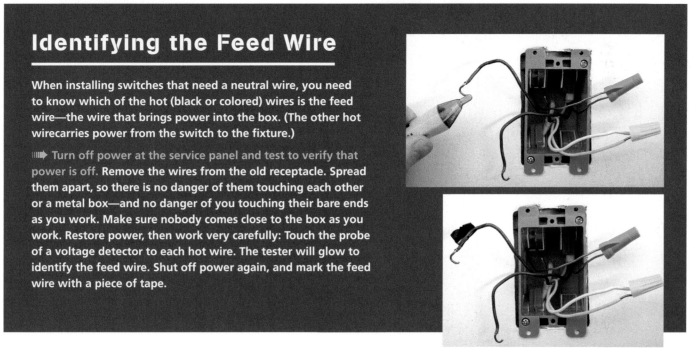

Two ways to use a switch/ receptacle

A switch/receptacle, also called a switch-outlet, can be used in two very different ways. For either use, the box must have two cables entering, so there is a separate neutral wire.

- You can replace an existing receptacle or switch with a switch/receptacle so that the receptacle is controlled by the switch. That way, you can plug in, say, undercabinet lights and use the switch to turn them on and off.
- You can replace a switch with a switch/receptacle whose receptacle is always hot (not controlled by the switch). This will give you another usable outlet for plugging into.

DIFFERENT STYLES AND CONFIGURATIONS. The two switch/receptacles shown here not only look different but also have terminals in different places. When wiring, pay attention to the location of the connecting tab, which joins the switch and the receptacle. If you supply power to the terminal on the side with the connecting tab, then the receptacle will be always hot. Connect it on the other side and the receptacle will be controlled by the switch.

▶ For either installation type, be sure to shut off power at the service panel. Test several times to verify that power is off, as shown on pp. 8–9. For double protection, use electrician's tools and work as if the wires were hot.

RECEPTACLE ALWAYS HOT. Determine which of the hot wires is the feed wire that brings power into the box (see p. 109). Connect the grounds. Connect the feed wire to the switch terminal on the side with the connecting tab. Connect the other hot wire to the brass terminal on the other side. Use a pigtail to connect the neutral wires to the silver terminal.

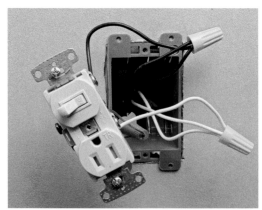

RECEPTACLE CONTROLLED BY THE SWITCH. Connect the grounds. Connect the two hot wires to a pigtail and the pigtail to the switch terminal on the side that does not have the connecting tab. Use a pigtail to connect the neutrals to the silver terminal.

Pilot-light switch

A pilot-light switch can serve either of two different purposes:

- If the switch controls a remote fan or other fixture that you cannot see and you'd like to know when the fixture is on, install a pilot-light switch that will glow when the switch is turned on.
- If a switch is located in a place that is often dark—say, a garage—and you sometimes need a bit of help finding the switch, wire it so its little light always glows. In a bedroom, this wiring arrangement creates a small night-light.

PILOT-LIGHT SWITCH

SWITCH CONTROLS LIGHT

If you want the light to come on only when you flip the switch, connect the grounds. Splice the neutrals to a pigtail and connect the pigtail to the silver screw on the side without the connecting tab. Connect the feed wire to the dark brass terminal by the switch on the side with the connecting tab. Connect the other black or colored wire (load) to the terminal near the switch on the other side.

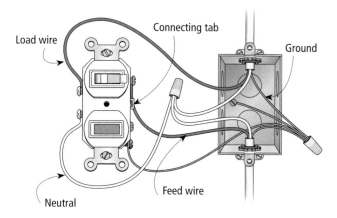

Load wire

Connecting tab

Ground

Neutral

Feed wire

LIGHT ALWAYS ON

If you want the light to always be on, wire it in the same way as shown but reverse the black wires: The feed wire goes to the terminal by the switch on the side with no connecting tab, and the load wire goes on the side with the connecting tab.

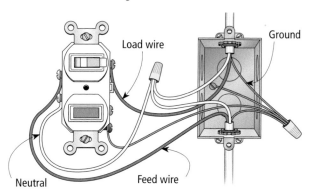

Load wire

Ground

Neutral

Feed wire

➠ For all the specialty switches on these pages, be sure to shut off power at the service panel. Test several times to verify that power is off, as shown on pp. 8–9. For double protection, use electrician's tools and work as if the wires were hot.

The Connecting Tab on a Switch

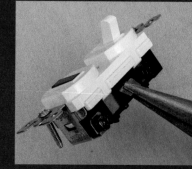

With some switch installations you may need to identify, and maybe even remove, the "connecting tab." On a receptacle a connecting tab joins the two hot terminals (see p. 113). On a specialty switch a tab joins two functions: for example, the receptacle and the switch on a switch/receptacle, or (as shown here) the small light and the switch on a pilot-light switch.

Motion-sensor switch

Also called an "occupancy sensor," this switch does what it says, turning on when motion in the room is sensed. Some also have a daylight sensing feature, which prevents the switch from turning on when the room is already lit. Switches like this often give you the option of use for either two-way or three-way switching.

WIRE FOR SINGLE SWITCHING. If the switch will be a normal two-way, cap the blue lead by cutting off any bare wire and screwing on a wire nut. Splice the two neutral wires together and connect the grounds to the green lead. Splice the black lead to the feed wire (which is black or colored) and the red lead to the other black or colored wire, which is the load wire.

A Couple More Specialty Switches

There are plenty of other special-duty switches, and here are two examples. With a countdown timer (left), you can press any of the top four buttons to make a fan or light stay on for a preset number of minutes. Following instructions, you can use the buttons to set the timer for other time intervals.

A humidity sensor/fan control (right) turns a fan on when a room reaches a predetermined level of humidity, and shuts the fan off when the humidity drops.

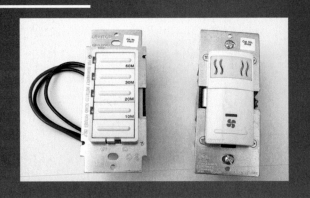

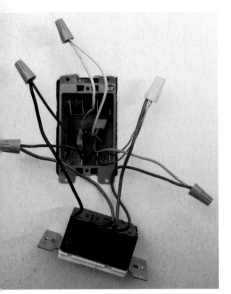

WIRE FOR THREE-WAY SWITCHING. The switch can be wired for three-way switching in several different ways, depending on the wiring configurations; see pp. 211–212 for the possibilities. The sensor switch can be partnered with a standard three-way switch or with another three-way sensor. Here, the red and blue leads are spliced to traveler wires (see p. 211), and the black lead is spliced to the feed wire. Follow manufacturer's instructions, which should cover every wiring possibility.

PROGRAM THE SWITCH. Use a small Phillips screwdriver to make adjustments. If your switch has a daylight sensor, you can program it for the level of light sensitivity. You can also program how long the light will stay on once motion has been detected.

Replacing a Receptacle

This is a fairly easy project, so go ahead and replace a receptacle if it is damaged in any way, if it has paint splotches, or if you just want a change of style. To peruse the various types of receptacles available, see pp. 28–29.

If a receptacle fails to deliver power, first try plugging in a receptacle analyzer. If that does not reveal a problem, ▐▌➡ **shut off power,** remove the receptacle, and test it, as shown on the facing page. If the receptacle passes the test, check the wires and connections. If you have an older box, see pp. 128–130 for ways to repair wiring.

Install the correct type of receptacle. If its circuit is on a 20-amp breaker or fuse with 12-gauge wire, install a 20-amp receptacle. If the circuit is 15 amps with 14-gauge wire, install a 15-amp receptacle (see pp. 24–25).

The steps shown here are for wiring a mid-run receptacle, where the wires lead to other receptacles downstream. If you have an end-run receptacle, there will be only one cable (two wires plus the ground) in the box.

▐▌➡ **Be sure to shut off power at the service panel. Test several times to verify that power is off, as shown on pp. 8–9. For double protection, use electrician's tools and work as if the wires were hot.**

TIP Should the grounding holes be positioned up or down on a receptacle? Electricians and inspectors differ on the subject. If your inspector has an opinion, follow that. Otherwise, choose the arrangement you like and stick with it for a pleasing consistency of appearance.

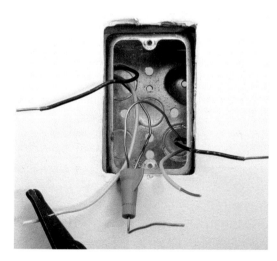

1 **TEST, REMOVE, AND INSPECT.**
With the power off,
remove the receptacle. Note the
configuration of the wires so you
can install the new one in the same
way. Also check out the wires to
be sure none of them are nicked or
otherwise damaged.

Split Receptacle

If a receptacle has its connecting tab on the hot side removed, then
either the outlets are on different circuits (which often happens with
kitchen counter receptacles) or one of the outlets is controlled by
a wall switch (which is sometimes the case in a bedroom or living
room). Mark one of the hot wires to indicate where it goes. Use a
small slot screwdriver or a pair of long-nose pliers to remove the tab
on the new receptacle, and wire the receptacle.

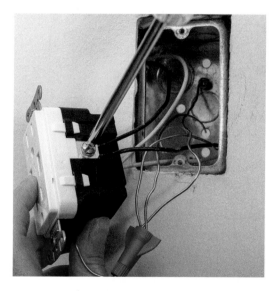

2 **DISCONNECT AND PREP THE WIRE ENDS.** As
discussed for replacing a switch (p. 102), if
the wires are long enough you can cut them near
the receptacle and then restrip the wire ends. If
the wires are a bit short, back off the terminal
screws and remove the wires. Try not to bend and
rebend the bare wires too much, or they could
break. In the example shown, the wire ends are
left straight to insert into poke-in terminals.

3 **WIRE THE NEW RECEPTACLE.** Connect the
grounds; you may need to upgrade the ground
connections (see pp. 52–53). Connect the neutral wires
to the silver terminals and the hot wires to the brass
terminals. (This receptacle has poke-in terminals that
are captured with a screw-in connector.)

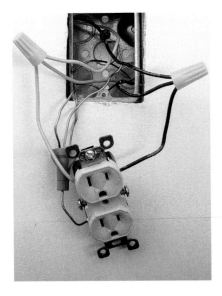

WIRING WITH PIGTAILS. Some inspectors prefer mid-run receptacles to be wired with pigtails, as shown, rather than connecting to all four terminals. When wired this way, you can remove one receptacle and the other receptacles on the circuit will stay energized.

4 WRAP. Many pros skip this step, but it provides extra protection. Wind electrician's tape around the body of the receptacle to cover the terminals and any exposed bare wires. Take care not to trap the mounting screws as you wrap.

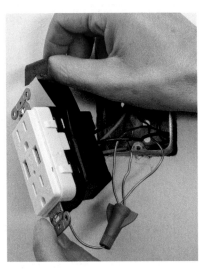

5 MOUNT. Gently push the wires back into the box and push the receptacle into position. Drive the mounting screws most of the way. Hold a level next to the receptacle and finish driving the screws when it is plumb. Replace the cover plate. Restore power and test with a receptacle analyzer.

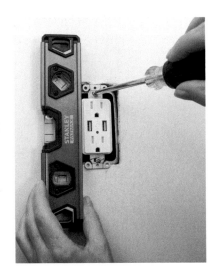

Installing a GFCI and/or AFCI Receptacle

A ground-fault circuit interrupter (GFCI) senses when electrical current takes a wrong path. For instance, if the current travels to metal in an appliance or fixture or to another conductor such as a human body rather than traveling back to the service panel via the neutral wire, a GFCI will sense an imbalance between power out (via the hot wires) and power in (via the neutral wires) and will instantly shut off, preventing a potentially dangerous situation. GFCIs are required in areas that tend toward dampness, like bathrooms, kitchen countertops, and outdoor areas.

An arc-fault circuit interrupter (AFCI) detects when power jumps in an arc from a hot wire to a neutral wire. The most common cause of an arc is a cord with damaged insulation, so that its hot and neutral wires touch each other. An AFCI shuts off power immediately when an arc is detected.

GFCI and AFCI protection can be supplied with receptacles, as shown on these pages, or with circuit breakers, which protect entire circuits. (If you install a GFCI and/or AFCI breaker, standard receptacles on the circuit will all be protected.) Nowadays it is common to have receptacles and circuit breakers that are both GFCI and AFCI protected.

Whether you install a GFCI, AFCI, or a combo GFCI/AFCI receptacle, the wiring is the same. You can install one for single- or multiple-location protection.

⮕ **Be sure to shut off power at the service panel. Test several times to verify that power is off, as shown on pp. 8–9. For double protection, use electrician's tools and work as if the wires were hot.**

TIP If you are replacing a mid-run receptacle, you'll need to identify the feed wire, which brings in power (see p. 109).

GFCI RECEPTACLE, MULTIPLE-LOCATION PROTECTION

A GFCI receptacle can protect devices* downstream if wired as shown. Attach wires from the power source to terminals marked "line." Attach wires continuing downstream to terminals marked "load." As with any receptacle, attach hot wires to brass screws, white wires to silver screws, and a grounding pigtail to the ground screw. Note: Here, only ground wires are spliced; hot and neutral wires attach directly to screw terminals.

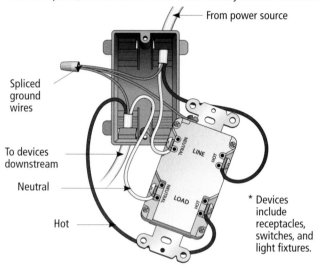

From power source

Spliced ground wires

To devices downstream

Neutral

Hot

* Devices include receptacles, switches, and light fixtures.

GFCI RECEPTACLE, SINGLE-LOCATION PROTECTION

This configuration provides GFCI protection only at the GFCI receptacle. All devices downstream remain unprotected. Here, splice hot and neutral wires so the power downstream is continuous and attach pigtails to the GFCI's "line" screw terminals. With this setup, receptacle use downstream won't cause nuisance tripping of the GFCI receptacle.

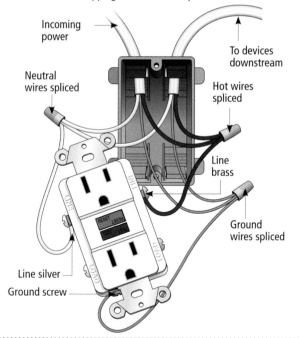

Incoming power

To devices downstream

Neutral wires spliced

Hot wires spliced

Line brass

Ground wires spliced

Line silver

Ground screw

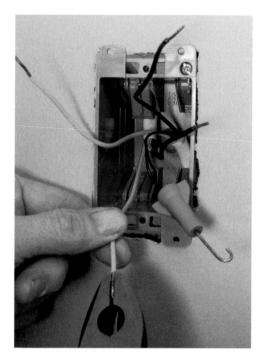

1 PREP THE WIRES. Disconnect the existing receptacle. If the wires are long enough, cut and restrip them, as shown on pp. 46–47. If not, back off or remove the terminal screws. To prepare wires that were wrapped around terminal screws for poke-in terminals, straighten them with lineman's pliers as shown.

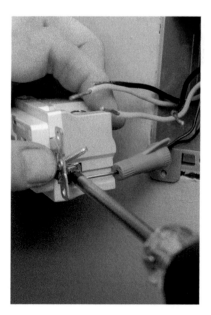

2 CONNECT THE GROUNDS. Attach ground wires to suit your electrical box; upgrade them if needed, as shown on pp. 52–53.

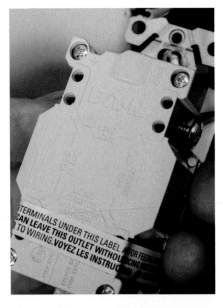

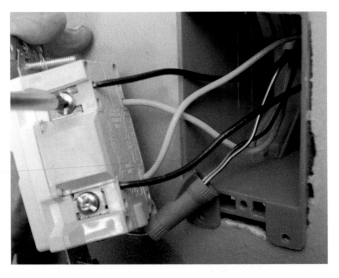

3 **DETERMINE LINE AND LOAD.** The back of the receptacle tells you which terminals are "line" and which are "load." If you want to protect other receptacles downstream from the one you are installing, you will connect the feed wire and its neutral to the line terminals. Then you will connect the other wires, which lead to other receptacles or a fixture, to the load terminals.

4 **WIRE THE GFCI.** Attach the feed wire and its neutral to the line terminals and the wires leading out of the box to the load terminals.

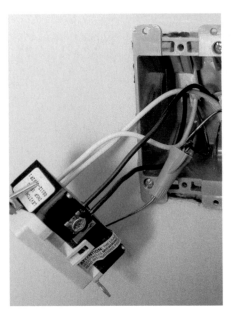

SINGLE LOCATION WIRING. If you want to protect only this one receptacle, attach wires to the load terminals only.

5 **MOUNT AND TEST.** Drive screws to mount the receptacle, add the cover plate, and restore power. Test the receptacle by plugging in a receptacle analyzer (p. 33). Press the TEST button; the receptacle should no longer supply power. To restore power, press RESET.

High-Voltage Receptacles

High-voltage receptacles and appliances are anywhere from 220 volts to 250 volts. The numbers all mean the same thing: Voltage may vary a bit from house to house, but that does not affect installations. (We'll just refer to them as 240 volts, for convenience.) Electric water heaters, central air-conditioning and heating units, cooktops, and other appliances are often "hard wired," meaning there is no receptacle; see p. 239 and pp. 242–243 for hard wiring. Electric ranges, dryers, individual air conditioners, and some other appliances use 240-volt receptacles.

High-voltage receptacles serve specific purposes. Some deliver 30 amps, some 40 amps, and some 50 amps. The wires that supply power to them need to be thick enough: 10-gauge for 30 amps, 8-gauge for 40 amps, and 6-gauge for 50 amps or 55 amps. They have different slot and hole arrangements to prevent plugging an appliance into the wrong receptacle.

Receptacles are sometimes described according to the purpose they usually serve:

- 20-amp or 30-amp air-conditioner receptacle
- 120/240-volt (also called 124/250-volt) 30-amp dryer receptacle, which supplies high voltage for the heater and motor and low voltage for the control panel
- 120/250-volt 50-amp or 40-amp range or cooktop receptacle (high voltage for the heating units and low voltage for the clock and controls)

In some cases, an older receptacle will be configured to receive only three wires—red and black hots and a white neutral—but newer codes and newer appliances call for four-wire receptacles. The newer plug cannot be inserted into the older receptacle, which must be changed. To run new wires or cable for a four-wire receptacle, see p. 223.

Warning! High Voltage!

Working with wiring for high-voltage receptacles does not call for much in the way of new skills. But because it is more dangerous, work even more carefully than usual. A 120-volt shock can harm you, but a 240-volt shock may kill. Test carefully to be sure power is off.

▥▶ Be sure to shut off power at the service panel. Test several times to verify that power is off, as shown on pp. 8–9. For double protection, use electrician's tools and work as if the wires were hot.

Stripping Thick Wires

To strip thick (10-gauge and thicker) stranded wire, use a knife with care. Roll the insulation against the knife, bearing down enough to slice most but not all the way through the insulation. Bend and twist the insulation with your fingers to pull it off, and then twist the stranded wires to consolidate any frayed ends.

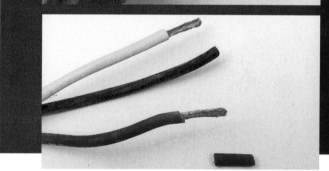

TESTING FOR POWER. Use a multitester to test for power in several ways. Hold the prongs of a tester well back from the metal ends. Insert one probe into a side (hot) slot and one into a top or bottom (neutral or ground) slot. Try this with several combinations of side plus top/bottom slots. Also hold one probe against the metal casing (which should be grounded) and insert the other probe into each of the slots. Then insert the probes into the two side (hot) slots. Of course, the tester should not glow during any of these tests.

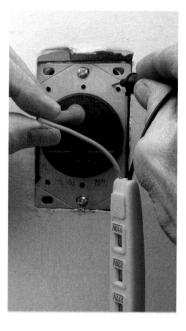

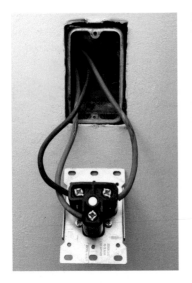

FLUSH WALL RECEPTACLE. To replace a faulty wall receptacle, follow the procedures shown on pp. 112–113. Make sure you know which wire will go where on the new receptacle; you may need to mark one or two of them with a piece of tape. Make sure that the wires are the correct gauge for the receptacle. These thick wires are usually stranded rather than solid, and in most cases the connection is made by poking the bare ends into holes and tightening screws.

ENCASED RECEPTACLE. This type of receptacle may be mounted on a floor or wall. Remove the screws that mount the old unit and detach the wires. Mount the new plate to the floor or wall, attach the wires, and add the cover.

AIR-CONDITIONER RECEPTACLE

A typical large-BTU window air conditioner requires a 240-volt, 20-amp receptacle. Two-wire 12-gauge cable runs from a double-pole 240-volt circuit breaker to the receptacle box. The white wire is marked black at either end to show that it is hot.

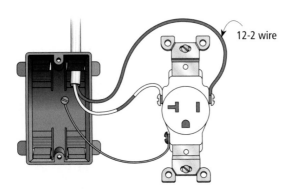

12-2 wire

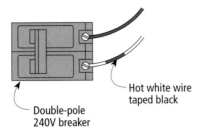

Hot white wire taped black

Double-pole 240V breaker

Running Raceway Wiring

Here's a way you can run wiring for new services without threading cable or conduit through walls. Raceway wiring is also called surface-mounted for obvious reasons. Wires run through channels made of plastic or metal and then into boxes that protrude from the wall.

Most people would not want to see a lot of raceway channels and boxes on their walls, but this system makes for an appropriate look in a utility room, basement, or laundry room. And if installed neatly and painted the same color as the wall, it is not obtrusive.

PAINTING MAKES IT RECEDE. Metal raceway can be easily painted to match the wall. Plastic raceway can be painted if you sand it first and/or first apply an alcohol-based primer, but there is no guarantee it will not peel.

Before installing, make sure that you will not overload a circuit. Find out which circuit the starter receptacle box is on, and see pp. 154–155 for calculating load. If you're adding only a switch and a light, as shown here, and if the light will use an LED bulb, the added load will be minimal. However, if you're also adding a new receptacle, factor in the sorts of things that will be plugged into it and add that to your calculations.

Plan the job in a detailed way. Determine where you want each switch, fixture, and receptacle box and note every place where you will need to make an inside or sideways turn. Channels generally come in 5-ft. lengths, which you can cut as needed. Plan to avoid end-to-end joints as much as possible.

➠ **Be sure to shut off power at the service panel. Test several times to verify that power is off, as shown on pp. 8–9. For double protection, use electrician's tools and work as if the wires were hot**

TIP Here we show a simple installation with two-wire (plus the ground) wiring for a switch and light. With raceway you can also run three-wire cable, and you can install almost any wiring configuration that is shown in Chapter 8.

Buy enough wire—black, white, and green for the ground—to suit the circuit and the devices and fixtures. (The most common type of wire, suitable for most uses, is labeled THHN, meaning the insulation is thermoplastic high-heat-resistant nylon.) Use 12-gauge wires for a 20-amp circuit and 14 gauge for a 15-amp circuit. Buy enough of each wire to run the total length of the installation, plus 10 percent.

1 STARTER BOX. You will attach all the channels and box plates, then run the wire, and then install devices and fixtures. At the box where you will grab power, pull out the receptacle and install the starter box plate—which has a large opening—by driving the screws that you would use to mount the receptacle.

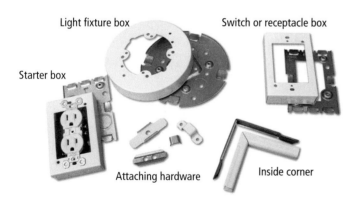

Light fixture box

Switch or receptacle box

Starter box

Attaching hardware

Inside corner

LOTS OF PARTS. Here are some of the parts you may use. In addition to these, you may want a deep box if you are installing a bulky switch or receptacle, or an angle turn for rerouting on a wall or ceiling. Of course, you'll also need wires and channels. You could also buy plastic raceway, which is less expensive. However, plastic is bulkier and a bit dowdy in appearance; plus, it cannot be painted as well as metal and is more easily damaged.

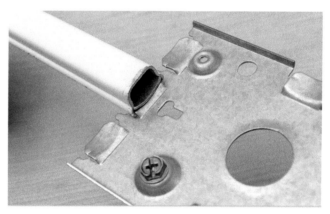

INSERTING CHANNELS. At many points you will slip a channel into a plate or other hardware piece. It's easy to get this wrong, so work carefully. The tab on the hardware must slip behind the back of the channel, as shown, for a tight connection and to ensure that wires will not get damaged when you run them.

TIP Some installers also install clips a few inches away from box plates. This does add rigidity but is not necessary, because a proper connection to the plate will hold it securely.

2 MARK FOR CLIPS AND CHANNEL LENGTH. If a channel run is longer than 4 ft., install one or more clips to help secure it to the wall or ceiling. First slip a channel into a plate, as shown on p. 119. Use a level on a wall and a square on a ceiling. Mark alongside where the channel will go. Here, the channel has also been marked for cutting to length, to end up with a switch box at a standard 50 in. or so above the floor.

3 INSTALL CLIPS. Install a clip alongside the line you drew in step 2. The clip's plate is alongside the layout line, while its "arms" are outside. Unless you can hit a wall stud or ceiling joist, use a plastic anchor to secure the screw (p. 76).

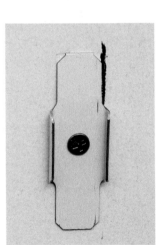

4 CUT A CHANNEL. Use a hacksaw or a reciprocating saw with a metal-cutting blade to cut channels to length. After cutting, use a slot screwdriver or a small rasp to remove any burrs that could damage the wires as they pass through.

END-TO-END CONNECTION. Where you need to extend a straight run, use a coupling connector and cover the joint with a two-hole strap.

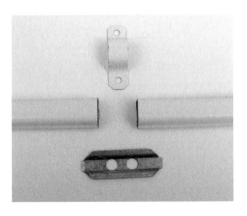

5 ASSEMBLE A PLATE AND CHANNEL AND ATTACH. Slip a plate into a channel, and then insert the channel into a plate or fitting at the other end. If there is a clip, snap the channel into it. You can probably push it in by hand, but you may need to tap it. Use a block of wood rather than a hammer, to keep from marring the channel.

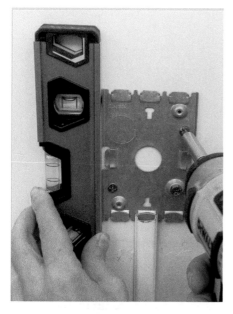

6 **ATTACH A PLATE.** Check that the channel is fully inserted into the plate and drive screws to attach it to the wall. Use plastic anchors if you do not hit a framing piece.

7 **INSTALL A CHANNEL UP TO AN INSIDE CORNER.** Whether running up to a ceiling or over to another wall, slip an inside corner plate into one end of a channel. Hold it in place and mark for a cut that is about ¼ in. shorter than a tight fit. Cut the channel.

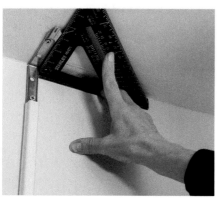

8 **INSTALL THE CORNER.** Slip the cut end into the plate. At the other end, position the corner plate up against the other surface; you may need to slide the plate slightly to make a tight fit. Check that it is square and drive screws to attach. At an inside corner you are likely to hit a framing member. If not, use plastic anchors.

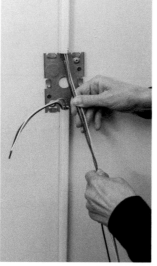

9 **PREP FOR A LIGHT.** This may take a bit of noodling. Before you attach a fixture plate to a ceiling, learn how all the pieces go together. Prep the plate by installing studs up through the back side so you can attach the cover later. Make sure your fixture will fit over the cover.

10 **RUN OVER TO A FIXTURE.** To install a ceiling fixture, use the same method as for running from the starting plate to a wall plate. Instead of using a level, use a large square to guide the run. If the channel runs across joists, use a stud finder to locate joists and position clips there. If the joists run parallel and you do not run across a framing member, use toggle bolts, as shown in step 6 on p. 72.

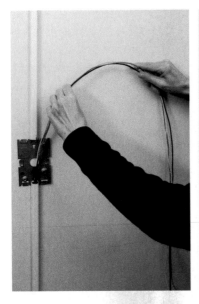
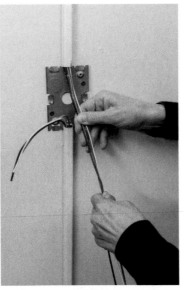
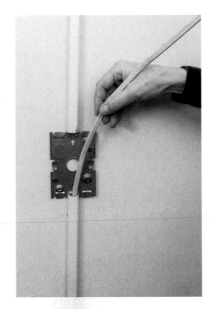

11 **RUN WIRES TO PLATES.** Tape the wires together at one end and push them up from the starter plate to the first box plate or corner plate—or the other direction, as shown at left. At each plate, leave about 10 in. of wire protruding through the channel, cut, and start a new run to the next plate (right).

RUN CABLE INSTEAD. Rather than running individual wires, you could run cable. Strip the sheathing at one end, run the cable, and cut the cable 11 in. past the end of the channel. Then strip sheathing there as well.

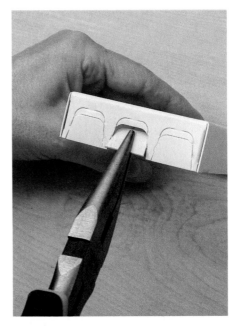

12 **RUN THROUGH CORNERS.** At a corner, pull a foot or so of wire length through, and then push the wire in the other direction.

13 **REMOVE KNOCKOUTS.** Use long-nose pliers to remove the side knockouts on boxes so they can slip over the channels.

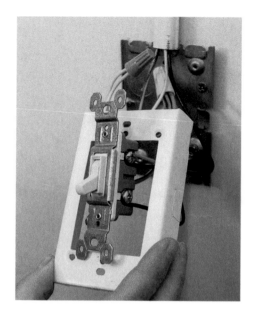

14 **WIRE DEVICES.** Attach a switch or receptacle to its box, then strip wires and wire the device as shown on pp. 50–51. Attach the box with screws to the plate and add the cover plate.

15 **INSTALL A FIXTURE.** Attach the cover and then attach the strap to the cover. Wire the fixture (see p. 64) and attach it to the strap.

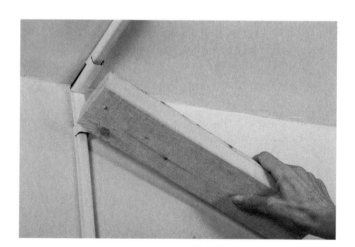

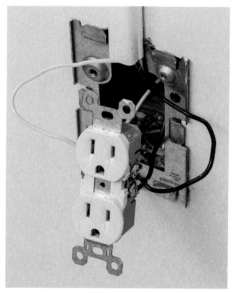

16 **SNAP ON COVERS.** Covers for corner fittings, end-to-end couplings, and other fittings all snap on. You may need to tap gently with a piece of wood or with a hammer.

17 **WIRE THE STARTER UNIT.** Attach wires to grab power. Connect the grounds (see p. 13 and pp. 52–53). Here, we show an end-run receptacle, so you need only attach the wires to the open terminals. If a receptacle is mid-run, use pigtails to connect the wires (see p. 53).

Electrical Repairs

IT IS A FACT OF LIFE that people repair things less often today than in years past. And if a fixture is not operating, there's a good chance that you would rather replace it with something more attractive anyway. But there are still definitely occasions for making repairs to an electrical system. Many of these repairs are pretty simple, so you can save money by doing them yourself even if you have little experience.

Here are a few examples:

- If your receptacle or switch cover plates do not lie flat on the wall or do not cover their openings, you can fix the problem in several different ways.

- Old wiring may have damaged wires, or it may be difficult to attach a fixture in an old box. Often (though not always) there are simple solutions.

- A cherished but defective old lamp or antique chandelier can almost always be made to work like new for a small outlay of cash and time.

- If there is a circuit that often overloads and shuts down when you have two or more appliances running, there may be easy ways to solve the problem.

Work safely when making repairs. Unplug any lamps before working on them, of course. Shut off power and test to verify that power is off before working in boxes. Also, approach repairs methodically, and prepare an organized workspace so you will not lose any small parts as you proceed.

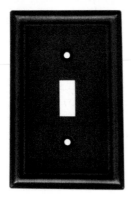

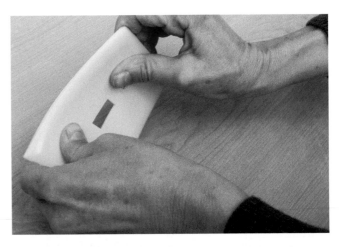

FLEXIBLE PLATES. If a cover plate cracks when you tighten the mounting screws, buy a higher-quality plate that is almost unbreakable. The extra flexibility may allow the plate to hug the wall more tightly.

DECORATIVE COVER PLATES. At a home center or from online sources you can buy decorative cover plates in almost any style and design. You can also paint a cover plate: First rough it up a bit with some sandpaper and apply a coat of alcohol-based primer to ensure the paint will stick.

Cover Plate Problems

If a cover plate (also called a wall plate) is cracked or even dingy, replace it. Plates are usually available in white or ivory, but some come in a sort of light ivory that may be called "light almond." Black, gray, brown, and metallic plates are also available, but you may need to special-order them. You can also buy decorative plates.

If a plate does not lie flat against the wall, either the wall is not flat, the device (switch or receptacle) protrudes out from the wall, or both. Some solutions to these problems are shown here.

▬▶ Before working on a switch or receptacle, be sure to shut off power at the service panel. Test several times to verify that power is off, as shown on pp. 8–9. For double protection, use electrician's tools and work as if the wires were hot.

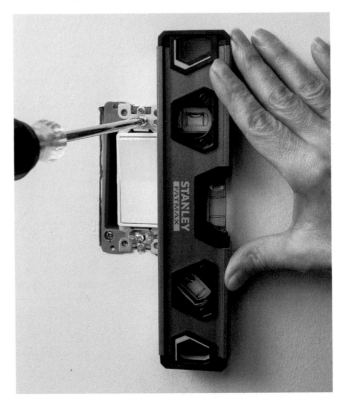

STRAIGHTENING OUT. If a device is slightly tilted, remove the cover plate and slightly loosen the two mounting screws. Push one or both ends sideways, check for level or plumb, and then retighten the screws. If this does not solve the problem, the box is seriously out of alignment. You may be able to drive a screw sideways into a stud to realign it, as shown on p. 129.

Plates that protrude

If a plate stands proud of the wall so you can see a gap between it and the wall, sometimes clipping the device's tabs will solve the problem. But if clipping does not solve the problem, you have a couple of other options, as shown.

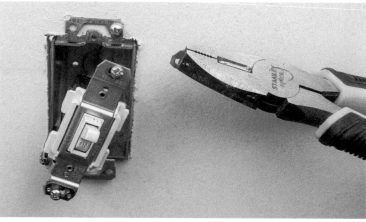

REMOVE DEVICE TABS. In this situation, the device has "ears" at the top and bottom that hold the switch away from the wall. Twisting off the tabs from the switch will allow the switch to come a good ⅛ in. closer to the wall (above right).

BUILD OUT THE WALL. If the wall surrounding the device is wavy, use joint compound or spackle and a taping knife to straighten it out. If the box protrudes, you can also build out the wall using the same method. You may need to apply two or three coats, scraping and sanding between coats, to achieve a smooth surface. Apply primer, then paint.

FOAM BACKING. This product, sold as "sealer," serves as weatherstripping to keep the device box sealed against cold air. It can also work to fill in small gaps between the cover plate and the wall. You may need to apply two or more layers of the backing. Its color blends well with ivory cover plates.

Problems in Boxes

Problems with electrical boxes are simple to fix when the framing is exposed, but usually the walls are finished with drywall or plaster. Fortunately, most modern boxes are in good shape. Older wiring, on the other hand, has its challenges.

▥➡ **Before working inside a box, be sure to shut off power at the service panel. Be aware that it is possible for there to be two circuits present in the box, so shutting off one breaker may not remove all power. Test several times to verify that power is off, as shown on pp. 8–9. For double protection, use electrician's tools and work as if the wires were hot.**

Common Issues with Old Wiring

Even when they do not use knob-and-tube wiring (see p. 34), very old homes often have distinctive wiring characteristics and problems, which can include the following:

- *Switch-loop wiring.* Although through-switch wiring is the norm in older homes, switch-loop wiring, in which the power goes first to the fixture box and then to the switch, was the norm in the old days of electrical installations. That means that when the switch is turned off the hot wire in the fixture box stays energized—so by all means, shut off power at the service panel, rather than just turning the switch off, before working on a fixture.

- *Neutral switching.* For complicated reasons we can't go into here, in many old homes switches control not the hot wire but the neutral wire. In most cases, you can leave the wiring as it is with no danger, as long as the fixture is not removed. But again, be aware that the box may be hot even if the switch is turned off.

- *Hard-to-identify wires.* Much old wiring (especially in cold-weather areas where coal was used for heating for many years) has blackened over time. That means you may not be able to tell a white neutral wire from a black or red hot wire. If you wipe a small section of wire with a cloth dampened with a soap solution, you can usually see the original color.

- *Pancake boxes.* Ceiling boxes in old homes are often very shallow, and sometimes a number of cables run through them. This means that wiring can get very crowded and cramped inside a "pancake" box. It's usually a good idea to buy a ceiling fixture with a fairly large canopy so you don't have to tightly cram all those wires back into the box.

- *Cracked insulation.* Where wires run inside cable, they can stay in good shape for a very long time. But where they emerge in a box and are exposed to air, the insulation can become brittle and cracked. Follow the instructions on the facing page for repairing damaged insulation.

- *Old fixture hardware.* Old switch and receptacle boxes usually have screw holes in the same places as newer boxes, so installing a new device is no problem. You can even replace an old push-button switch with an exact replacement or with a standard switch. But old fixture boxes often have much more difficult arrangements. (In some cases, pancake boxes are actually attached to old gas pipes.) See p. 131 for attaching new to old.

- *Taped splices.* In the days before wire nuts, wires were spliced together using friction tape, which has a rough texture. Done correctly, these splices are secure and safe. They are also very difficult to remove.

- *Grounding methods.* Some older homes are ungrounded (see p. 131), but many employ metal conduit or the metal sheathing of BX cable as the ground path. Test receptacles with a receptacle analyzer to be sure they are grounded—and correctly polarized as well (see p. 12). If your system is ungrounded, consider having it thoroughly updated.

- *Possible mistakes.* Any home may have wiring mistakes, but they are often an issue in an old home, especially when a do-it-yourselfer has done some remodeling work. Be wary, continually testing for power and grounding, and if you see something that you don't completely understand, call in a pro for evaluation.

SECURING A BOX. To firm up or realign a box, use a stud finder to find which side of the box the stud is on. Detach the device and move it as far as possible over and out of the way; it may be necessary to remove the device altogether. Using a drill bit that is about the same thickness as the screw you will drive, drill a pilot hole sideways through the box. Then drive a screw. Drive tightly if the box is metal. If the box is plastic, avoid pushing too hard, which could crack the box.

Box that's loose or crooked

If a box is less than firmly attached or leaning noticeably, it should be reattached. It may be necessary to cut a hole in the wall, reattach the box, and then patch the hole you cut—a pretty tedious process, but within the reach of a do-it-yourselfer. However, because boxes are usually attached to the side of a stud, you can firm one up to a certain extent by driving an additional screw or two. Drill a pilot hole through the box first.

Repairing damaged wires

Check that all wires are protected. If armored cable enters a box, there should be a red plastic bushing to protect the wires from rubbing against metal, or a special connector that contains a bushing. If the wiring is old, its insulation—which may be cloth—can get cracked, exposing bare wires. And if insulation is cracked in one place, it is brittle enough to crack elsewhere as well. So even if the wiring is in working order, it's a good idea to wrap the wires to protect them.

The example below shows a common situation in old homes, where a thin lead wire is attached to a thicker house wire with rough-textured "friction tape" rather than a wire nut. Unwrapping friction tape is very difficult. You could cut the house wire just short of the friction tape and restrip it, but often that will leave you with a wire that is too short. Shrink-wrap tubing, available at home centers and hardware stores, is a good solution.

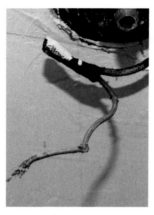

1 SLIP ON A SHRINK-WRAP TUBE. Purchase shrink-wrap tubes for your thickness of wire. They should fit a bit snugly, so you don't have to shrink them too much. Identify a section of wire that needs protection and slip the tube over it.

2 HEAT TO SHRINK. Use a hair dryer set on high to shrink the wrap. Hold the dryer very close to the wrap and wait until it starts shrinking before moving on to another section.

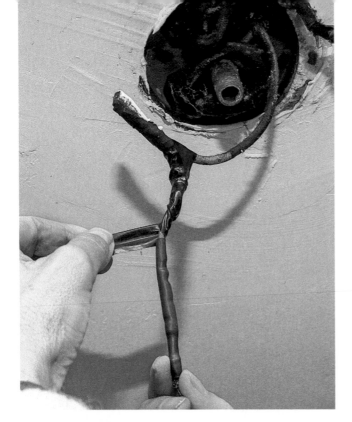

HARDWARE OPTIONS. A number of adaptive hardware pieces can be used to anchor a strap or center stud. If you live in a neighborhood with old houses, you may be more likely to find these at a hardware store than at a home center. A gas pipe typically has a ⅜-in. diameter; a simple nut can hold a strap. Electrical center studs are usually ³⁄₁₆ in., so you may need a reducer fitting.

3 **FINISH WITH TAPE.** Use professional-quality electrician's tape to cover areas you can't reach with the tubes. Work carefully, so the sticky side consistently faces inward while you wrap.

Adapting old boxes for new fixtures

An older fixture box, like the pancake box shown here, may need some adaptive hardware before it can accept a standard strap or center stud.

CHANDELIER FITTING. For a pendant (or chandelier) you will need a gizmo like this. It reduces from ⅜-in. gas pipe to a ³⁄₁₆-in. electrical stud and has space for the wires to emerge inside the box.

Watch Out for Gas

Many older boxes are attached to old gas pipes. (For a time in the early 20th century, some homes had gas lights. When homes were retrofitted for electricity, the pipes were used for attaching hardware.) In most cases the gas to the pipe was shut off when wiring was installed. But in rare cases it wasn't, so it's possible that if you remove the cap, gas will come shooting out. If you hear and/or smell it (which you will, immediately), screw the cap back on and call in a plumber to shut off the gas. If you smell only a slight odor, it may just be gas that remained in the pipe. Wait a day, checking often, and if the smell goes away you should be fine. But it's a good idea to call in a plumber anyway.

CENTER STUD. Here, a simple reducer fitting allows you to screw on a center stud.

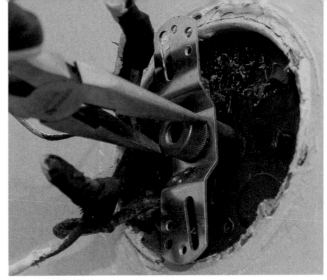

NUT AND STRAP. A ⅜-in. nut (in this case, the same nut as used in the left photo) can be used to secure a standard strap.

Replacing an Ungrounded Receptacle with a Grounded Receptacle

If you have an old ungrounded receptacle, it's possible that the metal box into which it is mounted is actually grounded, using conduit or armored cable as the ground path. Remove the cover plate and insert one prong of a voltage tester into the smaller (hot) slot while you touch the metal box. If the tester glows, the box is grounded.

You could simply install a grounded receptacle; its mounting tab will make good contact with the box.

Use a receptacle analyzer to be sure it is grounded. For a more secure connection, ➡ Shut off power. Move wires off to the side, drill a hole in the back of the box, and drive a screw to install a grounding pigtail. Attach the pigtail to the receptacle's grounding screw when you install it. (In this example, the wires had minor insulation damage, so we wrapped them with electrical tape.) Test with a receptacle analyzer (p. 33).

Cord and Plug Replacements

If a lamp or small appliance cord is damaged near the plug, or if the plug itself is damaged, you could replace the entire cord with plug, as shown on pp. 137–138. Or save money and trouble by snipping the cord (unplug it first, of course) and attaching a replacement plug. Plenty of them are available, to fit almost any cord.

Working with cords

A cord is like a cable in that it contains several insulated wires. However, the wires are almost always stranded rather than solid and the insulation and sheathing are made of a very flexible rubber, so it can be bent many times without cracking. Zip cord is pulled apart, then stripped. Three-wire cord must have its sheathing removed first.

If a cord for a lamp or small appliance is damaged so that exposed metal wires show or may touch each other, you could unplug the cord, strip the ends, splice them together carefully with electrician's tape, and then tape over the whole repair. But that is a temporary repair at best, not to mention unsightly. It is far better to replace the entire cord. You can buy replacement cords with plugs attached, or you can install a new cord and attach a plug, as shown on p. 134.

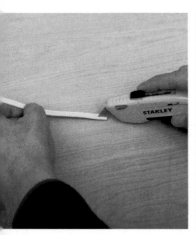
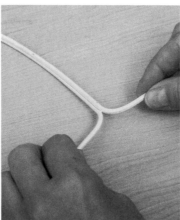

1 **ZIP APART.** On a zip cord, insert a knife in the center of the cord between the two wires, about an inch from the end. Pull on the cord to complete a short cut. Then pull the two wires apart to the desired length. (Or pull them apart a short distance; you can always separate them more later.)

The Right Cord for the Job

Many lamps and small appliances use ungrounded cord, with only two wires. This is typically called "zip cord," because it can be pulled apart (see the three cords at left, below. Cords with a ground wire are cased in sheathing. Cords come in a variety of sizes and types. If you look very closely at some cords, you will see designations like "HPN" or VSVT." Choose a cord that matches the designation, or choose one that is the same size. If a cord gets hot during operation, replace it with a larger one.

Three-wire cord uses the same color designations as cable. Much two-wire zip cord has one wire with ribbed insulation; that's the neutral (far right in the photo below). The wire with smooth insulation is the hot wire. It's important to attach these correctly: Commonly, the ribbed neutral wire goes to the silver lamp terminal and the wider prong on the plug and the smooth hot wire goes to the brass terminal and the narrower plug prong. If you attach them to the wrong terminals, polarization will be incorrect (see p. 12), which means that power will be present in the lamp or appliance even when it is turned off.

Small-gauge zip cord may be nonpolarized, with both wires having smooth insulation; it attaches to a plug that has two prongs of the same size.

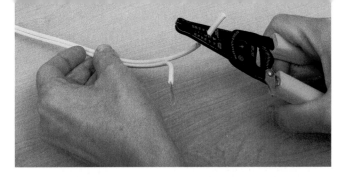

2 **STRIP THE WIRES.** Experiment with wire strippers to find the right hole to use. When working with cord, you may need to use a larger stripping hole than expected: For instance, in this example the 12-gauge hole works best for this 16-gauge wire.

3 **TWIST AND FORM THE STRANDS.** Stranded wire takes a bit of care. Twist it tightly so there are no loose ends. Depending on the type of terminal, you may also need to form it into loops.

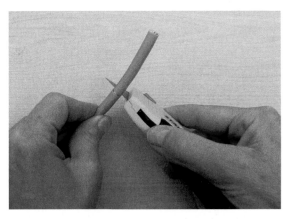

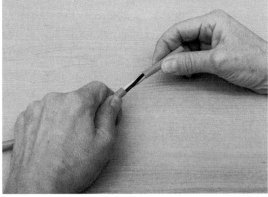

REMOVING ROUND CORD SHEATHING. If the cord has three wires and round sheathing, carefully cut through the sheathing only by rolling the cord against a knife. You don't actually need to cut all the way through the sheathing; most of the way will do. Pull the sheathing off and look closely to be sure you haven't cut into any wire insulation. If you have, snip the cord and try again.

Replacing plugs

Replace a plug if it is cracked, if a prong is loose, if you see sparks when you plug it in or pull it out, or if it is damaged in any way. Fortunately, plug replacement is quick and inexpensive. Here, we show a few of the more common types; more styles and clamping methods are possible.

Choosing a Replacement Plug

A good variety of replacement plugs can be found at a hardware store or home center. As seen on the following pages, a "butterfly" replacement plug, like the yellow and white plugs shown at top left, opens up to receive the cord. With other types, you insert the cord into the plug body. Choose one that suits the amperage of your lamp or appliance—usually 15 amps, but sometimes 20 amps. Also check its back hole to see that it will grab your cord firmly without pinching it too much. A unit with poke-in terminals is a good deal easier to work with than one requiring you to bend stranded wire ends into loops.

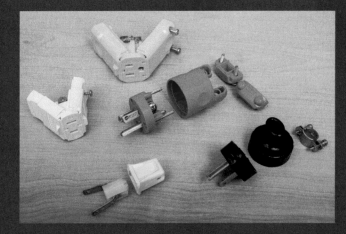

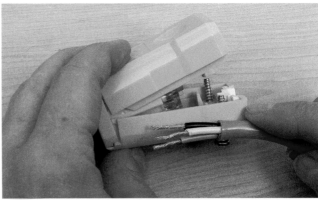

NO-STRIP PLUG. This replacement plug works only with thin lamp cord, and it is not polarized—both prongs are the same width, and it doesn't matter which wire attaches to which prong. Separate the two parts of the plug and open the two prongs wide apart. Slide the cord through the hole in the cover and poke it into the prong casing. Squeeze the prongs together; doing this causes the prongs to pierce the wires and make electrical contact. Then slide the cover onto the prong casing until it snaps into place. You're done.

THE RIGHT LENGTHS. For most replacement plugs, you'll need to cut and strip sheathing and wires to the right lengths. Usually you have ¼ in. or so of wiggle room, but that's not much. Start by stripping a bit too much sheathing; then hold the cord in place or take measurements and cut the wires to the right length. Then strip the wires.

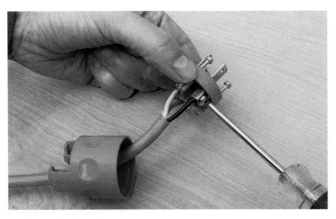

TYPICAL INSTALLS. Replacement plugs differ in style and attachment types, but methods are pretty similar: Disassemble the plug, attach wires to terminals, and reassemble the plug. In this example, the cord is stripped so that the wires will reach all the way into the terminals and none of the wires will be exposed once the plug is assembled. Slide the plug's casing onto the cord. Attach the stripped wire ends to the terminals. Be sure there are no stray strands that are not captured. Tug to test that the connections are firm, then slide the casing up and drive three screws to hold the two parts together. (With some types, you simply push the two parts together until they snap tight.) Tighten screws to clamp the cord tightly.

Cord switches

A cord switch may offer a convenient way to control a lamp or small fan if its existing switch is in an awkward place. A cord switch may not last for many years if it is used constantly; use these instructions to replace a broken one with a new one or to upgrade from a small rotary switch to a more reliable switch with a rocker toggle. Of course, ⮕ **Unplug the cord first.**

TIP To install a pull-chain or other type of switch on a fixture or lamp, see p. 139.

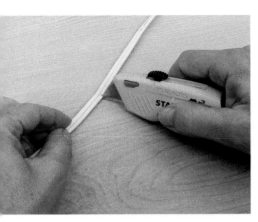

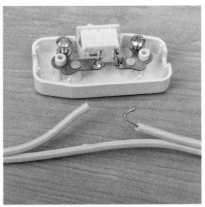

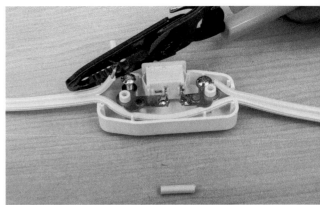

1 **CUT THROUGH THE HOT WIRE.** Choose a spot on the cord that will be easy to reach when you want to turn the lamp on and off. Use a utility knife to cut through only the wire with smooth insulation, which is the hot wire.

2 **ZIP, THEN STRIP ONE END.** Disassemble the cord switch. Make a short slice through the center of the cord on each side of the cut you just made. Pull the wires apart slightly. Strip one of the ends of the hot wire, twist the strands together, and form into a partial loop.

3 **POSITION THE SWITCH, CUT, AND STRIP.** Push the cord into the body of the switch. Wrap the stripped wire end around a terminal, taking care to keep all the strands consolidated, and tighten the terminal screw. Cut the other end of the hot wire to length so it will wrap around the terminal, and strip the wire end.

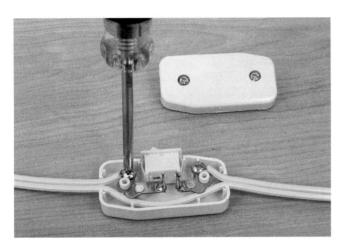

4 **FINISH.** Attach the wire to the other terminal as you did the first. Reassemble the switch, taking care to tuck all the wires snugly in place. Plug in and test.

Rotary Cord Switch

This inexpensive little switch actually works well, and it's mighty easy to install. It's a good option if you don't expect to use the switch constantly. There is no stripping or attaching to terminals. Cut through the hot wire and zip the wires apart an inch or so. Push the wires into the body of the switch as shown, and then reattach the other part of the switch. A couple of metal barbs will pierce the hot wire to make the electrical connection as you screw the parts together.

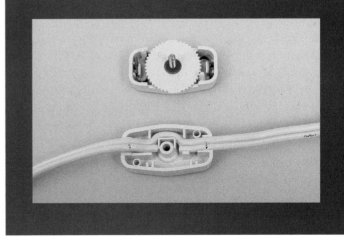

Lamp Repair

You can refurbish most lamps by installing new wiring and a new socket, as long as the lamp's body is in sound condition. These repairs are inexpensive and pretty simple, so go ahead and make them to solve even cosmetic flaws. This is rarely difficult.

➠ Be sure to unplug the lamp before beginning any tests or repairs.

THE PARTS. A lamp's socket may have a switch that you pull, slide over, or twist. Or it may have no switch, in which case it is probably controlled by a cord switch (see p. 135). The socket consists of a socket cap, which screws onto the lamp at the bottom; the socket itself, with terminals and perhaps a switch; and a socket shell, which slides over the socket. The shell has an inner sleeve made of cardboard.

A SIMPLE REPAIR. If the bulb does not come on or if it flickers, try this. Use a small screwdriver to pull up on the socket tab, which needs to make solid contact with the bulb's base. If the tab is rusty, scrape it until the brass shines. Also clean out any dust and debris from inside the socket. If this does not solve the problem, move on to the following repairs.

Testing sockets and cords

To find out what the problem is, you can easily test a socket or cord.

1 DISASSEMBLE. If there is a tiny screw near the socket tab, unscrew it. Press on the shell where it says **PRESS HERE** and pull out the shell and socket. Unscrew the terminals and remove the two wires.

2 TEST THE CORD AND PLUG. Clamp one end of a continuity tester (or multitester, see p. 45) to the bare hot wire (with smooth insulation), and touch the probe to the narrow (hot) prong. Also test with the neutral (ribbed insulation) wire and the wide prong. If the tester does not glow or register for continuity in each case, replace the cord and plug.

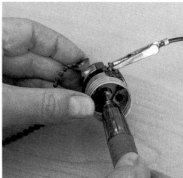

3 TEST THE SOCKET. Clamp a continuity tester's clip to the socket's metal threads and touch the probe to the silver (neutral) terminal screw (left). The tester should glow or show continuity when the switch is on and not glow when the switch is off. Also test the hot connection: Clamp to the brass terminal screw and touch the socket tab (right) and test in the same way. If the socket fails any of the tests, replace it.

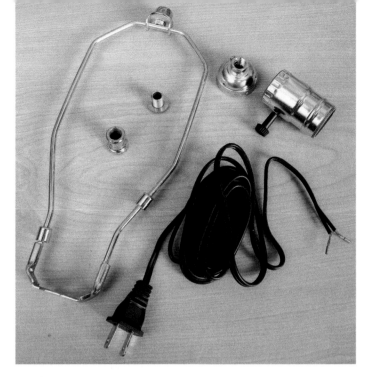

LAMP REPAIR KIT. As long as you're replacing one thing, consider spending a bit more time and money to completely overhaul your lamp. A kit like this allows you to replace the socket, cord with plug, harp, and other hardware.

Replacing a cord and plug

Rather than repairing a damaged cord, replace the whole thing with a cord that has a plug. The new cord should be at least as thick as the old one—thicker, if the old cord or plug got hot during operation.

1 **TAPE NEW CORD TO THE OLD ONE.** Cut off the old cord fairly close to the lamp's base. Use electrician's tape to attach the old cord to the new one. Wrap tightly and take care not to create a joint that is much thicker than the cord itself.

2 **PULL THROUGH.** At the top of the lamp, pull the cord through until the new cord comes out the top 2 in. or more. With some lamps you will need to use pliers to loosen the cord where it passes through a tight spot (left).

Replacing a socket

Replace a socket if it fails a test (step 3 on p. 136), if the switch doesn't work, if the cardboard insulation is damaged, if the light flickers, or if it is wobbly. When replacing, you may choose to change the type of switch; they are all interchangeable.

3 **WIRE THE SOCKET.** Attach the neutral wire (with the ribbed insulation) to the silver terminal, and attach the hot wire (with smooth insulation) to the brass terminal.

1 **SCREW ON THE SOCKET CAP.** Slip the socket cap through the wires and screw it onto the lamp. If your lamp has a harp, first slip on the harp's holder (right). Tighten the socket cap's setscrew to hold it firmly.

4 **FASTEN THE SOCKET SHELL.** Align the shell's heavily marked indentations with the small holes in the socket cap, as shown, and push firmly until it attaches tightly to the cap. You may need to pull on the wire at the other end as you do this. Screw in a bulb, plug in the cord, and test.

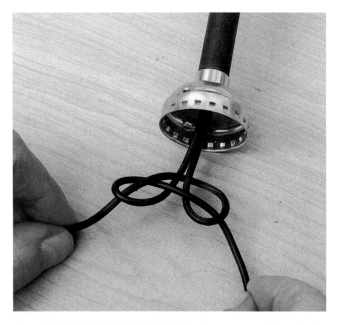

2 **TIE AN UNDERWRITER'S KNOT.** Create an underwriter's knot with two loops, as shown. Pull the knot tight. You may need to cut the wires to length afterward.

5 **HARP.** If your lampshade uses a harp, squeeze it and insert the prongs into the holder below the socket cap. Slide the sleeve holders or use other hardware to hold the harp in place.

Replacing or Installing a Pull-Chain Switch

A pull-chain is the most common type of fixture switch, but toggle switches are also available and are installed the same way. These switches are most often installed in fan or light fixture canopies. Unfortunately, pull-chain switches are notoriously short lived if they are used often, and you may find yourself replacing one every couple of years or so.

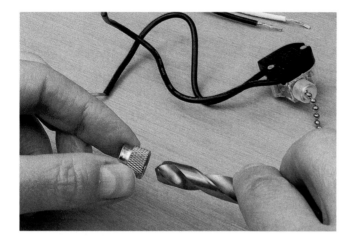

1 DRILL A HOLE. If you are installing a new switch where there was none before, carefully select a place on the canopy where there will be room for the switch and where the chain will be easy to access. Select a drill bit that is just slightly larger than the switch's threads and slightly smaller than the nut that holds it in place. Drill a hole in the canopy.

2 ATTACH THE SWITCH. Insert the switch's threads through the hole. Screw on the nut to fasten it securely.

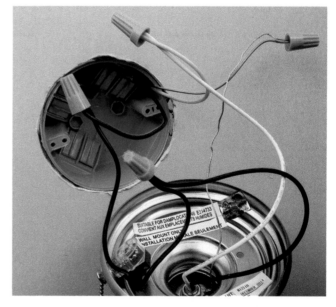

3 WIRE THE SWITCH. If you are replacing a switch, wire the new one just like the old one. Wire so that power passes through the switch: The house's hot wire is spliced to one switch lead, and the other switch lead is spliced to the fixture.

Dealing with Lost Power

Household electricity is generally quite reliable. If you do lose power to all or part of your system, proceed cautiously and systematically. Sometimes the problem is with the service entering your home, and sometimes it is with a particular switch, receptacle, or fixture. Quite often, a circuit is overloaded.

Power loss to all or much of your system

If power is suddenly lost to your whole house, the problem is most likely not with your home's wiring. Chances are there is a power outage in your area, which may affect a few homes or a much wider area. Call your electric utility, which should have outage information as well as an estimate of when power will be restored.

If power is lost to your home only, or if about half of your power is suddenly lost, call your utility. They should send someone out quickly. The most common cause is damage to one or both of the service wires that bring power to your home. Do not try to solve this problem yourself; in fact, don't go anywhere near the wires or your service entrance (see pp. 14–15). If the problem is not with the service wires, they can help you find the cause. You may need to call in a professional electrician to work on your service panel.

Loss of power to a single fixture or device

If a light does not come on even after changing a bulb, see pp. 44–45 for testing and replacing a switch or fixture. If a receptacle stops working, test with a receptacle analyzer.

➡ **Shut off power and check that the wires are all firmly connected and that none of them are damaged. See pp. 112–114 for replacing a non-working receptacle.**

Short circuit, overload, or bad breaker?

If a circuit breaker trips off or a fuse blows, there are three possible causes:

- A short circuit occurred due to faulty wiring. It will likely happen when a certain fixture, lamp, or appliance is used, or when a certain receptacle is plugged into. Often you will see a spark when the short circuit occurs, or you may see black smudges indicating that there was a spark. There may be a whiff of smoke in the air. In this case, you need to find the faulty wiring, fixture, or appliance and fix or replace it.

- An overload occurred even when all the wiring is in sound condition, but too much electrical power is being drawn on a single circuit. If there is an overload, you must take steps to lighten the load on the circuit. See pp. 154–155 for calculating how much power a circuit can safely supply.

- The circuit breaker may be defective, causing it to overload too easily, or to not supply power even after you try to reset it. The solution is to replace the breaker.

Tracking down the problem

If a circuit goes dead and nothing happens when you reset the breaker, test the breaker, as shown on pp. 142–143.

If the breaker flips off or the fuse blows almost immediately after you turn it back on, you likely have a short circuit. With the circuit turned off, check for dark burn spots near devices, fixtures, cords, and appliances. Two common causes are cords with damaged insulation or a loose wire inside a box. If you cannot see the source of the problem, work systematically: Turn off all switches and unplug all lamps and appliances. Restore power. If the breaker trips immediately again, the problem is probably loose wiring inside a box. If power stays on, turn on switches and plug in lamps and appliances one by one until you find the culprit.

If it takes a few seconds or longer for a circuit to blow, chances are the circuit is overloaded. With the breaker off or the fuse unscrewed, turn off everything. Restore power, and start turning things on one by one and wait ten seconds or more each time. You may find that when two big users are on at the same time—say, a toaster and a microwave—the circuit will blow. Now you know that those two things running together present too large a load for the circuit.

What to do

If the problem is a short circuit, take steps to make repairs, as shown earlier in this chapter.

If the circuit is overloaded, you may be able to fix the problem easily: Perhaps plug an appliance into a receptacle that is on another circuit. It's possible—especially with receptacles above kitchen counters—that your receptacles are "split," with the two outlets on separate circuits. In that case, simply moving a plug from one to the other outlet may solve the problem. It may help to switch from incandescent to LED bulbs, which use much less energy. Check the information plates on appliances: You may be able to fix things by buying a newer microwave or toaster that uses less power than the old one.

If simple solutions do not address the problem, you may need to install a new circuit with its own receptacles (see Chapters 6–8).

Dedicated Circuits

Appliances and fixtures that have heating elements or fans not only use a good deal of power, but they also "surge" when they first come on, meaning that they use extra juice for a second or two. For this reason, modern codes require that refrigerators, large fans, air conditioners and receptacles that supply air conditioners, heating units, and other big-use items be on "dedicated" circuits, meaning that the circuit should supply that one thing only.

Do You Have a Problematic Service Panel?

Most service panels and their breakers (usually, a panel can use breakers made by the same company) are trustworthy, but some models have proved unreliable. Sometimes this is mostly a nuisance: Breakers may trip too easily. But in other cases, a bad service panel can create a dangerous situation, because its breakers may fail to shut down during an overload or short circuit, which could result in shocks or even fires.

If your panel is not made by a well-known manufacturer with a reliable reputation, consult with your building department or with an electrician who has been working for years in your area. Also do an online search for your panel, ignoring results that are run by the manufacturer or that are advertisements. If your panel is notorious for problems, you will quickly find a site that tells about it. Or search for "unsafe service panels." Zinsco and Federal Pacific Electric panels have bad reputations, and these panels should probably be replaced.

If your breakers are "pushmatic" types, with buttons that you press rather than toggles that you push to the side, get professional advice. Some of these are considered sound, whereas others are untrustworthy and should be replaced. See pp. 225–227 for replacing a service panel.

TIP Add up wattages/amps and use the calculations on pp. 154–155 to make sure a circuit is not using more than "safe capacity."

Testing and Replacing Circuit Breakers

Circuit breakers are usually reliable, but they do go bad occasionally. A malfunctioning breaker may fail to turn the circuit on when you flip its switch. Or it could shut off even when there is no overload or short circuit. If you suspect a breaker has gone bad, or if you want to see if it is the problem (and not your wiring), you can easily test it. Replacing a faulty breaker is not a difficult job.

Testing a breaker

You can test with an inexpensive neon voltage tester, a multimeter, or, as shown at right, a four-level voltage tester. Remove the service panel's cover as shown on p. 20.

FIRST TEST. Touch one of the tester's probes to the breaker's terminal screw, where the hot wire attaches to the breaker. Touch the other probe to the neutral bus bar. The meter should glow or indicate around 115 volts to 125 volts when the breaker is flipped on and not glow or indicate volts when the breaker is shut off. (You can also perform the test by touching one probe to the terminal screw and one to the panel's metal housing.) If it fails either test, replace the breaker.

1 SECOND TEST. ⟱ Shut off power at the main breaker, which will leave the whole service panel (and the house) without energy. Use a voltage detector to make sure there is no power in the service panel: Touch it to wires and breakers throughout the panel.

2 PULL OUT WIRES. On the suspect breaker, loosen the terminal screw and pull the wire out. Do the same for a nearby breaker that is working and is of the same amperage. Put a wire nut on the wire from the working breaker, to be sure you remember which wire goes where.

3 INSERT WIRE INTO THE OTHER BREAKER. Insert the wire from the suspected breaker into the breaker that is working and tighten the screw. Turn on the main breaker. Now turn on all the lights and plug in lamps or tools into the receptacles that were on the suspected breaker. If everything works fine and the breaker does not trip off, then the suspected breaker is faulty; replace it.

Replacing a breaker

Purchase a breaker of the same make and amperage as the one you are replacing. In rare cases, you may be able to find a breaker from another manufacturer that is made for your service panel.

1 **DISCONNECT THE BAD BREAKER.** ⟫ Shut off the power at the main breaker and use a voltage tester to verify that power is off, as shown in step 1 on the facing page. Remove the old breaker. You probably need to pull on one side, then the other. Wiggle it out, then loosen the terminal screw and remove the wire.

2 **INSTALL THE NEW BREAKER.** Insert the wire into the new breaker and tighten the terminal screw to hold it firm. Push the breaker into place in the reverse order you used for removing it. It should snap firmly in place and should be as fully inserted as the neighboring breakers. Turn the main breaker back on and test the users on the circuit.

Double-Pole Breakers

A double-pole breaker connects to two hot wires. It may supply 240 volts, or it may supply two circuits with 120 volts each.

To test one (right), flip the breaker on and touch the probes of a multitester or a multi-level voltage detector (do not use a simple neon tester). You should get a reading of around 220 volts to 250 volts. You can also test the individual terminals in the same way as you would a 120-volt breaker, using the steps shown on the facing page.

To replace one (far right), follow the same instructions for replacing a breaker, but remove and reinstall two wires instead of one.

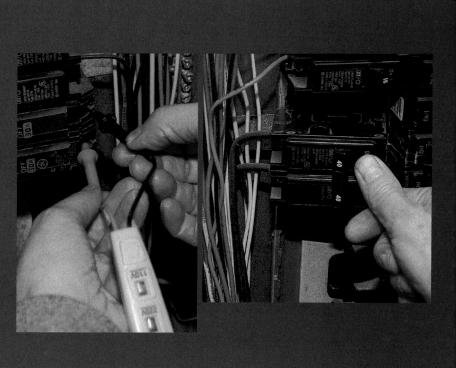

Planning for New Electrical Service

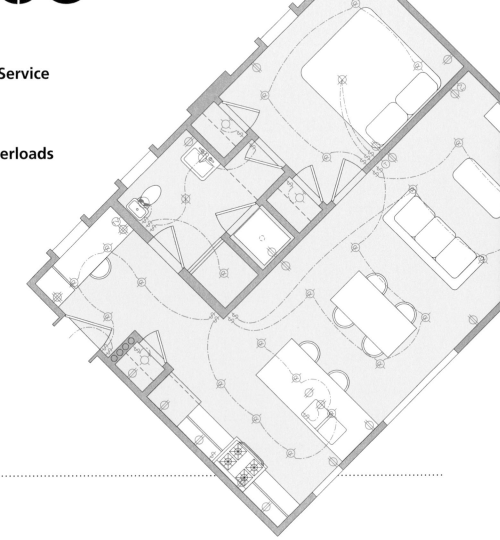

UP TO THIS POINT, the projects in this book have not required running new wiring and installing new outlets. (The exception was the raceway on pp. 118–121.) "New electrical service," which the rest of the book deals with, may be as simple as adding a new light fixture or receptacle, or it may be as complicated as installing all new wiring for an addition or upgrading a service panel.

Look through the projects carefully and make a sober decision: Should you attempt this work yourself or should you hire a professional electrician? Do not start any project unless you are certain you understand all that's required and are confident you can do the work.

Much of the "grunt work" of installing new boxes and cable does not call for special skills; we'll show how to run new wiring in open framing and behind finished walls. But making sure that the wiring is correct—the right amperage and correct loading for the outlets you will install—may require knowledge that pros know better than you. As a result, people sometimes hire pros to help plan and then inspect their work, while they do much or all of the drilling, cutting, attaching, and connecting themselves.

With any new service, the first question is this: Will it overload the circuit it is connected to? A single light fixture using LED or other low-voltage fixtures or bulbs will add only a small amount of electrical load. Often you can simply add these by tapping into an existing circuit. Larger users often require installing new circuits.

Building departments usually want you to pull a permit and schedule inspections whenever you install new wiring, and want you to follow local codes to the letter. Be sure to check with your building department before you execute any work. They may require that you hire a professional rather than doing it yourself.

Tools for Running New Service

Start with the tools shown on pp. 40–43, which you need for electrical replacements and repairs. You'll need them for more advanced projects as well. Then add the tools shown on these pages as you need them. The tools you need depend on the project and the type of material. For instance, if you will run only NM cable, you won't need conduit tools or an armored-cable cutter.

see pp. 40–43

VDE screwdrivers

These deluxe electrician's screwdrivers combine chrome vanadium steel, precision-machined hardened tips, special handles to increase torque, and ultra-insulated handles and shafts, rated to withstand up to 1,000 volts. They represent more screwdriver than you probably need, but because you'll use them so often you may want to pay extra to buy a few.

More testers

A tester that clamps around wires or cables, often called a snap-around tester, acts as a sort of pro-level voltage detector. It tells you a line's voltage without touching any bare wires. The model shown below also has probes and can do almost anything that a multitester can do; it requires batteries. A solenoid voltage tester is a pro-level multitester, and it also can test DC current. It doesn't need batteries but doesn't perform as many functions as a battery-operated tester. It will cause a GFCI receptacle to trip and so cannot be used to test one.

use a cable ripper, which neatly slices through the center of the sheathing without touching the insulated wires inside. For some types of NM cable you may need to use a utility knife; buy a high-quality tool and make sure its blade is sharp.

If you are working with armored cable (either MC or BX), it is possible to use a hacksaw, but an armored cable cutter is much easier to use, and—more important—it reliably cuts through the armor without damaging the wire insulation.

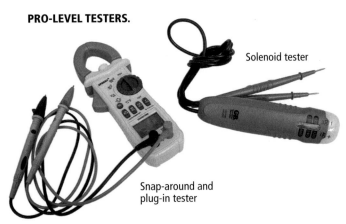

PRO-LEVEL TESTERS.

Solenoid tester

Snap-around and plug-in tester

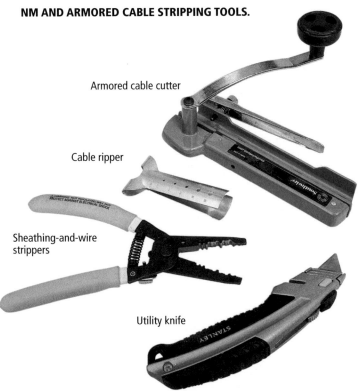

NM AND ARMORED CABLE STRIPPING TOOLS.

Armored cable cutter

Cable ripper

Sheathing-and-wire strippers

Utility knife

NM cable stripping tools

To strip nonmetallic cable's outer sheathing without damaging the wire insulation inside, you have several options, as shown on pp. 168–170. One is to use a pair of sheathing-and-wire strippers, which, for the most common sizes of cable and wire, quickly remove the sheathing, then the wire insulation. Or you may choose to

as shown on pp. 168–170

TOOLS FOR CONDUIT.

Conduit bender

Hacksaw

Cement for PVC conduit

Electrician's tubing cutter

Conduit reamer

PVC cutter

Tools for conduit

Metal and PVC conduit have their own tools. To cut metal conduit, use a good-quality hacksaw with a sharp blade. Cutting will create burrs inside the conduit, which can damage wire insulation. You can remove burrs with pliers or another metal tool, but a reaming tool is faster and does a better job. Alternately, you can use an electrician's tubing cutter, which cuts neatly without creating burrs. However, some people find it slow and difficult to use. The only way to bend conduit is with a tool made for the purpose. Get one made for your size conduit—usually ½ in. or ¾ in.

Cut PVC conduit cleanly, with no burrs, using a PVC cutter. Glue the parts together using gray PVC cement made for electrical work.

Fishing tools

A pair of fish tapes is often used to run wires through metal or PVC conduit. Fish tape is also sometimes used to run cable behind finished walls or ceilings, but often a fishing rod, which is stiffer, is handier to use. A typical rod comes in three parts that screw together. In many behind-surface situations a three-part fishing bit—including a long bit, a bender to aim the bit, and a mesh pulling attachment—is the best solution, allowing you to bore holes in a joist or stud without having to cut into the wall.

FISHING TOOLS.

Three-part fishing bit

Fishing rod

Fish tape

Tools for cutting and attaching

Running cable usually means cutting holes in wood framing or making openings in wall surfaces. A right-angle drill (see p. 148) cuts holes in tight spots and is much easier to use between studs or joists than a regular drill. Here, we show a 20-volt cordless model that cuts with surprising power and speed. If you have lots of holes to drill, consider renting or buying a heavy-duty ½-in. right-angle drill. An auger bit is the traditional choice, but high-quality spade bits can cut just as quickly, though they may not last as long.

For general demolition and heavy-duty cutting, a reciprocating saw works great. Nowadays, 20-volt cordless models provide plenty of power. A sabersaw cuts neat holes in walls. A standard cordless drill often speeds the work of assembling and attaching appliances, fixtures, and boxes. A set of nut drivers will help you drive hex-head fasteners.

CUTTING AND ATTACHING TOOLS.

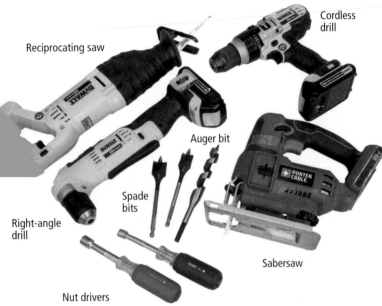

Reciprocating saw

Cordless drill

Auger bit

Spade bits

Right-angle drill

Sabersaw

Nut drivers

Tool Bag with Light

This tool bag not only holds plenty of tools in a way that makes them easy to find, but also has a built-in light that can come in mighty handy when working with the power shut off. The light can be pointed out into the room, or turned inward to shine on tools inside the bag.

Electrical Boxes

All electrical connections—splicing wires together and connecting wires to terminals on devices, fixtures, or appliances—must be made inside a code-approved electrical box. Some fixtures and appliances have built-in boxes, but for the most part you will use separate boxes. There are many boxes to choose from, but your local home center, electrical supply store, or hardware store will likely carry the types that are common (and code-approved) in your area. These pages show some of the more common boxes.

Box names are sometimes a bit misleading. A "switch box" can often be used for a receptacle and vice versa. Ceiling boxes (or the mud rings that attach to metal boxes) are usually round or octagonal; wall boxes are usually square or rectangular. A single-gang box has mounting holes for one device; a double-gang box holds two devices, and so on.

Metal or plastic

The first choice is between metal and plastic. Do as instructed by your inspector and local codes. If you run non-metallic cable, you may be allowed to use plastic boxes, but in some areas metal boxes are required. When running armored cable or metal conduit, metal boxes are always required. Metal boxes are stronger, and they receive a ground wire for extra-secure ground connections. Plastic boxes are not as sturdy but are certainly strong enough when installed behind drywall, and a tightly attached connection between the ground wire and the device or fixture will remain firm and reliable. Where boxes are exposed, as is often the case in a basement or garage, metal boxes are usually required, although some types of plastic may be allowed.

New- and old-work boxes

New-work boxes attach directly to studs or joists when the framing is exposed, before the drywall is installed (see pp. 175–176). If the walls are already finished with drywall or plaster, use old-work (also called cut-in) boxes. You will typically cut a hole for the box, then run cable into the box, then install the box (see pp. 188–192).

The right depth

It's important that the front of a box (or the mud ring that attaches to a metal box) be flush or nearly flush with the surrounding wall surface. Most new-work boxes have built-in guides that make it easy to install them ½ in. out from the framing to accommodate ½-in. drywall. If your wall surface will be thicker than ½ in., be sure to install the boxes with their edges farther out from the framing. Old-work boxes come flush with the wall when you install them.

Large enough

Be sure your boxes are large enough inside that wires and devices will not be crowded. See the chart below, but if there is any doubt, install a larger box—either deeper or larger in area.

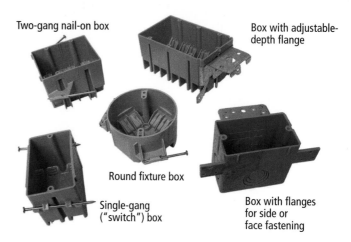

Just Go Large

Unless you have limited space inside a wall, save yourself calculating time and installation trouble by simply buying big boxes. With plastic boxes, that means boxes that are at least 2½ in. deep—preferably even 3½ in. deep. With metal boxes, a square box 4 in. by 4 in. by 1½ in. with a mud ring, as shown on p. 150, gives plenty of room for one device; if you have two devices, use a 4×4 box that is at least 2¼ in. deep.

NUMBER OF CONDUCTORS ALLOWED IN A BOX

BOX SIZE	WIRE SIZE			
	14	12	10	8
ROUND/OCTAGONAL BOXES				
4 in. × 1¼ in.	6	5	5	4
4 in. × 1½ in.	7	6	6	5
4 in. × 2⅛ in.	10	9	8	7
SQUARE BOXES				
4 in. × 1¼ in.	9	8	7	6
4 in. × 1½ in.	10	9	8	7
4 in. × 2⅛ in.	15	13	12	10
4¹¹/₁₆ in. × 1¼ in.	12	11	10	8
4¹¹/₁₆ in. × 1½ in.	14	13	11	9
RECTANGULAR BOXES				
3 in. × 2 in. × 2¼ in.	5	4	4	3
3 in. × 2 in. × 2½ in.	6	5	5	4
3 in. × 2 in. × 2¾ in.	7	6	5	4
3 in. × 2 in. × 3½ in.	9	8	7	6
4 in. × 2⅛ in. × 1½ in.	5	4	4	3
4 in. × 2⅛ in. × 1⅞ in.	6	5	5	4
4 in. × 2⅛ in. × 2⅛ in.	7	6	5	4

Notes: Count each wire that does not have a wire nut—including the grounding wire—as well as any pigtail, as one conductor. Each device (receptacle or switch) counts as two conductors. Count a large device, such as a GFCI or AFCI receptacle, as four conductors. If there are any bulky fixture hardware items, such as a stud or hickey, count them as one conductor each.

NEW-WORK PLASTIC BOXES. The most common plastic boxes attach to studs or joists via pre-attached nails for quick and easy installation. Other types have flanges through which you drive screws for a firmer attachment. Most have gauges to position the front of the box ½ in. out from the framing; a box with an adjustable flange can be moved in or out by turning a screw.

Two-gang nail-on box

Box with adjustable-depth flange

Round fixture box

Single-gang ("switch") box

Box with flanges for side or face fastening

Old-work single-gang box

Round old-work box

OLD-WORK (CUT-IN) PLASTIC BOXES. These have tabs that tighten the box to the drywall when you drive face screws (see p. 189).

METAL BOXES WITH MUD RINGS. Install square or rectangular metal boxes with their front edges flush with the front of studs or joists. After running wiring into the box, attach the appropriate mud rings.

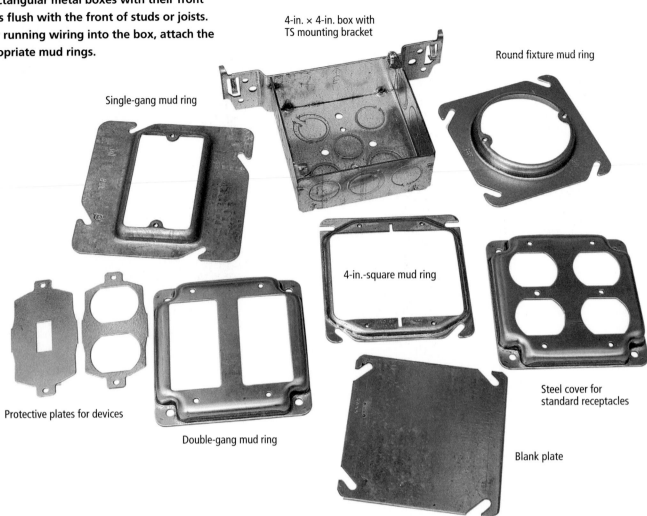

4-in. × 4-in. box with
TS mounting bracket

Round fixture mud ring

Single-gang mud ring

4-in.-square mud ring

Protective plates for devices

Double-gang mud ring

Steel cover for
standard receptacles

Blank plate

Box with plaster ears

Box with expanding flanges

OLD-WORK METAL BOXES. Old-work, or cut-in, metal boxes may have flanges that grab the inside of the drywall when you drive a mounting screw. When working with old lath-and-plaster walls, you can use a box with plaster "ears" that can be adjusted for depth; drive small screws through the ears and into the lath.

TIP To install a ceiling fan or a heavy chandelier, use a fan-rated box, as shown on pp. 84–88.

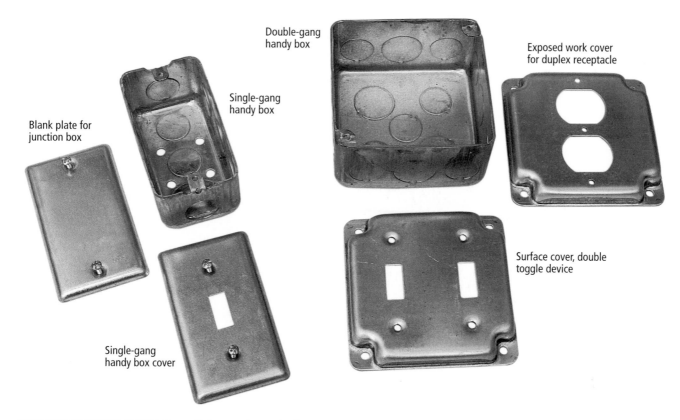

Blank plate for junction box

Double-gang handy box

Single-gang handy box

Exposed work cover for duplex receptacle

Single-gang handy box cover

Surface cover, double toggle device

HANDY BOXES WITH COVERS. Install these where the boxes will be exposed. They have round corners and holes in the back through which you can drive screws for attaching to a wall. Complete the installation with metal cover plates.

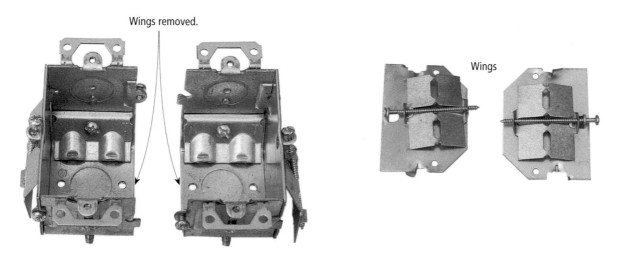

Wings removed.

Wings

GANGABLE BOXES. These single-gang boxes can be partially disassembled and then joined together to create boxes that have two or more gangs. The type shown is an old-work box; remove the "wings" from one side of each box before ganging them together.

Meeting Codes

Whether you are just adding a new receptacle or fixture or are installing new circuits for a major remodel, it is of primary importance to (1) avoid overloading any circuit and (2) comply with local codes. Often taking care of (1) will satisfy (2), but not always.

The last decades have seen the growth of two conflicting trends. On the one hand, many appliances, as well as fixtures and light bulbs, now use less energy than older models. Today's window air conditioners, toasters, microwaves, dishwashers, and so on use a good deal less wattage than older models. On the other hand, electrical codes have generally gotten stricter. For instance, four or even three circuits used to be considered plenty for a medium-size kitchen; nowadays, six circuits is often the minimum.

So whether you are doing work yourself or hiring a pro, planning the service means both calculating to make sure your circuits are under "safe capacity" and also learning and following local codes.

If a project requires new circuits, see p. 224 to learn whether your service panel (and your service wires) can handle the new load.

Working with Your Building Department

Resist the temptation to install new electrical service without working with your local building department. Although this may seem like a big hassle, the inspection process makes sure that your installations will be safe and secure. And you can get into big trouble if it is discovered that you are working without a permit. When it comes time to sell your home, work done without inspection may come to light, and you may have to redo much of the work.

As a general rule, building departments want to inspect and approve any new electrical service—be it a single receptacle or multiple new circuits. Your building department may require that you hire a licensed electrician, or you may be allowed to do the work yourself. In some cases you can do some of the work yourself, but you'll have to hire a licensed pro for installing new circuits. Or for a fee a licensed pro may agree to let you do most or all of the work, which he or she will supervise and inspect. The pro will be ultimately responsible for code compliance, so the fee may be hefty.

The National Electrical Code (NEC), which gets updated every three years, provides codes that are followed by most building departments. However, codes can vary quite a bit from area to area—sometimes even from town to town.

The inspector's job is simply to inspect, not to advise you. Some inspectors are friendly and willing to offer advice. Others are not happy working with homeowners; they are used to working with pros and do not have time to educate do-it-yourselfers. (Many are overworked.) If you will perform the work, approach the department with as much knowledge and information as possible. Learn about their codes; the department may have some literature you can consult. Make drawings that are clear and that use accepted symbols (see p. 156). Supply a list of materials.

If you are at all unclear as to how certain aspects of the job should be done, first study as much as you can, and perhaps consult with an electrician. Ask the inspector as few questions as possible.

You will probably need to pull a permit (and pay for it). Post the permit on a window or door where it is clearly visible. Usually there will be two inspections: one for the rough-in of cables and boxes and one for the finished job after the fixtures and cover plates have been installed. Be sure not to drywall over any rough wiring until after the rough inspection is completed; otherwise, you may have to tear out the drywall. If a service panel has been added to or replaced, there may be a separate inspection for that.

Typical electrical codes

There are thousands of national and local electrical codes covering every aspect of residential wiring. However, the codes you need to worry about will probably be more in the tens. Here are some of the more common issues. (For more codes that are specific to kitchens, bathrooms, and laundry rooms, see pp. 158–160 and pp. 162–164.)

Positioning of light fixtures, switches, and receptacles

- Every bedroom and living room must have at least one overhead light that is controlled by a light switch. Or there can be one outlet of a receptacle that is controlled by a switch; once you plug in a lamp, it will be controlled by the wall switch.
- In living areas (bedrooms, living rooms, dining rooms, dens, etc.) there must be a receptacle every 12 ft., so that at every point in a room a receptacle is no farther away than 6 ft. Every wall wider than 2 ft. must have at least one receptacle.
- Switches must be positioned where they are easy to reach.
- Where a light should be controlled from two different places, such as a stairway light or a light in a large room, a pair of three-way switches should be installed.
- Above a kitchen counter there must be 20-amp receptacles spaced so that no point is farther than two horizontal feet from a receptacle.
- Receptacles are usually required to be 12 in. to 18 in. above the floor; switches should be 45 in. to 50 in. above the floor.
- Smoke and carbon monoxide (CO) detectors are required at least on every floor. In many areas they are required to be hardwired with battery backup. Consult local codes for exact positioning.

Boxes and cables

- All splices and connections to terminals must be made inside a code-approved electrical box.
- To support a ceiling fan or a heavy chandelier, a fan-rated box must be securely attached to framing (see pp. 84–88).
- Boxes must be installed with their front edges within 1/8 in. of the finished wall (which may be drywall, plaster, tile, or paneling).
- In exposed framing, cable must be stapled every 3 ft. to 4 ft. (see pp. 177–182 for more requirements).
- For wiring and boxes that will be hidden behind walls and ceilings, you may be allowed or required to use plastic boxes with NM cable, metal boxes with NM cable, metal boxes with armored cable, or metal boxes with conduit.
- Codes for boxes that will be exposed are generally different. Most commonly, conduit and metal boxes are required.
- Cable must be securely attached, either to an approved clamp in the box or by stapling it to a framing member within 8 in. of the box.
- Cable and conduit must be protected from nails or screws driven into framing members. This can be done by running it through framing members at least 1½ in. from the finished wall surface or by attaching protective nail plates.

WHEN A CABLE HOLE IS WITHIN 1¼ IN. of the edge of a stud, code requires nail plates to prevent drywall fasteners or finish nails from damaging the cable.

- For outdoor underground cable runs, codes can vary widely. Underground-feed (UF) cable is almost always required. In many areas, UF cable should run inside rigid metal conduit where it is exposed or above a certain underground depth. You may have to run the cable at a certain depth, or run it in inside plastic conduit, or protect it with a board on top.

Wiring requirements

- All switches, receptacles, and fixtures must be grounded in a way that meets local codes (see p. 13 and pp. 52–53).
- Wires must be correctly sized for the circuit's amperage. In most areas, a 15-amp circuit should use 14-gauge wire, a 20-amp circuit should use 12-gauge wire, and a 30-amp circuit should use 10-gauge wire.
- Wire that emerges into a box should be at least 6 in. long—8 in. in some areas.
- Only one wire may be connected to a terminal. If you need to connect more wires, use pigtails (see p. 53).
- All splices (wire-to-wire connections) must be made using wire nuts, never tape.
- Each receptacle that supplies a refrigerator, air conditioner, or other heavy-use appliance should be on a separate, dedicated circuit.
- Appliances that use 240-volt service almost always are on separate, dedicated circuits.

- GFCI protection—with either GFCI receptacles or GFCI circuit breakers—is required for damp areas like kitchen counters, bathrooms, and garages.
- AFCI protection—with either AFCI receptacles or AFCI circuit breakers—is required for all living-area receptacles.

Service panel and circuit distribution

- A service panel should have enough amperage for your home (see p. 224).
- A service panel should be balanced, so that roughly half the users are on each bus bar (see p. 19).
- If you will install a new service panel or subpanel, make sure it is of a model approved by local codes.
- A panel should be indexed with labels next to each breaker or on the inside door, so it is easy to find which users are controlled by which breakers.

Calculating to Avoid Overloads

Many circuits will be "automatically" determined. For instance, you probably need to have a separate circuit for a refrigerator, a dishwasher, and/or garbage disposal. For circuits that have multiple users, you should add up the wattages/amps for all the users to be sure you do not overload.

If you are hoping to add new service to an existing circuit, first be sure you know which devices and fixtures are on that circuit. Use the service panel's index; if you don't have an index, create one, as shown on p. 23. If you are planning for a new circuit, add up all the new users, including the appliances that may be plugged into its receptacles.

If adding new users to an existing circuit will cause it to overload past safe capacity, look for another circuit to tap into or install a new circuit. When planning new circuits, be sure none will have users that exceed safe capacity.

The math

Remember that amps = watts ÷ volts. (To put it another way, volts × amps = watts.) Check the labels on appliances, as well as wattages of bulbs, to figure how much power a circuit is being asked to supply.

- On a 120-volt circuit (by far the most common type), it takes 120 watts to equal 1 amp (240-volt circuits almost always supply a single user, so this type of calculation is not needed). This means that a 15-amp circuit can supply 1,800 watts and a 20-amp circuit can supply 2,400 watts.
- However, it is considered unsafe to completely load a circuit. For "safe capacity" (also called "safe usage"), circuits should supply no more than 80 percent of total capacity. So full capacity for a 15-amp circuit is 1,800 watts, but for safe usage, it should supply no more than 12 amps, or 1,440 watts. A 20-amp circuit can safely supply no more than 16 amps, or 1,920 watts. A 30-amp circuit's safe capacity is 24 amps, or 2,880 watts. Causing a circuit to supply more than safe capacity is often considered a code violation.

Gathering wattage and ampere information

Figure in the wattages of light bulbs (be sure to use the actual wattages of LED bulbs, which are significantly less than the equivalent incandescent wattages) for fixtures and for lamps plugged into receptacles. Also figure in wattages or amps of appliances, whether they are plugged in or hardwired. Some items will list watts, and others amps. Add up all the wattages and/or amps. (For 120-volt users, convert wattage to amps by dividing watts by 120; multiply amps times 120 to find the watts.)

Reading Rating Plates

On most appliances and tools, information about wattage or amps may be found on an attached metal or plastic plate, or it may be etched into plastic housing. Almost all will say "120V" or "120VAC," meaning 120 volts or volts alternating current, as well as "60 Hz," which tells the standard oscillation of the alternating current. Look for a number followed by "W" meaning watts or "A" meaning amps.

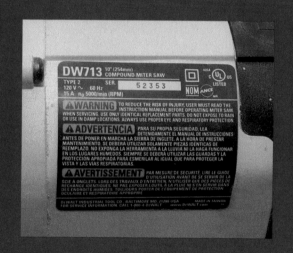

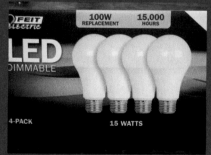

Drawing Plans

If your project involves running new lines and installing new circuits, your building department will likely require professional-looking electrical plan drawings. Depending on the inspector and the scope of the project, you may need to have them drawn by a licensed electrician. But with some practice you can make drawings that will at least help you calculate the job and gather materials—and they may be good enough to satisfy a building department as well.

Inspectors usually want to see plan, or overhead view, drawings. But at least for a kitchen or a bathroom, you may also find it helpful to make an elevation, or side view, drawing (see p. 160). That will help you position receptacles and switches at the correct heights—for instance, receptacles at 5 in. above a countertop, or whips (short lengths of cable) for lights just under cabinets.

A drawing should indicate the locations and types of lights, switches, and receptacles, as well as the types and wire sizes for cables.

In addition to a drawing, make a list of materials, including the following:
- cable types, with wire sizes and number of wires
- box types—plastic or metal—and sizes (see pp. 149–151)
- number and grade (e.g., residential or commercial) of switches and receptacles
- model and make of fixtures
- wattages of fixtures

Though a professional may not include it, it's a good idea for you to color-code each circuit—not only the new circuits you will install, but also existing circuits that you will be reusing. A solid line indicates a cable that simply brings power to a device; a dashed line indicates a switch leg cable, bringing switched power to a fixture. An arrow on a solid line indicates that the cable will be running to the service panel in a "home run."

To keep your drawing from getting crowded and complicated, you may want to produce two plan-view renderings: one showing all the circuits, as shown on the following pages, and another indicating exact room dimensions and precise locations of fixtures and devices, as shown on p. 162.

Electrical Symbols

Standard electrical symbols are easy to draw and make things clear, so use them when you produce a plan. Here are some of the most common symbols, but don't be surprised if your building department uses different symbols in some cases.

Duplex receptacle	
Fourplex receptacle	
GFCI receptacle	GFCI
AFCI receptacle	AFCI
Weatherproof receptacle	WP
Split duplex receptacle	
240v dryer receptacle	D
240v range receptacle	R
Junction box—wall	J
Television cable	TV
Smoke detector	SD
Line-voltage thermostat	TL
Low-voltage thermostat	TLV
Telephone outlet	
Single-pole switch	
3-way switch	
4-way switch	
Dimmer switch	
Pilot-light switch	
Timer switch	
Ceiling light	
Sconce	
Recessed light	
Track lighting	
Undercabinet light	
Ceiling fan with light	
2-wire cable	
3-wire cable	
Home-run cable	
Switch-leg cable	

OVERALL PLAN

This overall plan does not indicate the various circuits that will supply fixtures and receptacles, but it gives detailed information on doorway locations (and door swing directions), windows, and room openings. It also shows where furniture will go. That helps you position all the devices and fixtures in exactly the correct positions.

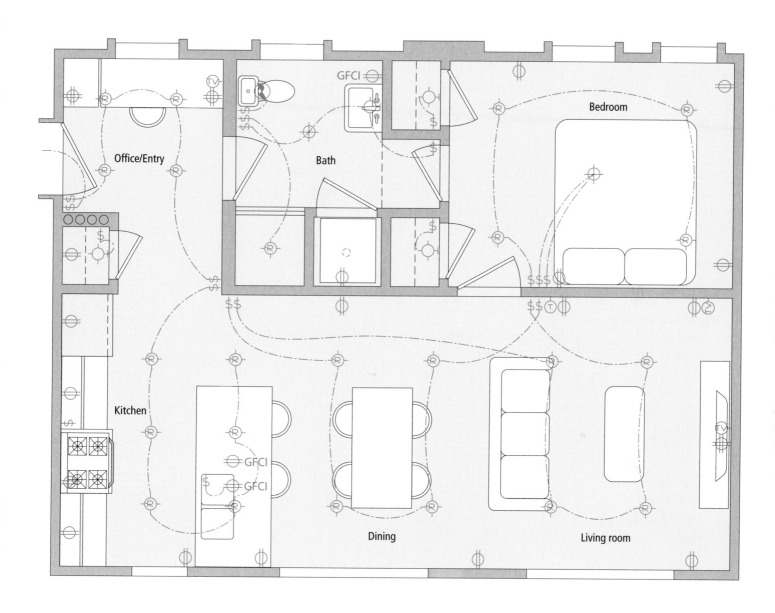

Kitchen Wiring

In most locales, small or mid-size kitchens are required to have at least five, and often six or seven, circuits. Though codes vary and configurations can change depending on layout, these circuits often include the following:

- A separate 15-amp or 20-amp circuit (depending on the size of the refrigerator) for the refrigerator receptacle. No other receptacles should be on this circuit, to ensure that the refrigerator will never be without power.
- Two 20-amp small-appliance receptacles that are GFCI protected. Most of these receptacles are typically above the countertops. Receptacles should be no farther than 4 ft. apart.
- A lighting circuit, to supply both overhead lights (which may be flush, recessed, or track) and undercabinet lights.
- A circuit to supply a garbage disposal and dishwasher.
- If you have an electric range, cooktop, or oven, a 240-volt circuit is required.
- A large microwave and/or a large range hood with vent fan may require another circuit.

Here are some other considerations:

- Most lighting nowadays uses little in the way of wattage. However, if you have a ceiling fan or other high-wattage fixtures, be sure to add up the wattages to make sure you do not overload a lighting circuit.
- In this plan, each of the small-appliance circuits supplies one area of the kitchen. However, some building departments require that receptacles alternate circuits, so that receptacles next to each other are on different circuits. Or they may require receptacles to be split, so that each (duplex) receptacle has each of its outlets on separate circuits. See p. 210 for these arrangements.
- Here we show the dishwasher and the garbage disposal on the same circuit, which is often accepted. However, you may be required to put each on a separate circuit.
- In this plan, the two small-appliance circuits are GFCI protected with GFCI circuit breakers. Another arrangement is to use GFCI receptacles. (If wired correctly, only one GFCI receptacle would be needed on each circuit; see p. 115.)
- If you have an electric range, cooktop, or oven, check the requirements carefully. In most cases, a 50-amp, 240-volt dedicated circuit is needed. Be sure to get a range receptacle, not one meant for a dryer.
- You may be allowed to put a microwave and/or a range hood with vent fan on a small-appliance circuit. A hefty combination microwave/hood should be placed on its own circuit.

KITCHEN ELECTRICAL NEEDS. A kitchen should be brightly lit, both with ambient overhead light and with undercabinet lights that clearly illuminate countertops without shining in peoples' eyes. Here, both recessed canisters and a memorable pendant supply both general and focused illumination. Lights both under and inside cabinets light up specific areas. A kitchen also has strict and very specific requirements for supplying power to the many appliances we've come to rely on.

KITCHEN WIRING PLAN

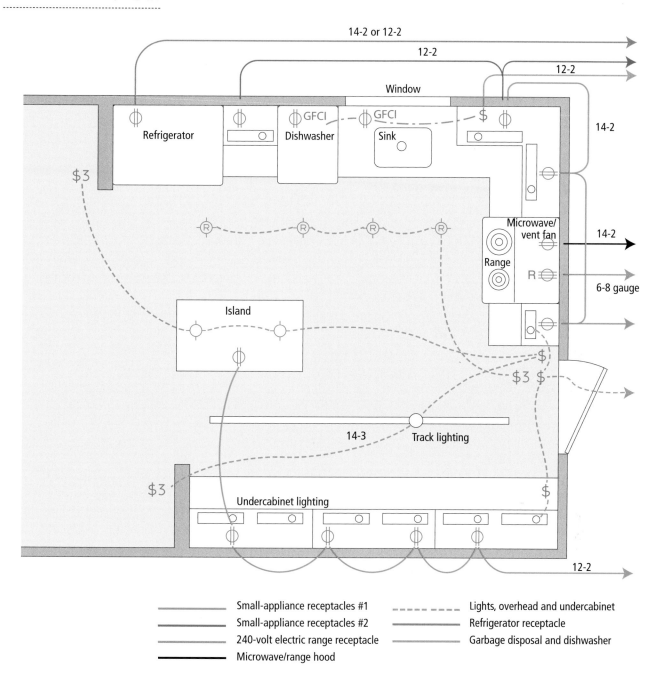

14-2 or 12-2

12-2

12-2

Window

Refrigerator

$3

Dishwasher

GFCI

Sink

GFCI

$

14-2

Microwave/
vent fan

Range

14-2

R

6-8 gauge

$

$3

$

Island

$3

$

14-3

Track lighting

$3

Undercabinet lighting

$

12-2

———— Small-appliance receptacles #1	– – – – Lights, overhead and undercabinet
———— Small-appliance receptacles #2	———— Refrigerator receptacle
———— 240-volt electric range receptacle	———— Garbage disposal and dishwasher
———— Microwave/range hood	

KITCHEN CABINETS

Here are standard dimensions for kitchen cabinets. Be sure to position whips for the undercabinet lights just below the wall cabinets. (If the cabinets have "lips" at the bottom, you can plan to notch-cut them.) Place receptacles so their cover plates will be an inch or so above the countertop back-splash, if there is one.

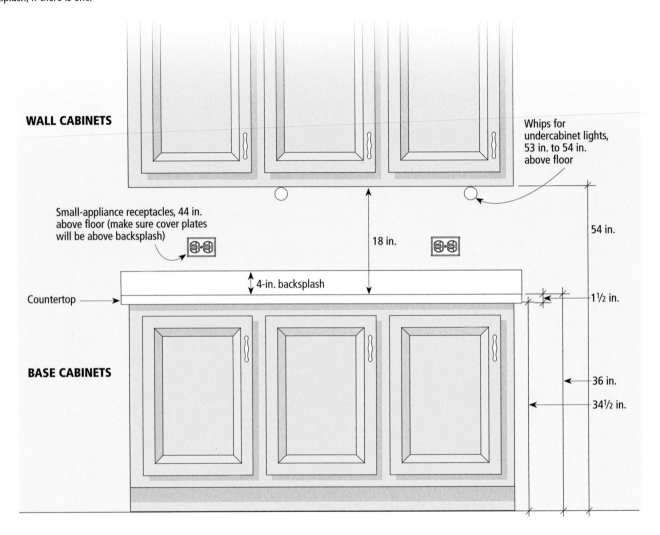

WALL CABINETS

Whips for undercabinet lights, 53 in. to 54 in. above floor

Small-appliance receptacles, 44 in. above floor (make sure cover plates will be above backsplash)

18 in.

54 in.

4-in. backsplash

Countertop

1½ in.

BASE CABINETS

36 in.

34½ in.

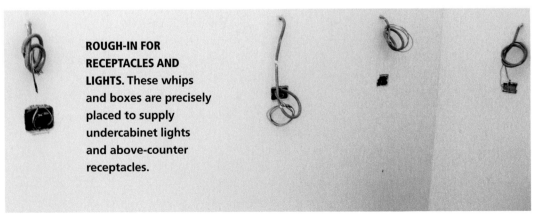

ROUGH-IN FOR RECEPTACLES AND LIGHTS. These whips and boxes are precisely placed to supply undercabinet lights and above-counter receptacles.

TIP Nowadays, the kitchen often flows seamlessly into a dining room and maybe even a living area. You may be allowed to put lights from another room on the same circuit as the kitchen lights, but chances are pretty good you will need to have a separate circuit for the receptacles. In any case, dining room and living room receptacles will probably need to be AFCI protected.

Bedroom Wiring

A bedroom is comparatively simple to plan. It must have either an overhead light or a receptacle outlet that is controlled by a wall switch, as well as AFCI-protected receptacles placed no farther than 6 ft. apart. If there is a closet, it must have at least one switch-controlled light, though a pull-chain light may be allowed.

The plan below features a ceiling fan/light that is controlled by two switches, one for the fan and one for the light; three-wire cable running from the switch to the fan supplies both switches (see p. 92 for ways to control a ceiling fan with a light). The lighting circuit also supplies two switched closet lights as well as two wall sconces positioned over where the bed will go. The receptacles are protected with an AFCI circuit breaker at the service panel. For a window air-conditioning unit, there is a dedicated 20-amp, 120-volt receptacle below the window.

BEDROOM WIRING PLAN

When planning bedroom wiring, you may want to add a few extra features, such as two ceiling lights for the closet and wall sconces for near the bed.

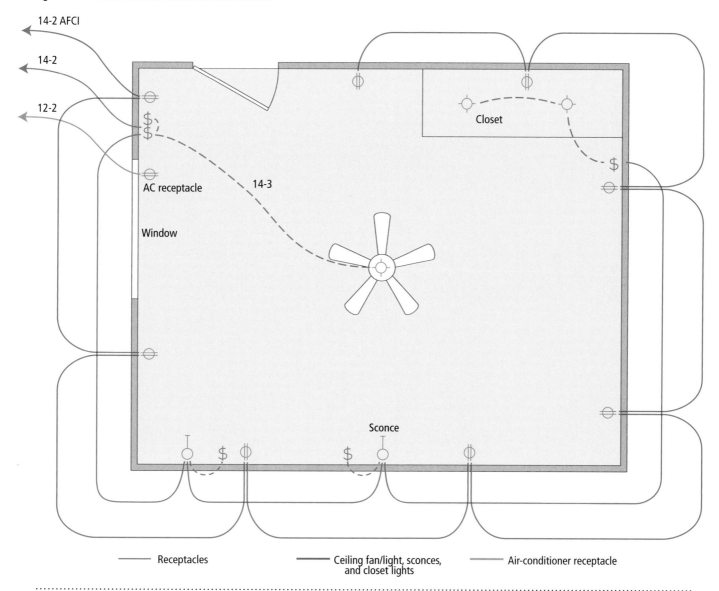

14-2 AFCI

14-2

12-2

AC receptacle

14-3

Window

Closet

Sconce

———— Receptacles   ———— Ceiling fan/light, sconces, and closet lights   ———— Air-conditioner receptacle

Bathroom Wiring

A bathroom is, of course, damp in some places and wet in others. Light fixtures and vent fans should be made to withstand moisture. In particular, a light over a shower or tub needs to be approved for wet-area use. Receptacles should be 20 amp and GFCI protected, either with GFCI receptacles or with a GFCI circuit breaker.

Bathrooms are also often small, but even if they are fairly large, the tub, shower, toilet, and sink are generally positioned precisely (see Taunton's *Stanley Plumbing* for specs on spacing the elements of a bathroom). For this reason, it's a good idea to make a drawing that shows the exact locations and sizes of the fixtures.

Plumbing should be finished before running the wiring. The drain and supply pipes may limit where you can position the electrical boxes. There should be at least one 20-amp GFCI-protected receptacle, positioned 12 in. away from the sink basin so it is unlikely to get splashed on, but within easy reach of a person standing at the sink. It should also be at least 3 ft. away from the tub/shower area, as shown in the drawing below.

This plan features two GFCI-protected receptacles, one near the sink and one near a towel heater. (Towel warmers generally use little power, and so this receptacle can be on the same circuit as the sink receptacle.) If you have a vent fan or a vent fan/light that does not pull too much power, you can likely place it on the same circuit as the other lights, so you may need only two circuits.

BATHROOM WIRING PLAN

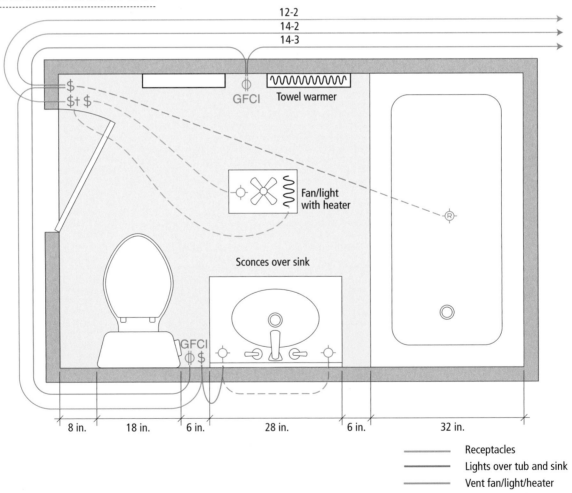

PLENTY OF LIGHTING OPTIONS. A good variety of lights makes a bathroom a cheery place.

BATHROOM RECEPTACLE PLACEMENT

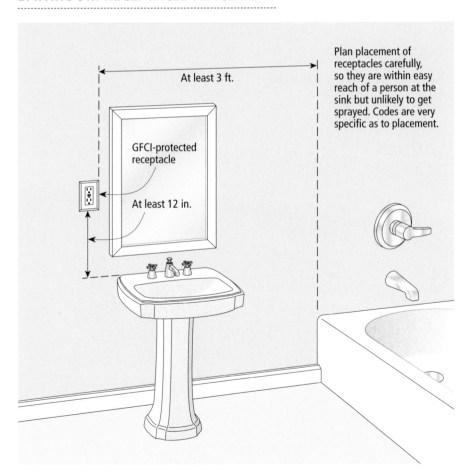

At least 3 ft.

Plan placement of receptacles carefully, so they are within easy reach of a person at the sink but unlikely to get sprayed. Codes are very specific as to placement.

GFCI-protected receptacle

At least 12 in.

Laundry Wiring

A typical laundry room contains at least a washer, a dryer, and a utility sink or a standpipe; a folding table and an ironing board are useful additions. If the dryer is electric, as shown in the drawing below, it requires a special 30-amp, 120/240-volt receptacle and circuit breaker. If the dryer is gas, you may be permitted to put the washer and dryer receptacles on the same circuit, or codes may call for separate circuits. Lighting is not extensive, so it is usually allowed for lights to be on a circuit that also supplies lights in other rooms.

Washer and dryer receptacles are typically positioned about 40 in. above the floor, so they can be easily unplugged without moving the machines. The same height usually works well for receptacles near a folding table or ironing board.

CAREFULLY PLANNED LAUNDRY. Washer and dryer receptacles are usually hidden behind the machines but positioned high enough so they can be easily reached. Make the room nice and bright with one or two overhead lights. General receptacles above a folding table or ironing board are useful.

LAUNDRY ROOM WIRING

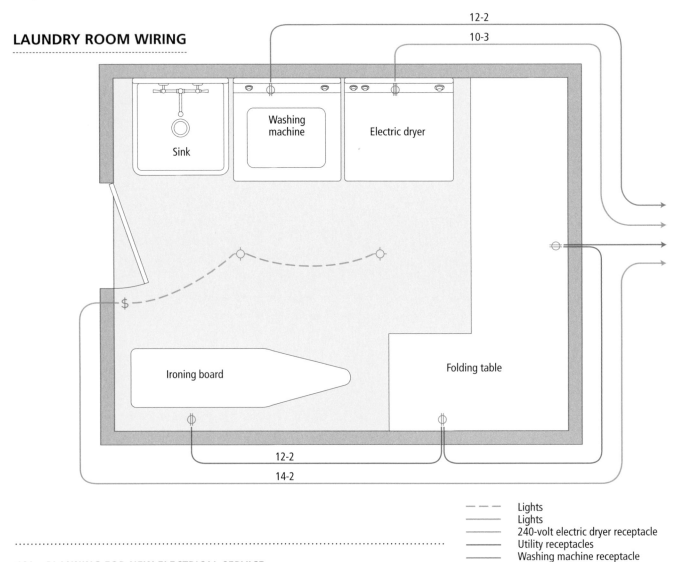

– – – –	Lights
———	Lights
———	240-volt electric dryer receptacle
———	Utility receptacles
———	Washing machine receptacle

Workshop Wiring

Workshops vary widely in size and electrical requirements. If you will have mostly modest-size shop tools like a tablesaw and chopsaw, the usual approach is to supply two 20-amp receptacle circuits, much like above kitchen countertops. Receptacles are often placed about 6 in. above the worktable, so you can plug in hand tools easily. Receptacles for stationary shop tools are often positioned near the floor. The two circuits may supply alternating receptacles, or the receptacles may be split so that a receptacle's two outlets are on different circuits. Large-use shop tools may need to be on separate circuits. Check the amperages.

The shop should be brightly lit but without glare. Plenty of overhead lights with diffuser lenses will spread the illumination pretty evenly. You may also want to hang shop lights near the wall and about 7 ft. above the floor, so they shine extra light on the worktable when someone is standing there.

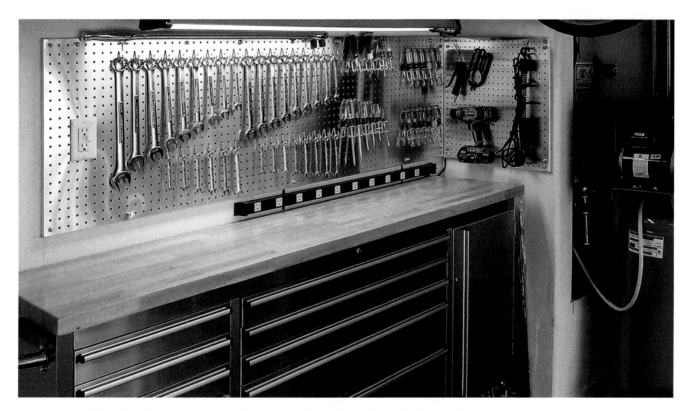

WORKSHOP. This strip of receptacle plugs above a workbench can be wired with alternating circuits, so you can plug tools into two adjacent plugs without overloading a circuit.

Installing Boxes and Running Cable

ONCE YOU'VE PLANNED where your new electrical boxes will go, have confirmed you will not overload a circuit with your new wiring, and have determined which type of cable and which size boxes you need, get approval from your local building department for your electrical project, as discussed in Chapter 6. You may need to hire a pro for at least some of the work.

Once you've figured out the wiring configurations, installing boxes and running cable are not difficult operations. It is important, however, to strip and run wiring so there is no chance that the wire insulation will get nicked, which can lead to a dangerous situation. As long as you follow the steps in this chapter, your wire installations will be safe.

This chapter will first show how to cut, strip, and install various types of cable and conduit. Once you have those techniques down, you can actually install the wiring in your walls and ceilings. Running wiring in new framing is quite straightforward, but if you need to install in finished walls the work becomes more challenging.

Stripping NM Cable

Nonmetallic (NM, also called Romex) cable is the most common type of cable used throughout the country, though in some areas and in some situations metal-clad cable (MC) or various types of conduit are required. The following pages show working with those materials. Here, we show how to strip NM cable and connect it to electrical boxes. To run cable through exposed framing, see pp. 177–182; through finished walls, see pp. 196–203. To understand the types of NM cable, see pp. 24–25.

On these pages we will show several techniques for stripping sheathing from NM cable. To strip wires, see pp. 46–47.

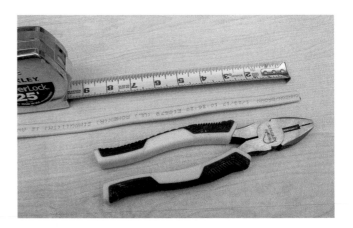

MEASURING THE LENGTH OF THE STRIP. Codes and general practice call for stripping 6 in. to 8 in. of sheathing so you have plenty of wire to work with when you attach devices and fixtures. It may seem excessively long, but you can always cut the wires later if needed. Using a tape measure for each strip would be tedious, so figure a quick way to gauge the length. In this example, the pliers are about 8½ in. long, making it pretty easy to figure a good length.

Avoid Knife Nicks

It's very important that you do not nick wire insulation as you strip the sheathing. If you do, you could create a very dangerous situation. For that reason, we do *not* recommend cutting across the cable with a knife. If you cut lengthwise, follow the instructions at right carefully.

Pros often find it quicker to poke unstripped cable into a box and then strip the sheathing inside the box. We show this technique on p. 170, but beginners should probably strip before poking into a box.

Cutting with the ground wire

This method makes it impossible to nick wire insulation inside the sheathing, and so is recommended. It's easier than it may look.

CUTTING CABLE TO LENGTH. You can probably cut two-wire 14-gauge cable easily using side cutters or lineman's pliers. When cutting 12-gauge or 3-wire cable, you may need to bear down with two hands. If you find the going rough, use a pair of shear-cut cable cutters.

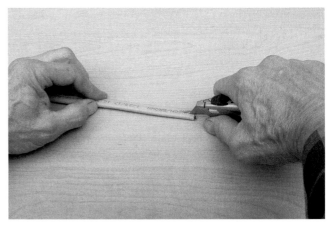

1 **SLICE A BIT OF THE END. Use a knife or cable rippers to make a ½-in.-long cut at the end of the cable. Cut in the exact center of the cable.**

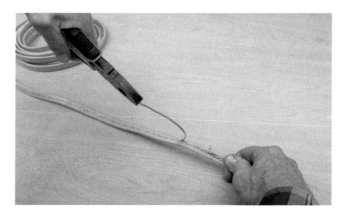

Slicing lengthwise

These methods are not difficult, but care should be taken not to damage any wire insulation as you work. For both methods, follow step 3 below left to finish the strip.

2 **PULL THE GROUND WIRE.** Pull apart the sheathing you cut and grab the ground (bare) wire with a pair of pliers. While holding the end of the cable with your hands, pull the ground wire, which will—with surprising ease—cut through the sheathing. Stop when you get to the desired length of the strip.

SLICE WITH A KNIFE. Practice this a few times on scrap pieces of cable until you get the hang of slicing the sheathing but not the wire insulation. Insert the blade of a knife into the exact center of flat NM cable, at the point where you want the strip to end. Push with enough pressure to cut through the insulation on one side and slice lengthwise to the end of the cable.

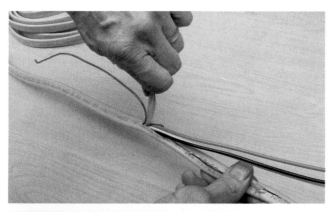

CABLE RIPPERS. This inexpensive tool almost automatically inserts into the center of the cable and makes only a shallow slice, to keep from damaging the hot and neutral wire insulations. Slip the cable through the hole in the bottom of the cable ripper, move up to the point

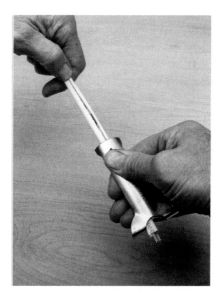

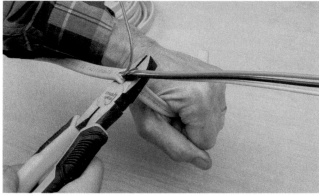

3 **PULL THE PAPER AND SHEATHING APART.** Disengage the insulated wires and pull out the paper wrapping. Pull back tightly on the sheathing and cut it off using lineman's pliers or side cutters. Cut the paper as well or simply rip it off.

where you want the strip to end, and squeeze. Then pull to create a sheathing slice.

Stripping inside a box

If you are confident of your skills, you can push and clamp unstripped cable into the box and then do the stripping.

Unfortunately, cable rippers cannot reach close enough to the insertion point, so you need to use a knife.

1 SLICE WITH A KNIFE. Starting about ¾ in. from the insertion point, use a knife to slice along the center of the sheathing. Work carefully so you don't damage any wire insulation.

2 TRIM THE EXCESS. Pull apart the sheathing, paper wrapping, and wires. Cut away the paper and sheathing as close as possible to where you started the center slice. Some electricians use a knife for this, but using side cutters ensures that you will not damage the wires.

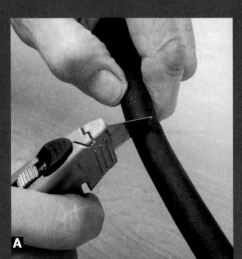

A

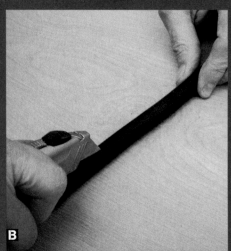

B

C

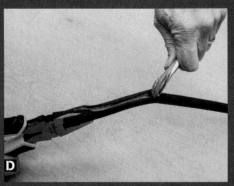

D

E

Stripping Thick Cable

Thick NM cable, which generally contains 10-gauge or thicker wires, is often round, and its sheathing can't be stripped using the methods for smaller cable. To ensure against damaging wire insulation, slice only partway through the sheathing, then use the wires to open it up.

Use a utility knife to cut a shallow slit around the cable at the end of the strip [A]. Cut only partway through the sheathing. Then make a lengthwise cut, again cutting only partway through [B]. At the end, make a short, deep cut so you can grab the wires [C]. Holding the sheathing with pliers, pull the wires out, which will finish the lengthwise cut [D]. Finish the strip by ripping the sheathing at the end [E].

Working with Armored Cable

Armored cable, also called metal-clad cable or "flex," is often used even in areas that allow NM cable, where it may be required for short runs that are at least partially exposed. Cutting the armor produces some sharp edges, so care should be taken when cutting it so you do not slice into wire insulation.

Stripping armored cable

These three steps apply to both MC and AC cable. Though it is possible to cut armored cable with a hacksaw, it is highly recommended that you buy and use a special rotary-type armored cable cutter.

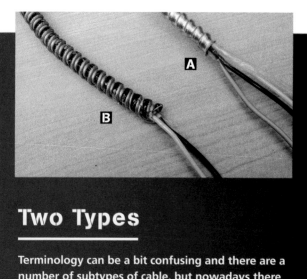

Two Types

Terminology can be a bit confusing and there are a number of subtypes of cable, but nowadays there are two types of armored cable. The most common—and most often approved—is MC, which has a green-insulated ground wire and a clear plastic protective wrapping around the wires [A]. You can also buy type AC, which has no grounding wire, but a thin bare aluminum "bonding wire" instead [B]. AC has paper, rather than protective plastic, wrapping around the wires. Type AC uses the sheathing, rather than a ground wire, as the grounding path.

TIP Older metal-clad cable was called BX, and nowadays armored cable of any type is sometimes called BX as well. However, all of today's armored cables protect the wires and have better insulation than older BX.

1 CUT WITH A ROTARY TOOL. Slip the cable into the tool's channel and adjust the cutting wheel so it touches the cable (top). Squeeze the tool's handle firmly and turn the crank several times to make a small lengthwise slice through the metal sheathing (above).

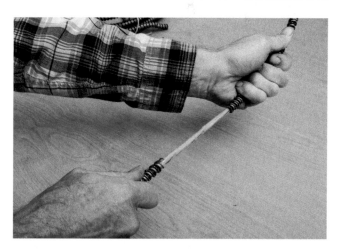

2 TWIST AND PULL OFF. Give the waste portion of the sheathing a twist, then pull it off. If the sheathing does not come off, repeat step 1, but adjust the wheel so it grabs the sheathing more tightly.

3 **CUT OFF SHARP EDGES.** Use diagonal cutters to snip away any sharp, pointy edges. Carefully examine the wires to make sure the insulation has not been damaged.

USING A HACKSAW. If you have only a few strips to make and if you work carefully, cutting with a hacksaw may make sense. Cut just barely through the metal, then bend the cable over, and finish the cut with side cutters. Look carefully to be sure you did not nick any wire insulation.

Protecting the wires for MC cable

Once the sheathing has been removed, take steps to ensure that the wires will be protected against sharp edges. (The steps are different for AC and MC cable.) Note that if you use the type of cable connector shown on p. 182, which has an integral bushing, you do not need to follow these steps.

1 **SLIP IN A RED BUSHING.** Slide a bushing over the plastic sleeve and into the metal sheathing. It should seat nice and tight.

2 **ADD A CONNECTOR.** Slide a metal connector over the bushing until it seats firmly against the end of the sheathing, then tighten the screws to hold it in place.

Protecting the wires and bonding for AC cable

Don't just snip off that thin metal wire or the little plastic strip; they are needed for a proper installation.

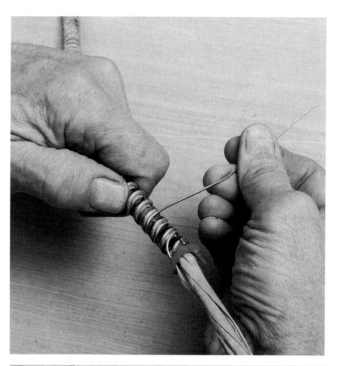

1 **PUSH IN A PLASTIC BUSHING.** Slide a red plastic bushing up along the wires so it goes around the paper sleeve and the thin metal wire. Press it firmly into the sheathing so it protects the wires from damage.

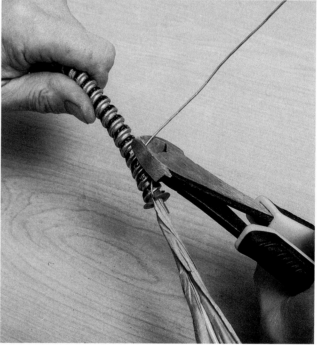

2 **WRAP THE BONDING WIRE.** Tightly wrap the thin bonding wire around the sheathing so it seats in the valleys. After a few revolutions, snip the wire.

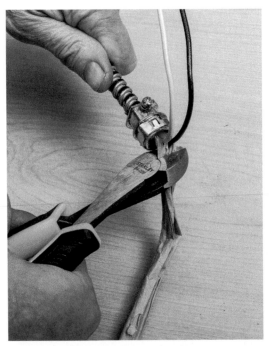

3 **ADD A CONNECTOR.** Slide a cable connector up firmly so it holds the bushing tightly against the sheathing, and tighten the setscrew. Pull to test that the connection is strong.

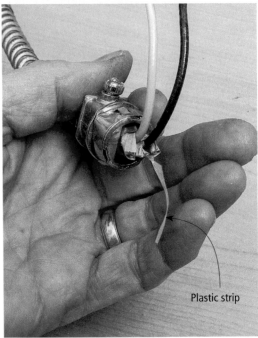

Plastic strip

4 **SHOW THE PLASTIC STRIP.** Separate the thin plastic strip out. Cut off the paper wrapping close to the connector, and then cut the plastic strip about 2 in. away from the connector. The plastic strip tells the inspector which type of cable you used.

Installing Boxes in Exposed Framing

If the framing is exposed, install the boxes first and then run the cable (pp. 177–182). (If the walls or ceiling surfaces are installed, you will install the boxes at the same time as the cable; see pp. 196–203.) This is usually straightforward work, but take care to install the boxes in the correct spots. Follow your electrical plan for the placement of boxes for receptacles, switches, and fixtures.

Receptacle boxes

Receptacle boxes are typically installed with their bottoms 8 in. to 14 in. above the floor. All the receptacles in a room should be at exactly the same height, but if heights vary slightly from room to room that is usually not noticeable. Exact horizontal placement is usually not a problem; putting them on the closest stud is usually close enough.

1 MEASURE FOR HEIGHT. Hammers are typically about 12 in. long, so many electricians use one as a height guide (right). To achieve another desired height, make a simple measuring jig out of two boards (far right).

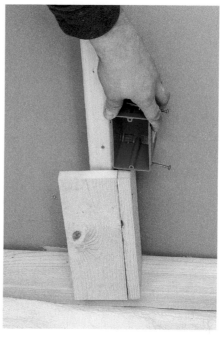

2 ATTACH. For a metal box, tap in the tabs that hold the box in place temporarily. Drive 1¼-in. screws to attach the box to a stud. Many single-gang plastic boxes are simply attached by driving their nails (see step 1).

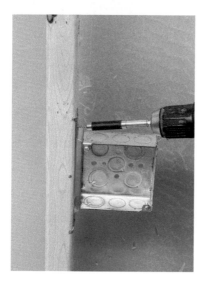

CEILING BOX. A simple box like this is nailed onto the side of a joist. For stronger boxes, or if you need to position a box between joists, see pp. 84–88.

Switch boxes

Switch boxes are typically installed with their bottoms 48 in. above the floor, though some people prefer lower or higher switches. A 4-ft. level makes an easy height gauge. Single-gang switch boxes can be attached like receptacle boxes, but larger boxes should be more securely anchored.

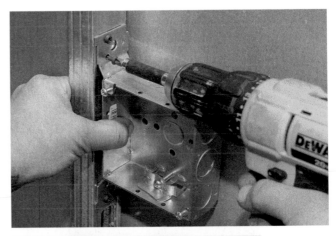

BOXES IN METAL FRAMING. If you have metal framing, attach boxes directly to the framing by driving self-tapping screws. Or attach a scrap of wood to the side of the framing and attach the box to that.

TWO METHODS FOR WIDE BOXES. This type of box has a metal bracket that attaches to the front of a stud, and it also has tabs for driving screws into the stud's side. This makes for a firm box. Another method uses a box with a plastic side flange. Apply construction adhesive to one edge of a 2×4 scrap (or 2×6, if the studs are that size) and slip it behind the flange. Drive screws and nails to attach the box on each side.

TIP Before you begin running cable, take time to be sure all the boxes are in good locations. Switches and receptacles should be placed so that they will not be too close to floor or wall trim. They should also be placed so they will be easy to reach even when a door is open.

Running Cable through Exposed Framing

If the studs or joists are not covered with drywall, running cable from box to box is straightforward. Of course, be sure to use the correct cable for your devices or fixtures. Cable should run through the centers of studs and should be slightly loose rather than tautly stretched; this helps protect the cable from being damaged by a nail driven after drywall is installed.

Drills and Bits

Use a right-angle drill, which enables you to drill straight holes between studs. In the steps below, we show a 20-amp cordless drill with a fast-cutting spade bit, which makes quick work of small projects. If you have a large project—with, say, over 100 holes to cut—it's a good idea to rent a ½-in. right-angle drill along with a heavy-duty bit, as shown here.

THE RIGHT SIZE BIT. Drill holes that are ⅛ in. to ¼ in. larger than the width of the cable you will run. This will allow them to be pulled through easily, at the same time minimizing weakening of the framing.

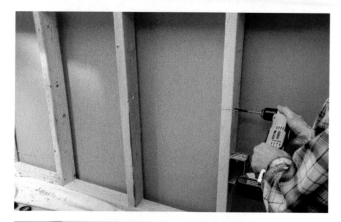

1 MARK FOR HOLES. Holes should be drilled 8 in. to 12 in. above the tops of the boxes. To keep them in a straight line, use a long level to mark the fronts of studs. Some pros find it is accurate enough to hold the drill at thigh or just-above-the-knee height.

2 DRILL HOLES. Drill holes using a right-angle drill. Holes should be in the centers of 2×4s (so a 1⅝-in. screw will not be able to reach the cable once ½-in. drywall is installed). You should be able to eyeball the centers, but check with a tape measure to be sure you are at least close to correct. To be sure, mark each hole with a sliding square.

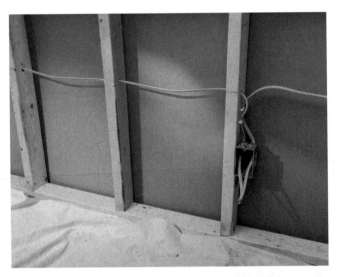

3 **SPOOL OUT CABLE.** If you just start pulling coiled cable through holes, it will twist and perhaps even kink—things you want to avoid. Feed the cable out from the coil first, and then pull the cable. If you have a lot of cable to pull, use a spool like the one shown for wires on p. 187.

4 **PULL AND STAPLE.** Pull the cable through the holes, taking care to avoid twisting or kinking. The cable should droop slightly between the studs, so it is not taught. Staple the cable within 8 in. of a box. You may choose to strip sheathing either before or after inserting into a plastic box (see pp. 168–169).

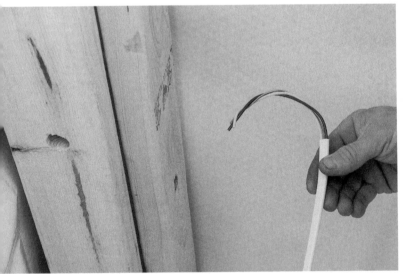

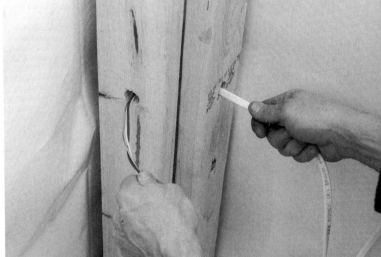

TURNING A CORNER. Where you need to turn an inside corner, drill holes on each side. Strip sheathing from the cable and bend it into a half circle, so it will be better able to thread through the holes, and then poke it through.

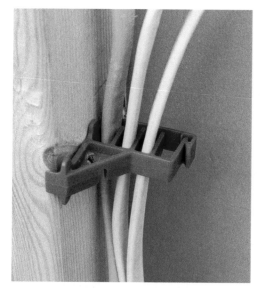

MULTI-CABLE STAPLES. Also called a cable stacker or cable standoff, a multi-cable staple allows you to secure several cables out of reach of stray nails.

Insulate Carefully

On an exterior wall, or if you want to add some soundproofing on an interior wall, add fiberglass insulation. Cut the insulation with a fair level of precision so there will be no air gaps.

Running Cable through Metal Framing

Metal framing has openings for running cable or conduit, but it also can have sharp edges. To prevent damage to cables while pulling them through, use snap-in plastic bushings, designed for the purpose. There is no need to attach cable to the sides of metal studs; just be sure the cable is securely clamped inside the box.

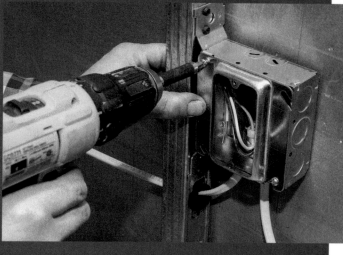

Connecting NM Cable to Boxes

Cable must be firmly connected to a box in a way that will not damage the sheathing or wires. There are various methods.

Plastic boxes

Most plastic boxes have openings for cable that are like trap doors, with little flaps that hold the cable in place pretty firmly; it is much easier to push the cable in than to pull it out. In addition, it's easier to push unstripped cable than cable with its sheathing stripped, but neither option is difficult.

Metal connector with nut

Connector with locking tab

Button push-in connector

CONNECTORS. Here are some of the most common cable connectors (also called box connectors or cable clamps) for NM cable. Other options generally work in much the same way as these.

Metal boxes

Metal boxes cost more than plastic boxes, and it will take more time to remove a knockout slug and install a clamp, but many pros prefer metal boxes because they are stronger. (See pp. 150–151 for choosing metal boxes and their mud rings.)

PUSHING INTO A PLASTIC BOX. You may be able to simply poke cable into an opening, but more likely you will need to use a screwdriver to loosen the flap first. You may also use it to hold the flap open while you insert the cable. Push the cable in until about 1 in. of sheathing pokes into the box. (After poking in, you will fasten the cable to a framing piece within about 8 in. of the box.)

REMOVING A SLUG. Use a hammer or lineman's pliers and a screwdriver to tap on a knockout slug until you can grab it with pliers. Twist a couple of times, and the slug will come loose.

TIP Resist the temptation to break off a plastic box's flaps, which would of course make it easier to insert the cable. The flaps are required by code, because they hold the cable in place.

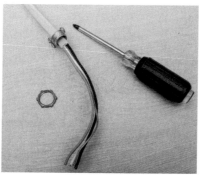

1 **ATTACH A METAL CONNECTOR.** Depending on the situation, it may be easier to first insert a metal connector into the box and loosely screw on the nut (left) or to attach the connector to the cable first (right).

2 **SLIP IN THE CABLE.** Slide the cable into the box. You may need to loosen the clamp first.

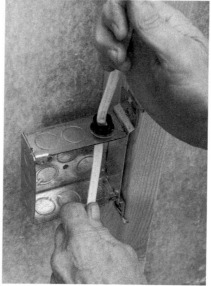

3 **TIGHTEN SCREWS AND THE NUT.** Use a screwdriver or a drill with a screwdriver bit to tighten the screws that clamp the cable. Hand-tighten the nut, then use a hammer or lineman's pliers with a screwdriver to tap on the side of the nut to tighten it as well. The connection does not have to be super tight, but the cable should not budge when you pull or twist it.

BUTTON PUSH-IN CONNECTOR. To use this type of clamp, push it up from the inside of the box. You might need to tap with pliers or a hammer to get it to click into place. Slip the cable down through the clamp, which grabs a little tighter than the plastic tabs of a plastic box.

 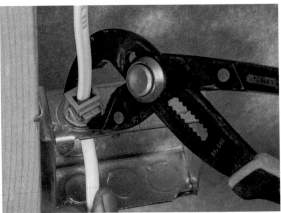 

CONNECTOR WITH LOCKING TAB. This type grabs the cable a bit more firmly. Tap or push the connector down from above into the knockout hole. Slide the cable in to the desired length, and then use pliers to squeeze the locking tab into place.

INTEGRAL CLAMP BOX. This type of box comes with a clamp inside. Push the cable in and tighten the screw to secure it.

Connecting armored cable to a box

Metal connectors (a.k.a. cable clamps) are used to attach armored cable to a box. Start by removing a knockout slug, as shown on p. 180.

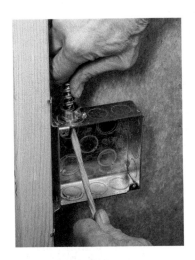  

STANDARD CABLE CONNECTOR. Install this type of cable connector either onto the cable first, or install it into the box first, then slip the cable in. Tighten the setscrew and test that the attachment is firm.

CONNECTOR WITH INTEGRAL BUSHING. To install this type of connector, which has its own bushing, push it into the knockout hole until it snaps in place. Slide the wires, with the plastic sleeve in place, through the connector until the metal sheathing seats firmly, and then tighten the setscrew. Cut back the clear plastic sheathing so no more than an inch protrudes into the box.

BOX WITH CLAMP. Don't use a box with an integral clamp like the one shown at top right, which is made for NM cable only. The type of clamp shown here holds the armored cable bushing snugly in place.

Working with Conduit

In many areas, metal or plastic conduit is required for locations where wiring is exposed, such as in basements, garages, and crawlspaces. In fewer locales, conduit is required for all wiring, even when it is hidden inside walls or ceilings. Conduit has two advantages: It protects wires from stray nails much better than NM cable, and even significantly better than armored cable. And conduit enables you to rewire for remodeling in the future without opening up wall surfaces; you can run new wires through the existing conduit.

TIP You can run standard solid-core wires through conduit, but as stranded wires are more flexible, they're easier to run, especially if you have a thicker strand of wires to push through.

Running EMT conduit

For indoor residential use, the most common type is electrical metallic tubing, or EMT, also called "thinwall." For outdoor jobs, intermediate metal conduit, or IMC, is a common choice. Plastic conduit is also often used outdoors.

Choose the right size conduit, so it will be easy to pull the wires through. Remember to take into account the ground wires when choosing:

- ½-in. EMT can hold up to twelve 14-gauge wires, nine 12-gauge wires, or five 10-gauge wires.
- ¾-in. EMT can hold up to twenty-two 14-gauge wires, sixteen 12-gauge wires, or ten 10-gauge wires.

These are the upper limits of capacity. If your project calls for almost as many as the upper limit, consider using ¾ in. instead of ½ in.

Install boxes first, then cut and bend conduit to fit between the boxes. If a conduit run (between two boxes or between a box and the service panel) has bends that add up to more than 360 degrees, install a pulling elbow (see below and p. 188) before you reach 360 degrees so you can pull the wires to that point, then start again. If there will be a place where wires branch off in two or more directions, install a junction box and cover it with a blank plate when you are done pulling wires.

Bending conduit takes some practice, but if you have a lot of conduit to run it is worth the trouble, because it saves money for fittings and allows the wires to run through smoothly.

1 **BENDING EMT CONDUIT. Measure for the place where the bend will start, and then move back 4 in. to 5 in. so the conduit will be a bit longer than needed. You will cut the pipe to length later (step 3). In most cases, it's easiest to bend on the floor: Slip the conduit into the bender (which should be made for your size of conduit) and slide it to the spot where the bend aligns with the mark on the bender. Step down on the footpad to make the bend.**

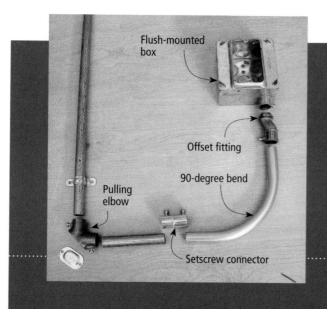

Flush-mounted box

Offset fitting

90-degree bend

Pulling elbow

Setscrew connector

Fittings Instead of Bending

If you have only a small job without too many bends, and if you have never bent conduit, it may make sense to do the job with fittings instead of bending conduit. Typical fittings, shown here, include a 90-degree bend, a pulling elbow, a setscrew connector, and an offset fitting for attaching to a flush-mounted box. On the downside, fittings are fairly expensive ($5 or so for a ¾-in. elbow, for example).

2 **MARK FOR CUTTING.** Hold the bent piece in place where it will go and check that the bends are correct. You may be able to correct small mistakes, but where bends are significantly misshapen you're better off cutting the conduit and starting again. Mark for cutting the conduit to length so it enters the connector by an inch or so.

3 **CUT CONDUIT.** The best tool for cutting conduit is a reciprocating saw with a metal-cutting blade, but a hacksaw works as well. Hold the conduit firmly in a clamp or with your foot so it doesn't vibrate as you cut.

4 **REAM THE CUT END.** It is very important to remove the burrs created by the saw, because they can cut into insulation when you pull the wires. You can use a pair of pliers that fit tightly into the pipe, but a reaming tool does a better job. Here we show a drill-attached reamer, but you can also use a hand reamer, as shown on p. 147.

5 **ATTACH TO BOXES, AND STRAP TO WALL.** Where the conduit and boxes will be exposed, use an offset fitting (or bend the conduit into an offset shape) so the conduit can rest flush against the wall. Attach the conduit to the wall with one- or two-hole straps every 4 ft. or less. On a concrete or block wall, use masonry screws.

WATERTIGHT COMPRESSION FITTINGS. For outdoor installations or areas that get wet, use watertight fittings.

Flexible metal conduit

Often called Greenfield, flexible metal conduit is frequently required for short runs of exposed wiring and for whips that attach to appliances like water heaters, cooktops, and dishwashers.

Cut Greenfield with a hacksaw or a reciprocating saw with a metal-cutting blade, as you would EMT. Ream away any burrs on the inside of the cut. Attach Greenfield to a framing member with a strap within 8 in. of the box and at least every 4 ft. along a run.

Greenfield tubing

Greenfield-to-EMT conduit connector

GREENFIELD PARTS. As with conduit, make sure your Greenfield will be large enough for the wires you plan to run. Use fittings made for conduit or flex; check that your Greenfield will easily fit into them.

Setscrew coupling

Setscrew connector

Clamp connector

Working with PVC conduit

Schedule 40 PVC is the most common type of plastic conduit for residences. It is fire-retardant and resists UV degradation, making it especially useful for outdoor wiring. It cannot be bent, so use fittings to make all the turns. As with EMT, install a pulling elbow if a run's bends total more than 360 degrees.

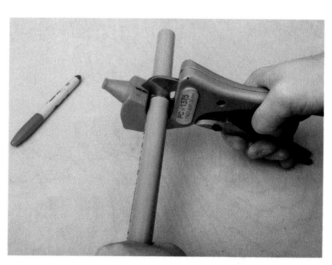

1 MEASURE AND CUT. Install the boxes first. Hold pieces in place to measure for cutting the conduit to length, and mark with a felt-tip pen. Cut with a cutter. (You can use a hacksaw, but that will be slower and will create more burrs to remove.)

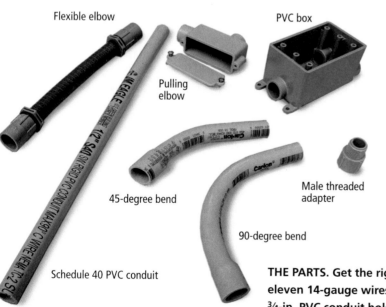

Flexible elbow

Pulling elbow

PVC box

45-degree bend

Male threaded adapter

90-degree bend

Schedule 40 PVC conduit

THE PARTS. Get the right size conduit: ½-in. PVC conduit can hold up to eleven 14-gauge wires, eight 12-gauge wires, or five 10-gauge wires; ¾-in. PVC conduit holds up to twenty-one 14-gauge wires, fifteen 12-gauge wires, or nine 10-gauge wires. Conduit comes with enlarged fitting openings at one end, so you usually do not need to buy couplings.

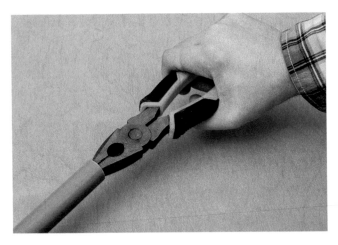

2 **DEBURR.** Use a knife or a pair of lineman's pliers to scrape away any burrs created by cutting. Plastic burrs will not damage wire insulation, but they will make pulling wires more difficult.

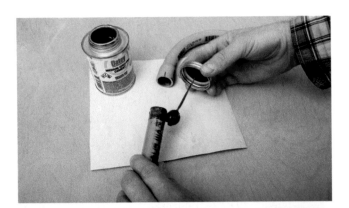

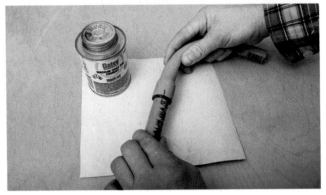

4 **CEMENT THE PARTS.** The cement dries quickly, so be prepared to assemble without delays. Apply electrician's PVC cement to the inside of the fitting and the outside of the conduit end. Push the conduit into the fitting with a quarter turn and hold in place for 10 seconds. Wipe away any excess cement.

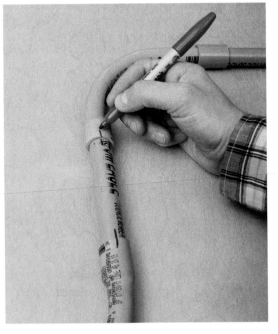

3 **DRY-FIT.** Assemble all the parts between two boxes, to be sure they will fit. (You cannot disassemble the parts after cementing.) Where needed, use a felt-tip pen to make layout marks so all the parts are facing in the right direction.

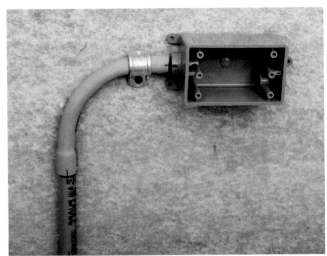

5 **STRAP.** Attach the conduit with PVC straps every 3 ft. or less. The strap shown here is made for use with masonry.

Pulling wires

Once the conduit has been installed, it's time to run wires through it. For a short run with one or two turns, you might be able to simply tape the wires tightly together at their ends, then push the wires through one box and into the other. However, if the run is longer than 8 ft. and has two or more turns, you probably need to use a fish tape.

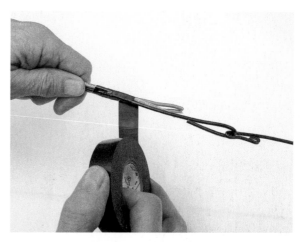

1 **THREAD A FISH TAPE.** Push a fish tape up through the box where the wires will end until it emerges in the box at the other end. On a long run you may need to jiggle the tape or push it back and forth until it slides smoothly.

2 **ATTACH WIRES TO THE TAPE.** Attach the wires to the fish tape in a way that does not create a large bulge that will be difficult to move through the conduit. Arrange the bent-over wire ends so they will not stack onto each other and so the taped joint will be fairly consistent in thickness.

WIRE SPOOLS FOR LARGE JOBS. If you have plenty of wire to run, a spool arrangement like this makes things go much more smoothly. If you don't have spools, feed the wires in carefully, so they don't get crimped or tangled.

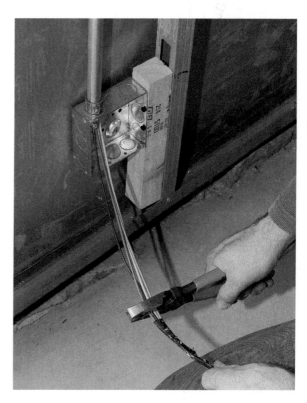

3 **PULL THROUGH.** You can now pull and reel in the fish tape until the wires emerge, then cut them off.

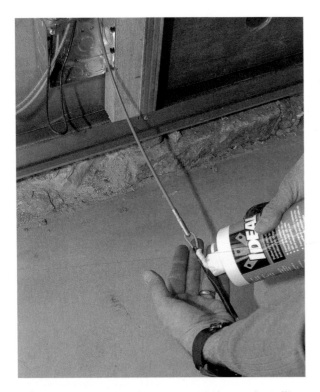

WIRE-PULLING LUBE. If things get tight, apply pulling lubricant to the front end of the wires, and apply more as needed while you pull. Lubricant makes pulling surprisingly easier.

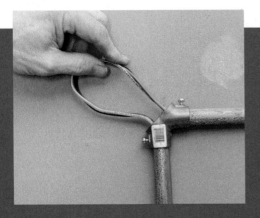

Using a Pulling Elbow

If the run is long, you may need to open a pulling elbow. If the wires have passed through the pulling elbow, have one person pull out the wires at the elbow while another person slowly reels in the fish tape. If things are really tight, you may need to pull the wires through one end of the elbow, then through the other end.

Remodel Boxes

Also called old-work or cut-in boxes, remodel boxes install into walls that are finished with drywall or plaster. They have ears or clips that clasp the box to the finished surface, so they are not as strong as boxes attached to framing members. But if the drywall or plaster (or the plaster lath) is in good shape, remodel boxes can be strong enough for receptacles, switches, and most ceiling fixtures (though not heavy chandeliers or ceiling fans). A number of remodel boxes are available; on these pages we show some of the most common.

The order of work when installing wiring inside finished walls and ceilings means that you may need to flip back and forth between the next 16 pages when installing a project. In most (though not all) cases, you will (1) cut the hole for the boxes, (2) run cable through walls and ceilings, (3) attach the cable to the boxes, and (4) make the electrical connections.

Sometimes You Should Use Standard Boxes in Finished Walls

If your wall or ceiling drywall or plaster is damaged, if you need to install a heavy ceiling fixture or a ceiling fan, or if running cable is difficult because of obstructions, it is probably a good idea to skip most of the steps on the following pages. Instead, cut a sizable hole in the drywall or plaster, install a standard box, and run cable as through exposed framing. Then patch the hole with drywall, tape, and joint compound. See pp. 86–87 for an example of this approach.

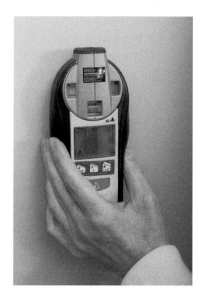

CHECK FOR OBSTRUCTIONS. Whichever type of box you use, first check with a multiscanner tool for obstructions inside the wall or ceiling. Check not only for wood or metal studs, but also for pipes, wiring, and ductwork. In particular, ductwork may mean that you need to move the box over a foot or more.

Plastic wall box

A plastic remodel box for switches or receptacles generally has two wings that flare out and then move forward when long screws are driven from the face of the box. This action clamps the box to the wall surface. The boxes also have fairly strong push-in tabs that hold the cable firmly in place. (You cannot staple cables to framing in a remodel situation, so these tabs are important.)

1 MARK FOR CUTTING. The remodel box may come with a cardboard template, which makes it easy to mark for the hole. If not, press the box against the wall using a small level to ensure it is at least close to plumb. Draw a line around the box's shape, but do not draw

around the "ears," which must rest against the wall (see step 4). The lines should outline an opening about ⅛ in. larger than the box.

2 CUT THE HOLE. To avoid roughing up the sides of the cut, first slice with a knife just outside the drawn lines. Then poke in a jab saw and cut to the inside of the knife line. Test to see that the box will fit into the hole.

3 RUN CABLES INTO THE BOX. Run cables through walls (pp. 196–203) and poke them into the box. You may choose to strip the insulation first, as shown here, or to strip it after the box is installed (see p. 170).

4 CLAMP THE BOX. Use a drill to drive the screws. (Working with a screwdriver will take a very long time.) This causes the box's wings to move out, then forward, to clamp the box against the drywall or plaster.

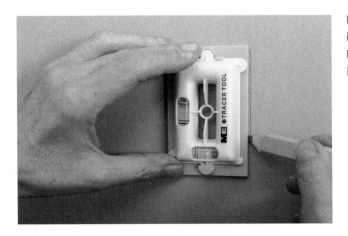

HANDY LITTLE TOOL. If you have plenty of boxes to install, this tool makes quick work of marking the holes. It will show that the box is plumb and level whether it's installed vertically or horizontally.

Plastic ceiling box

This works in the same way as a plastic wall box, with ears that move forward and grab the backside of the drywall or plaster. The difference is cutting a round hole.

1 MARK THE HOLE. These boxes really should come with cardboard templates, but often they don't. The hole must be cut precisely, because the lip is very narrow. You can press the box face-first against the ceiling, trace the outline of the lip, and then cut a hole that is about ⅜ in. smaller than the outline. Or use a compass set at half the diameter of the desired hole.

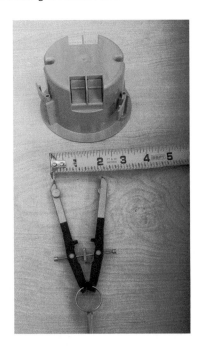

2 CUT THE HOLE. Test your drawing and cutting method on a scrap piece of drywall; the box should fit snugly, but not too tight. Slice through the drywall paper with a knife and then cut to the inside of the slice with a jab saw.

3 RUN CABLE AND CLAMP THE BOX. Run cable into the box, making sure that the tabs grab the cable firmly. Leave yourself at least 8 in. of stripped or unstripped cable. Check that the ears are not flared out, push the box firmly up into the hole, and drive screws to fasten the box.

Metal box with ears

Metal remodel boxes can be a bit trickier to install than plastic, but they do grasp the cable more firmly. And they may be required in your area.

1 **MARK AND CUT THE HOLE.** Hold the box face-side-out against the wall, check that it is fairly level, and trace its outline on the wall. Slice through the drywall paper with a knife and then cut with a jab saw. After cutting the rectangle, ream the sides to accommodate the box's ears.

2 **RUN CABLE.** Metal remodel boxes have integral clamps. With this type, you must strip the sheathing first. Thread the wires through the clamps and drive screws to tighten against the sheathing.

3 **ATTACH THE BOX.** Position the ears so they fit through the holes on the sides, and slip the box up against the wall. Drive screws to clamp the box to the wall.

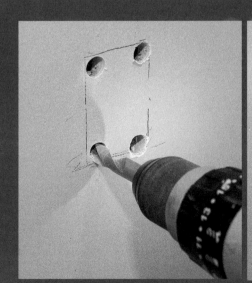

Cutting Holes in Plaster Walls

Plaster is easy to crack, making it difficult to cut clean holes. One method is simply to score repeated lines with a utility knife until you finally make it all the way through. Another is to drill holes in each corner and then score the lines several times with a knife. Then use a jigsaw to cut the hole. If you cause the underlying wood lath to vibrate, it will likely crack the plaster, so press very firmly against the wall as you cut, and move slowly.

Metal box with plaster ears

This is a tried-and-true remodel box, suitable for old plaster walls. It's somewhat fussy to install, but it works better than other boxes because the ears are not against the plaster—which does not indent as easily as drywall. That ensures against cover plate problems.

1 **CUT THE HOLE AND NOTCH FOR THE EARS.** Cut a hole for the box. Then cut strips of plaster only—exposing the wood lath—¾ in. wide above and below the hole. Wall plaster can be anywhere from ¼ in. to 1 in. deep. In most cases, you can cut a small section like this using only a utility knife.

2 **ADJUST THE BOX'S EARS TO THE PLASTER THICKNESS.** Measure the thickness of the plaster, without the lath. Use a screwdriver to adjust the box's ears so the box protrudes out from the ears the same thickness as the plaster. Test the fit and readjust the ears as needed so the box's front is flush with the wall.

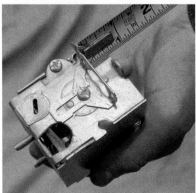

3 **DRIVE SCREWS TO ATTACH.** Run cable into the box. Drill pilot holes slightly smaller in diameter than the screws you will drive. (If you don't, the lath may crack, and the screws will not grab.) Drive four small screws to attach the box to the lath.

Grabbing Power from an Existing Circuit

If you need to add a modest number of electrical users, you may be able to get the power from an existing circuit. First, figure out which users are already on the circuit, and calculate to make sure the new service will not overload the circuit (see pp. 154–155). If there is no conveniently located circuit with enough space for your new service, you will need to run cable in a home run to the service panel and install a new circuit (see pp. 196–203).

The method shown on these pages is designed to minimize damage to the walls so you can patch them quickly. The small triangular holes can be filled in without attaching the drywall to framing. If you find this surgical approach difficult, you can cut out larger openings; in that case, you'll need to do some framing and more patching.

The main steps on these pages show tapping into a receptacle in a metal box. You'll also see instructions for tapping into a receptacle in a plastic box, a switch, and a junction box.

▐▶ Be sure to shut off power at the service panel. Test several times to verify that power is off, as shown on pp. 8–9. For double protection, use electrician's tools and work as if the wires were hot.

1 **PULL OUT RECEPTACLE AND CUT A TRIANGLE.** Shut off power and pull out the receptacle you want to grab power from. Use a multiscanner to make sure there are no obstructions above the box. About 4 in. above the box, cut out a triangle in the drywall, just large enough for you to insert four fingers (see step 5 on p. 194). Retain the triangular cutout for patching the wall later.

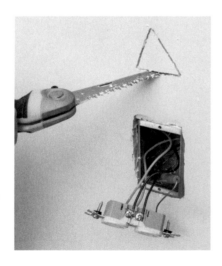

2 **REMOVE A SLUG.** Insert a screwdriver (not your best electrical screwdriver) down through the hole and tap with a hammer to loosen a knockout slug in the box. Reach up into the box with lineman's pliers, grab the slug, and twist it back and forth until you can remove it.

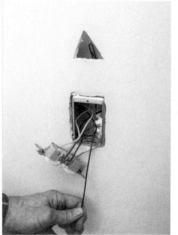
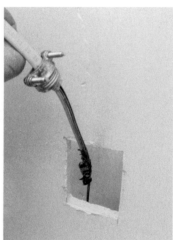

3 **RUN A FISH TAPE.** Cut the hole for a remodel box for your new service (see p. 189). From the cable you will use, strip about 10 in. of sheathing and several inches of wire insulation. Thread a fish tape up through the box where you will grab power and into the box for the new service. Attach a cable connector, without its nut, to the end of the sheathing. Tightly wrap the stripped wires around the fish tape, and then wrap tightly with tape.

4 **FISH WIRES DOWN INTO THE BOX.** Carefully pull and reel in the fish tape until the wires emerge in the box. Remove the tape.

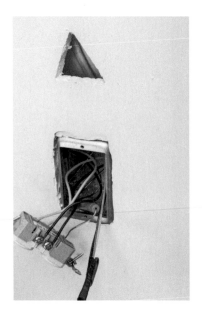

5 **SECURE THE CABLE CONNECTOR WITH A NUT.** Reach into the hole and push with your fingers as you pull the wires with your other hand. When you feel the cable connector inserting into the box's hole, hold it in place while you slide the clamp's nut up. Tighten the nut by hand, and then tap a screwdriver to tighten the nut (see p. 181). Make connections as shown below. Install a new box with a receptacle as shown on pp. 112–114 and p. 189.

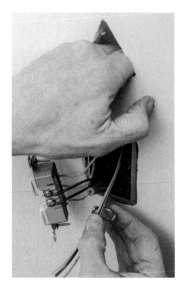

POWER-GRABBING CONNECTIONS

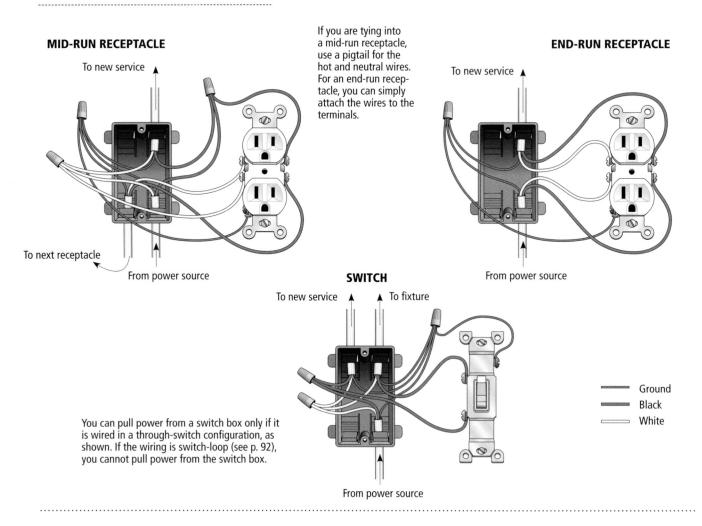

MID-RUN RECEPTACLE

To new service

To next receptacle

From power source

If you are tying into a mid-run receptacle, use a pigtail for the hot and neutral wires. For an end-run receptacle, you can simply attach the wires to the terminals.

END-RUN RECEPTACLE

To new service

From power source

SWITCH

To new service   To fixture

From power source

You can pull power from a switch box only if it is wired in a through-switch configuration, as shown. If the wiring is switch-loop (see p. 92), you cannot pull power from the switch box.

——— Ground
——— Black
——— White

RUNNING INTO A PLASTIC BOX. If you're tapping into a receptacle in a plastic box, the procedure is a little easier: Just poke the wires firmly through the tab connector. Make sure about 1 in. of sheathing pokes into the box.

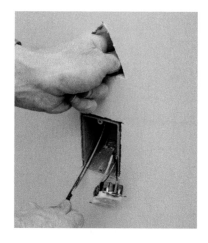

TYING INTO A JUNCTION BOX. If you have an exposed junction box, grabbing power is simple. ▧➤ Shut off power, and test for power carefully, because some junction boxes have more than one circuit running through them.

SWITCHING A PULL-CHAIN FIXTURE

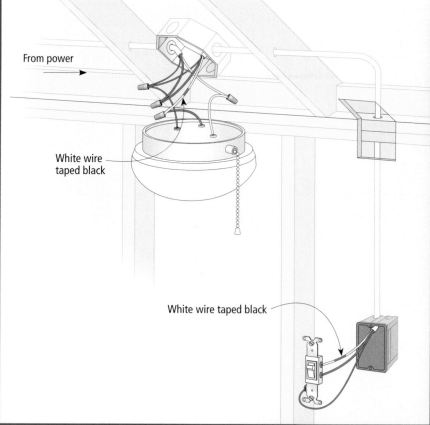

From power →

White wire taped black

White wire taped black

Putting a Pull-Chain Fixture on a Wall Switch

Pull-chain switches often need to be replaced and are inconvenient, so there's good reason to rewire so the light is controlled by a wall switch.

A pull-chain fixture has power running directly to the fixture, so the easiest way to wire for a switch is with switch-loop wiring. ▧➤ Shut off power and test that power is off. Remove the fixture and cut a hole for a remodel switch box in a nearby wall. Run two-wire cable from the fixture box to the hole, install the cable into the remodel box, and install the box.

Rewire the fixture as shown: Connect the ground wires together and run a pigtail to the box. Splice the black wire from the power source to the black wire running to the switch. Splice the white wire (marked with black tape) from the switch to the black or colored wire on the fixture. Splice the white wire from the power source to the white wire in the fixture. At the switch box, mark the white wire black and attach it and the black wire to the switch terminals.

Running Cable through Finished Walls

Fishing cable behind walls, above ceilings, and under floors is one of the most physically demanding and time-consuming wiring tasks. The goal is to minimize holes in the walls, which usually must be patched, taped, covered with three coats of joint compound (and each coat needs to dry and then be sanded smooth), primed, and painted. That's a lot of time-consuming work, so even if careful fishing costs you several hours of extra work, it will probably save you time in the long run.

Talk with your building department to learn if your inside-the-walls wiring will pass muster with them. Some inspectors may want you to staple NM cable near the box, meaning you will have to cut larger holes in drywall.

Learning about the obstructions

Make drawings that show the locations of all boxes for receptacles, switches, and fixtures. Your inspector may demand to see this, and it will help you plan the wiring route. Use a wall scanner (p. 45) to learn the locations of studs, joists, pipes, wires, and ductwork. If you have a duct, it likely fills the entire depth of the cavity inside the wall, meaning you cannot run through it.

Framing can be surprising. In a newer home, studs and joists are likely 16 in. on center (so there is a 14½-in. gap between them). But spacing can vary, especially near the end of a wall. In an older home, spacing can be irregular. There may be fire blocks—horizontal blocking pieces that span from stud to stud, usually about halfway up the wall height. An exterior wall in a newer home may have 2×6 rather than 2×4 studs. In a prewar brick home, the exterior wall may not have studs at all—just "furring strips" that may be ¾ in. or 1½ in. thick, nailed to the brick. That means you will have to run cable very carefully, and perhaps chip out holes in the brick for the boxes. You can also install special shallow-depth boxes.

Choosing the best route

If there is an unfinished attic above or an unfinished basement ceiling below, you can likely fish cable into the unfinished space without cutting holes in the wall or ceiling. Once there, it's easy to run cable across or along the joists.

In other cases you will have to cut holes in drywall or plaster. If possible, remove base trim or other molding and cut holes that will be covered up when you replace the molding. If that is not possible, cut channels or holes in drywall and reserve the cutouts, which will make neat patches.

Protecting the wiring

By code, and for your own peace of mind, electrical cable should be kept safe from stray nails. This means that where it runs through a stud or joist it should be at least 1¾ in. away from the finished wall or ceiling. If it is closer than that, a protective nailing plate must be attached in front of the cable (see p. 200).

TIP If you run armored cable instead of NM cable, the wires will of course be far better protected. Still, it is possible for a nail or screw to pierce the armor, so it is best to follow the same installation guidelines as for NM.

Cut to the Side of the Stud or Joist

When cutting a large opening, people often try to cut the drywall to the center of a framing member so they can attach the patch to half of the member's thickness. But making this cut is difficult, and you often run into fasteners. A better idea is to cut alongside the stud or joist, which is much easier to do and produces a neater patch. Before you install the patch, attach 2× cleats, as shown on p. 87. Then you'll have plenty of nailing surface for attaching the patch.

Common Routing Paths

When running cable inside walls and ceilings, the three methods shown below and on p. 198 often serve to make the job go smoothly.

FISHING THROUGH WALLS AND CEILINGS

In this example, power is grabbed from a receptacle. Base molding is removed so a channel can be cut in the wall near the floor. A fish tape is used to pull cables up from the floor to a switch box and to pull up and over to a ceiling fixture or box. Where the cable goes through the wall's top plate, either drill holes in the center of the plate or cut a notch and protect the cable with a wall plate.

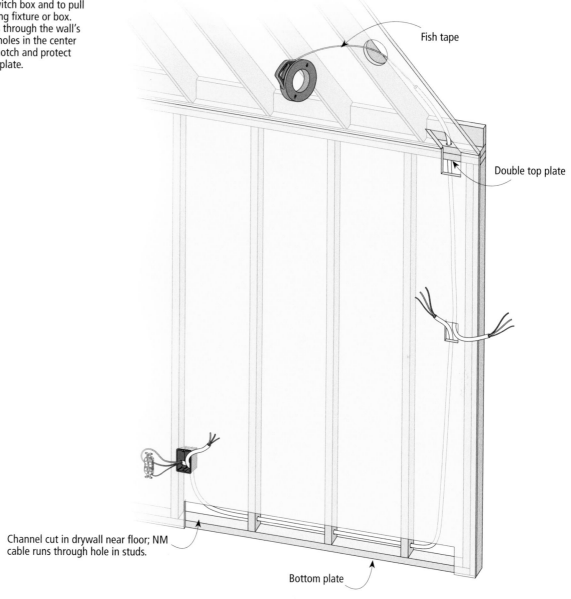

Fish tape

Double top plate

Channel cut in drywall near floor; NM cable runs through hole in studs.

Bottom plate

(continued on p. 198)

Common Routing Paths (continued)

FISHING THROUGH JOISTS

Where cable travels parallel to joists, fishing is usually simple. If you have to run cable across joists, use a fishing drill bit (see p. 147 and p. 203). You may be able to cut and fish through box- or fixture-size holes, as shown here, or you may need to cut larger holes and patch the ceiling afterward.

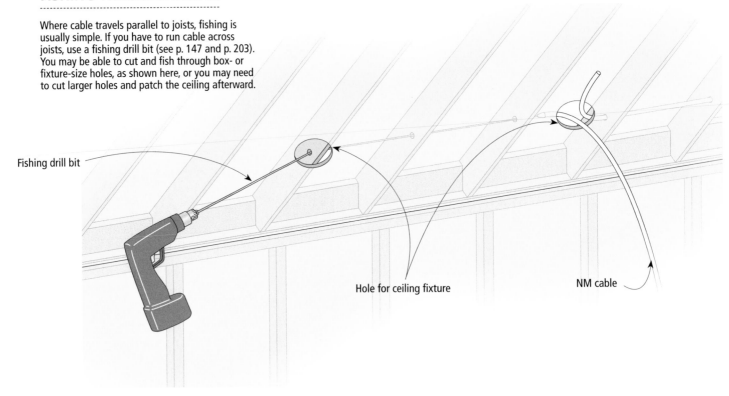

Fishing drill bit

Hole for ceiling fixture

NM cable

BACK-TO-BACK DEVICES

If a new receptacle or switch box will be installed on the other side of a wall, offset the new hole so the boxes do not bump into each other.

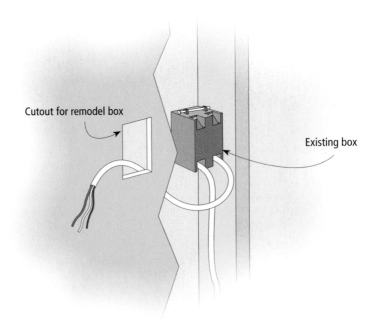

Cutout for remodel box

Existing box

Running near the floor

If your base trim is 3¼ in. or wider, you can usually run cable behind it so you don't need to patch the wall. If your molding is too narrow, or if it is not in great shape, consider replacing it.

1 **REMOVE THE MOLDING.** To avoid denting the wall or the molding, use one or two taping blades and a flat pry bar to pull the base molding away from the wall. Remove the trim nails by pulling them from the back side of the molding.

2 **CUT A DRYWALL CHANNEL.** Use a jab saw to cut a channel in the drywall or plaster. Take care not to cut above the top of the molding. Keep the cutout drywall pieces even if they are not in good shape; you'll use them just to back up the molding later.

3 **DRILL HOLES.** A small right-angle drill should fit into the channel you've cut. Equip it with a ⅞-in. bit and bore holes in the centers of the studs. Where boring holes is not possible, cut notches in the faces of the studs and plan to install nailing plates later.

4 **RUN CABLE.** Thread cable through the holes. Where cable is closer than 1¼ in. to the front edge of framing, add protective nailing plates.

5 **REPLACE THE BASE.** Replace the drywall, and nail it if needed to hold it in place. If the wall is plaster, install a spacer strip so the trim will rest flat against the wall.

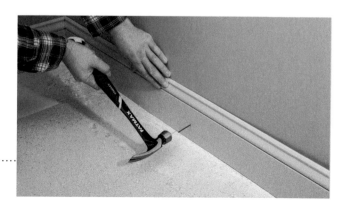

If You Must Notch

Sometimes you may run into nails, or a tight spot, and need to cut a notch in a stud's face instead of drilling a hole in the middle. Make two shallow cuts with a handsaw or reciprocating saw. After running the cable, add a protective plate. You will not be able to drive a nail here to attach the base molding.

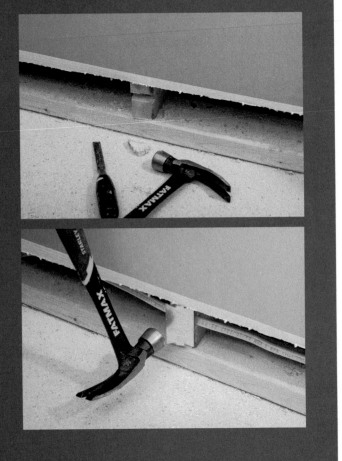

Running across a wall

Where running cable horizontally near the floor is not possible, cut a channel in the middle of the wall. This will necessitate replacing the cutout and patching and painting the wall after wiring is done.

1 **CUT A CHANNEL.** Use a wall scanner (p. 45) to make sure there are no ducts where you want to run the cable. Also check for pipes; you can usually run around them, but you don't want to damage them. Mark the wall for cutting a channel wide enough for your right-angle drill to fit into. As much as possible, choose a path where you will not run into nails. Use a jab saw to cut the channel. At the studs, you may find it easier to cut with a utility knife. Retain the cutout pieces for later patching.

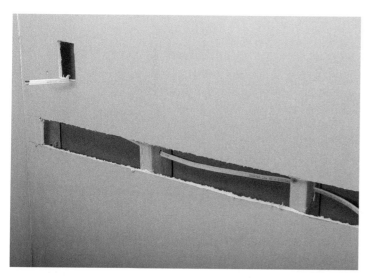

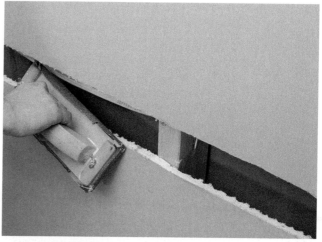

2 **CUT HOLES AND RUN CABLE.** Cut holes or notches, as shown on p. 199 and p. 200. Thread the cable through the holes. Run cable into boxes. The cable should be slightly slack, rather than taut.

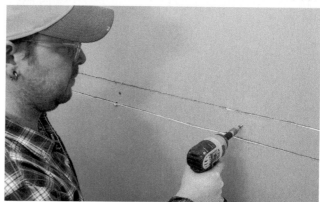

3 **REPLACE THE CUTOUTS.** Scrape and sand away any rough edges or shredded paper on the cutout pieces, so nothing will interfere with taping the patch (step 4). Press the cutouts back into the panel. Drive drywall screws to attach to the studs.

4 **PATCH THE WALL.** Press mesh drywall tape to cover the joints. Apply a layer of joint compound, using a blade wide enough to span across the entire patch. Allow to dry, scrape or sand, apply another coat, and repeat until the surface is even. Sand smooth and cover with primer and paint.

Channel in a Lath-and-Plaster Wall

The lath strips in an older lath-and-plaster wall are from 1 in. to 1½ in. wide and about ⅜ in. thick and are attached across studs or joints with ¼-in. spaces between them. If you remove two side-by-side laths, the resulting channel will be just wide enough for a small drill to fit into.

To cut a channel for running cable, first drill small test holes to find the gaps between laths. Strike chalklines along the gaps. Score the lines with a utility knife several times to ensure the plaster will not crack, then use a reciprocating saw to make shallow cuts on the inside of the knife lines (A). Tap away the plaster to reveal the lath (B) and pry it away (C). Save the lath for use later. Remove nails from the studs. Drill holes (D) and run cable (E). Patch the wall (F).

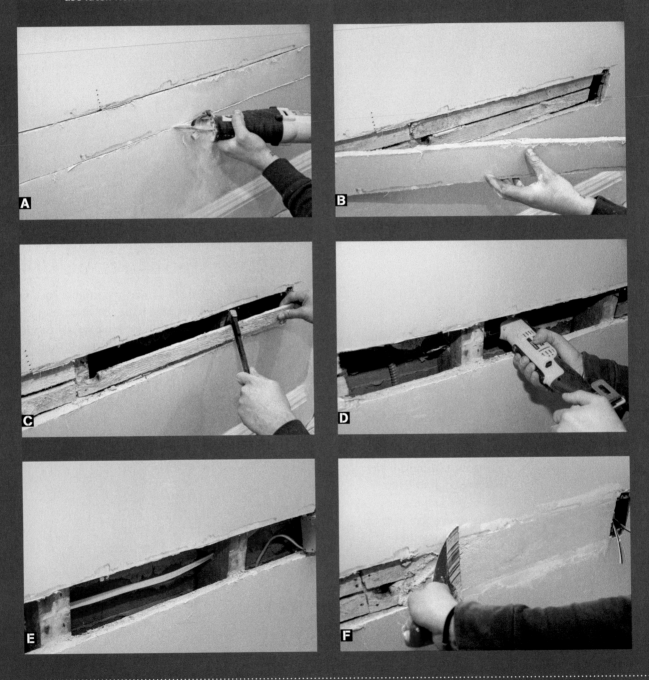

Fishing down to a basement or crawlspace

If the floor below has an unfinished ceiling, it's easy to run cable from a receptacle box hole near the floor down to the basement. From there, running cable through exposed joists is straightforward.

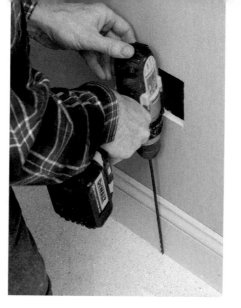

1 DRILL A LOCATOR HOLE. To run cable without a fishing bit, remove the base shoe and drill a locator hole. Use a long, narrow bit.

2 DRILL UP FROM THE CEILING. Down in the basement or crawlspace, drill a ⅞-in. hole up through the baseplate. If the wall is framed with 2×4, the hole should be about 2¼ in. over from the locator hole.

3 FISH UP. Push a fish tape up through the basement, and pull it through the box hole. Then attach another fish tape to it and pull it down into the basement. Attach the cable to the second fish tape and pull it into the basement.

Up into an Attic

To fish up into an attic with an unfinished floor, basically follow the steps for fishing down into a basement. Near the ceiling, cut out an access hole, saving the drywall cutout for patching later. In most cases there will be a single top 2× plate; bearing walls and exterior walls will have a double plate. Fish up through the plate either using a fishing bit (as shown) or using a locator hole, then fish tape as shown above.

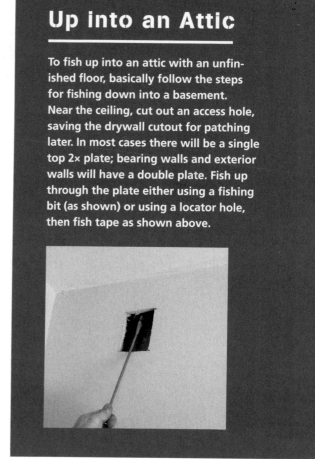

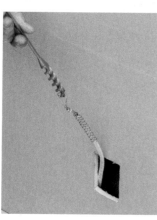

WITH A FISHING BIT. If you have a fishing bit, cut a hole for a box or remove an existing box. Guide the bit down the hole, through the wall's base plate, and into the basement. Attach cable to the bit's wire grabber (see p. 147) and pull the cable up through the hole.

Wiring for New Receptacles and Fixtures

UP TO THIS POINT, we have given instructions on working with cable and wire, installing boxes, running cable through unfinished or finished space, and generally planning for new service. Now we turn to specific instructions for installing new receptacles and light or fan fixtures.

We start with illustrations and descriptions of common wiring setups. You won't be able to use our wiring examples as your plans, because your setups will differ. But the plans shown will give you plenty of help in making your own drawings and installing your own wiring setups.

After installing the cable and boxes, you will most commonly connect ceiling and wall fixtures as shown in Chapter 3. However, some lights necessarily require running cable and have their own hook-ups. The two most common are recessed canisters and undercabinet lights, so we include them here.

Before running wiring, be sure to check that your service will not overload a circuit (see pp. 154–155). You may need to install a new circuit (see p. 214 and pp. 223–224).

Wiring Setups

The following pages show some of the most common wiring configurations used in homes. This book has already covered some basics; see the list at right for more setups shown elsewhere in the book.

The illustrations here show installation with NM cable and metal boxes. If you are using plastic boxes or metal conduit, grounding will likely be different. With conduit or armored cable, the ground wires will be green insulated rather than bare copper (see pp. 24–25).

➠ **For all wiring projects, be sure to shut off power at the service panel. Test several times to verify that power is off, as shown on pp. 8–9. For double protection, use electrician's tools and work as if the wires were hot.**

Other Wiring Setups in This Book

■ **Two ways to wire a switch and fixture (including wiring options for a ceiling fan)** p. 92
■ **Wiring for special-duty switches, including dimmers, timer, switch/receptacle, and pilot light** pp. 106–112
■ **Wiring GFCIs and AFCIs to protect other receptacles** pp. 114–116
■ **240-volt air-conditioner receptacle** p. 118

TIP Though not a hard and fast rule, many electricians follow this sequence when wiring in a box: First connect the grounds, then the neutrals, and finally the hots (black or colored). Working methodically and maintaining the same order will help you keep from getting confused as you work.

MULTIPLE RECEPTACLES

Connecting receptacles in a line is a matter of running two-wire cable between the boxes and connecting wires to terminals—black or colored hot wires to brass terminals and white neutrals to silver terminals. As you move away from the power source, the next receptacle is considered to be "downstream."

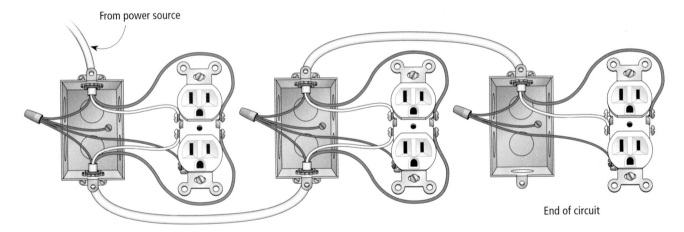

From power source

End of circuit

TWO RECEPTACLES IN A BOX

If you have two receptacles in one double-gang box, bring power to the box. Then use pigtails to connect to ground, neutral, and hot terminals as well as the outgoing cable to the next receptacle.

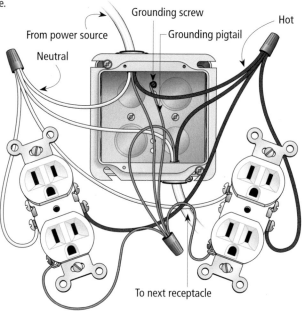

Grounding screw

From power source

Grounding pigtail

Hot

Neutral

To next receptacle

SWITCH CONTROLS MULTIPLE FIXTURES

THROUGH-SWITCH WIRING

If a switch will control more than one fixture, wire the switch as you normally would for through-switch wiring. Connect the first fixture—and all subsequent fixtures, until you reach the last one—with pigtails for the hot and neutral wires. At the last fixture, simply connect the hot and neutral wires to the fixture.

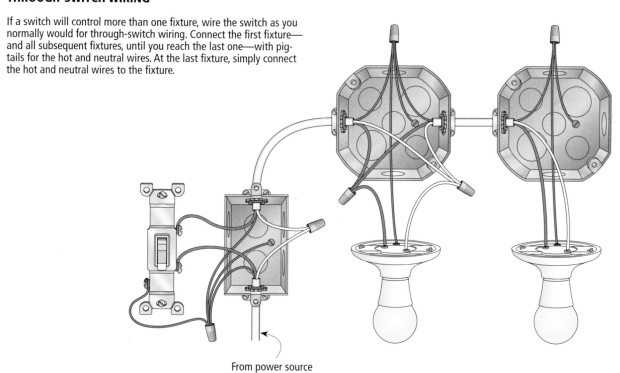

From power source

SWITCH CONTROLS MULTIPLE FIXTURES

SWITCH-LOOP WIRING

If power enters a fixture box first, run three-wire cable between it and any other fixture boxes that will be controlled by the switch. In the first and subsequent fixture box, splice the black wires together. Use pigtails to splice the neutral wires to the neutral fixture lead and splice the black lead to the red wire. In the last fixture box, splice the white wire to the white lead and splice the black wires together. Splice the black lead to the red wire and the white wire leading to the switch; mark the white wire black to indicate that it is hot.

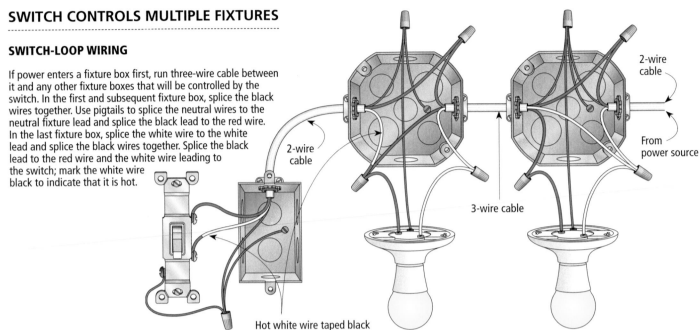

2-wire cable

2-wire cable

From power source

3-wire cable

Hot white wire taped black

MULTIPLE SWITCHES AND FIXTURES

THROUGH-SWITCH WIRING

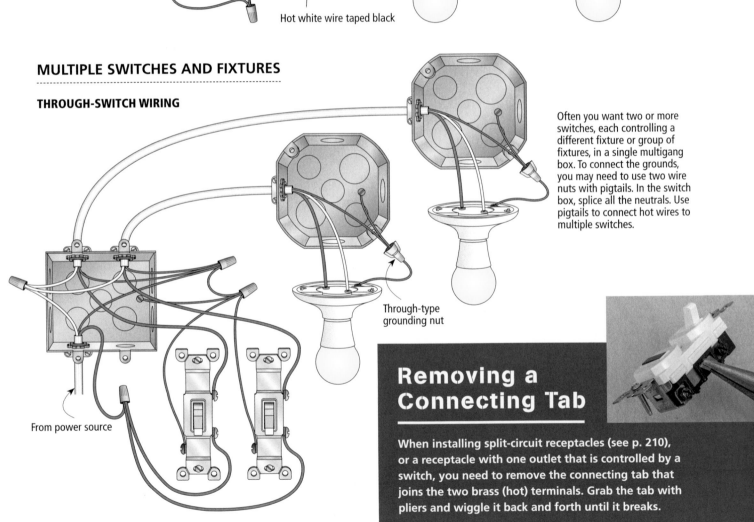

Often you want two or more switches, each controlling a different fixture or group of fixtures, in a single multigang box. To connect the grounds, you may need to use two wire nuts with pigtails. In the switch box, splice all the neutrals. Use pigtails to connect hot wires to multiple switches.

Through-type grounding nut

From power source

Removing a Connecting Tab

When installing split-circuit receptacles (see p. 210), or a receptacle with one outlet that is controlled by a switch, you need to remove the connecting tab that joins the two brass (hot) terminals. Grab the tab with pliers and wiggle it back and forth until it breaks.

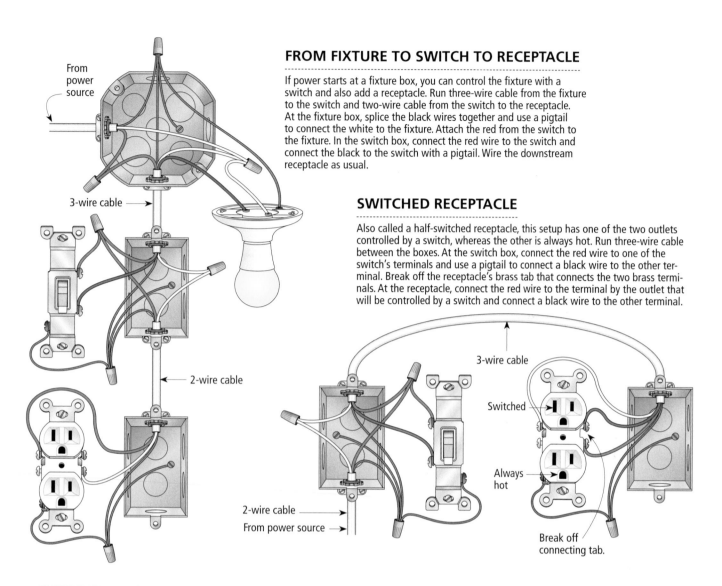

FROM FIXTURE TO SWITCH TO RECEPTACLE

If power starts at a fixture box, you can control the fixture with a switch and also add a receptacle. Run three-wire cable from the fixture to the switch and two-wire cable from the switch to the receptacle. At the fixture box, splice the black wires together and use a pigtail to connect the white to the fixture. Attach the red from the switch to the fixture. In the switch box, connect the red wire to the switch and connect the black to the switch with a pigtail. Wire the downstream receptacle as usual.

From power source

3-wire cable

2-wire cable

SWITCHED RECEPTACLE

Also called a half-switched receptacle, this setup has one of the two outlets controlled by a switch, whereas the other is always hot. Run three-wire cable between the boxes. At the switch box, connect the red wire to one of the switch's terminals and use a pigtail to connect a black wire to the other terminal. Break off the receptacle's brass tab that connects the two brass terminals. At the receptacle, connect the red wire to the terminal by the outlet that will be controlled by a switch and connect a black wire to the other terminal.

3-wire cable

Switched

Always hot

2-wire cable

From power source

Break off connecting tab.

SWITCHED RECEPTACLE, WITH MORE RECEPTACLES

If you will have more receptacles downstream from a half-switched receptacle, connect the wires to the first downstream receptacle in the same way, using three-wire cable, except that you connect the hot wire to the brass terminal with a pigtail. Connect the next receptacle as you normally would a mid- or end-line receptacle.

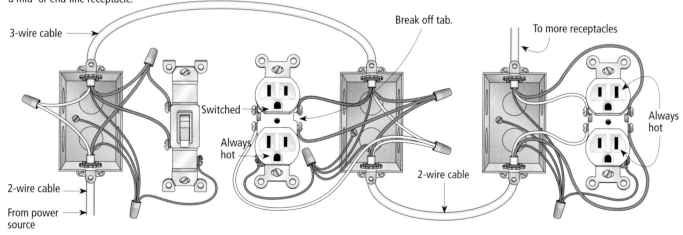

3-wire cable

Break off tab.

To more receptacles

Switched

Always hot

Always hot

2-wire cable

From power source

2-wire cable

SPLIT-CIRCUIT RECEPTACLES

In this arrangement, each receptacle has one outlet on one circuit and the other outlet on another circuit. That way you can plug two heavy-use appliances or tools into a single receptacle with little chance of overloading a circuit. In some areas, this arrangement is required for receptacles over kitchen counters instead of the more usual GFCI protection. (GFCI or AFCI receptacles may not be wired in this way; see below.) Start at the service panel with a double-pole circuit breaker, which supplies power from two circuits. Run three-wire cable from there and to all the receptacles. On all the receptacles, remove the tab connecting the two brass terminals. Use pigtails to attach a black wire to one terminal and a red wire to the other terminal on all the receptacles.

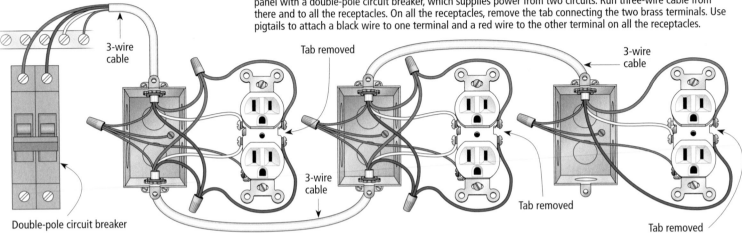

3-wire cable

Tab removed

3-wire cable

3-wire cable

Double-pole circuit breaker

Tab removed

Tab removed

RECEPTACLES ON ALTERNATING CIRCUITS

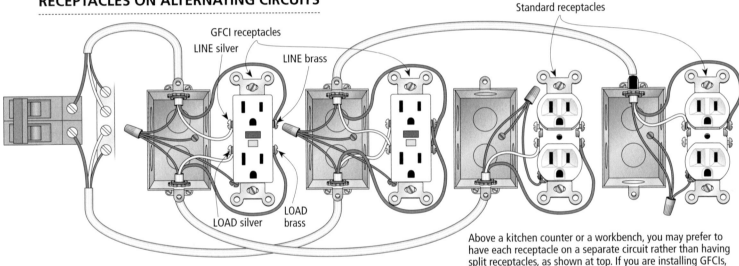

Standard receptacles

GFCI receptacles
LINE silver

LINE brass

LOAD silver

LOAD brass

Above a kitchen counter or a workbench, you may prefer to have each receptacle on a separate circuit rather than having split receptacles, as shown at top. If you are installing GFCIs, you cannot split the receptacles anyway. The solution is to run receptacles on separate circuits and simply alternate the locations of the receptacles.

GFCI RECEPTACLE PROTECTS FIXTURE

Where a light and switch are outdoors or in another location where moisture is a possibility, it's a good idea to provide them with GFCI protection. This is done the same as you would to protect downstream receptacles: Connect the incoming power wires to the LINE terminals and the outgoing wires to the LOAD terminals.

LOAD silver

LOAD brass

From power source

LINE silver

LINE brass

Three-Way Wiring

If you want to control a light or set of lights from two different locations, you need to do some three-way wiring. This means installing two special three-way switches in very specific ways, depending on the locations of the switches and fixture(s). If you want to control a fixture or fixtures from three different switches, you'll need a four-way switch and two three-ways (see p. 213).

A three-way switch has one brass or dark-colored terminal called the common terminal, two same-colored terminals called travelers, plus a grounding terminal.

Some general principles and procedures:
• Connect the hot "feed" wire that brings power into the box to the common terminal of one switch. (If power enters the fixture box first, it does not connect to the fixture but runs to a switch's common terminal.)
• Connect the hot wire from the fixture to the common terminal of the other switch.
• Run hot wires from the two traveler terminals of one switch to the traveler terminals of the other switch.

However, things get complicated, so the following pages show three-way wiring arrangements in detail.

⟹ **Before starting any wiring, be sure to shut off power at the service panel. Test several times to verify that power is off, as shown on pp. 8–9. For double protection, use electrician's tools and work as if the wires were hot.**

SWITCH–FIXTURE–SWITCH

Running cable from a switch to the fixture and then on to the other switch is the most common setup in a large room or long hallway. Two-wire cable brings power into the first switch box, and three-wire cable runs to the fixture and also to the other switch. At the first switch box, connect the feed wire to the common terminal. Splice the neutrals, and connect the black and red wires (from the fixture) to the traveler terminals. At the fixture box, splice the black wire to the white wire leading to the other terminal, and mark the white wire black. Connect the black and white wires to the fixture, and splice the red wires together. At the other switch box, connect the white-marked wire and the red wire to the traveler terminals, and connect the black wire to the common terminal.

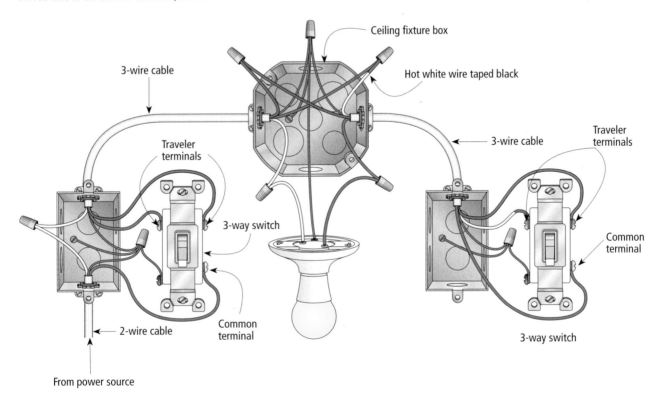

Ceiling fixture box

3-wire cable

Hot white wire taped black

3-wire cable

Traveler terminals

Traveler terminals

3-way switch

Common terminal

2-wire cable

Common terminal

3-way switch

From power source

SWITCH–SWITCH–FIXTURE

This arrangement is often used when installing switches at the bottom and top of stairs. Two-wire cable brings power into the first box, three-wire cable connects the two switch boxes, and two-wire cable runs from the second switch to the fixture. At the first switch, connect the feed (hot) wire to the common terminal. Splice the neutrals, and connect the red and black wires (that lead to the other switch) to the traveler terminals. At the second switch box, connect the red and black wires from the first switch to the traveler terminals. Splice the neutrals, and connect the black wire (leading to the fixture) to the common terminal. Wiring the fixture is straightforward.

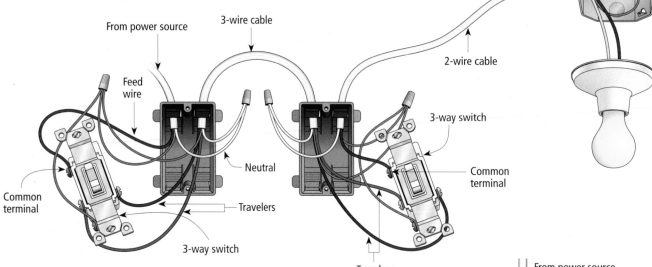

From power source

3-wire cable

2-wire cable

Feed wire

3-way switch

Neutral

Common terminal

Common terminal

Travelers

3-way switch

Travelers

FIXTURE–SWITCH–SWITCH

If you already have switch-loop wiring (see p. 92), with two-wire cable running to the fixture and between the fixture and the switch, here's a way you can add another switch. You will have to run three-wire cable from the first switch to the other switch box. At the first switch, connect the white-marked-black wire from the fixture to the common terminal. Splice the two black wires. Mark the other white wire black and connect it and the red wire to the traveler terminals. At the second switch, mark the white wire black and connect it and the red wire to the traveler terminals. Connect the black wire to the common terminal.

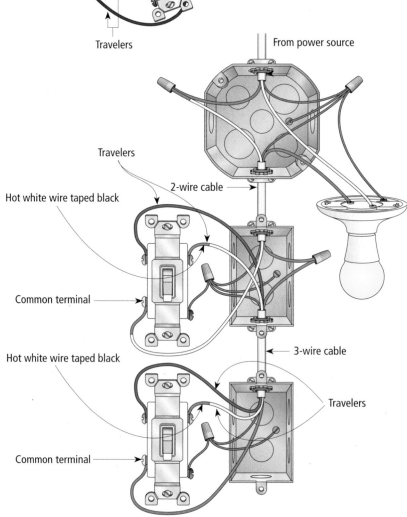

Travelers

From power source

Hot white wire taped black

2-wire cable

Common terminal

Hot white wire taped black

3-wire cable

Travelers

Common terminal

Four-Way Switching

A four-way switch can be added to a three-way setup for a third switch option. A four-way switch has two pairs of terminals, typically one with silver screws and one with brass screws. The four-way must be placed either between two three-way switches or between a three-wire switch and the fixture. The three-ways are wired as for a standard three-way setup. One pair of traveler wires, from a switch or fixture, is connected to one pair of terminals on the four-way; the other two travelers are connected to the other pair.

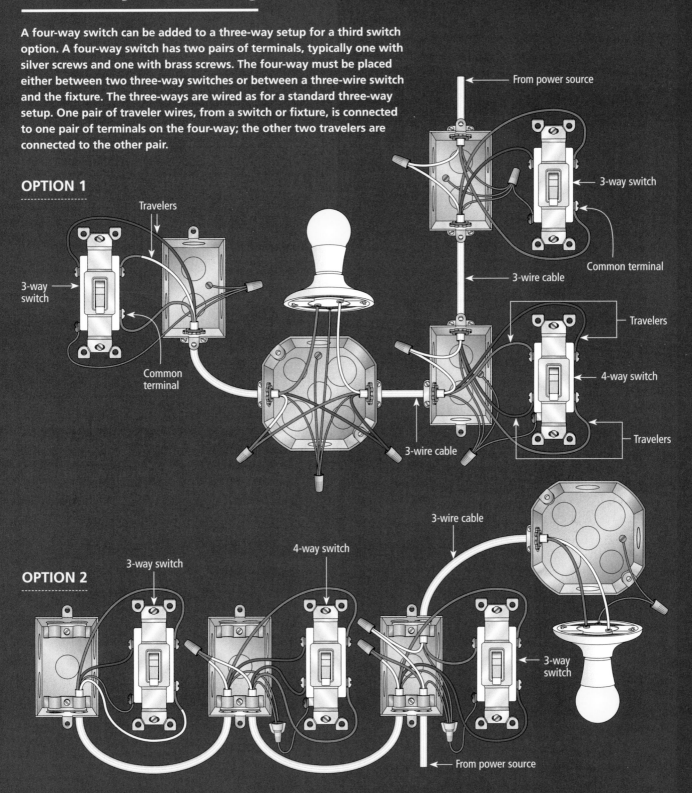

From power source

3-way switch

Common terminal

3-wire cable

Travelers

4-way switch

Travelers

3-wire cable

OPTION 1

Travelers

3-way switch

Common terminal

OPTION 2

3-way switch

4-way switch

3-wire cable

3-way switch

From power source

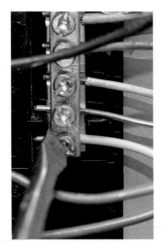

Wiring a Home Run for a New Circuit

Installing a new circuit sounds like a major, complicated task, but it's actually pretty simple. All of the operations—planning so as not to overload a circuit, running cable, removing a knockout, clamping cable, and connecting to a circuit breaker and a terminal—have already been well covered in this book; it's just a matter of putting them all together.

First, check that there is an open slot on your service panel for a new circuit breaker. (Or plan to replace a standard breaker with a duplex breaker.) Be sure that the service panel has enough capacity to handle the new service (see pp. 223–224). Run cable with 12-gauge wires for a 20-amp circuit or 14-gauge wires for a 15-amp circuit. To install a new 240-volt circuit, see pp. 222–223.

Install the new receptacles, lights, or appliances first. Run cable from the new boxes to the service panel, following the steps shown in Chapter 7. Make electrical connections to the new service users. Then shut off power and make connections in the service panel.

1 **PROVIDE PLENTY OF WIRE LENGTHS. At a** place near where the new breaker will go, remove a knockout. (Make sure it is the right size for the cable connector you will use.) Whether you are stripping cable sheathing or running wires in conduit, give yourself lots of wire length, because the hot, neutral, and ground wires all have to travel around the perimeter of the panel and to different places.

2 **CONNECT THE GROUND AND NEUTRAL WIRES.** Route the ground and neutral wires neatly around the panel's perimeter, and then cut and strip their ends so they can be inserted into an available hole in the ground/neutral bus bar. (Some panels have separate bars for the neutral and ground wires.)

➡️ **Provide yourself with adequate temporary lighting, then shut off the service panel's main breaker, which kills power to the entire panel and the entire house.**

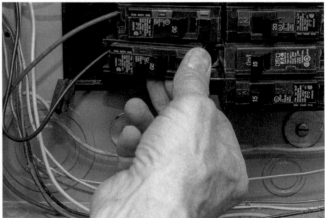

3 **CONNECT TO THE NEW BREAKER AND SNAP IN.** Run the hot wire in the same careful way. Cut the wire to fit, strip its end, insert into the breaker, and tighten the setscrew. Clip the plastic end of the breaker to the panel and then push the metal part onto the hot bus bar. Restore power and test.

Installing Undercabinet Lighting

Undercabinet lights that plug into a receptacle are easy to install but must be switched on individually. If you want the lights to be controlled by a wall switch, the wiring gets more serious. The solution shown in the steps on the following pages minimizes wall patching because it reuses a single-gang box.

Position the lights where they will light up the counter without shining in people's eyes. Often that means placing them to the rear, where they will cover up holes in the wall created by running wiring. If lights do glare, you may be able to solve the problem by installing a baffle—a strip of wood about 1 in. wide—on the underside of the cabinet near the front.

Adding these lights will probably not overload the circuit you tap into, because today's LEDs and other fixtures merely sip electricity. Still, look at pp. 154–155 to make sure the circuit can handle the extra load.

Installing lights controlled by a switch-receptacle

In this approach, a receptacle is replaced with a switch-receptacle so that its switch controls the light(s). The outlet of the switch-receptacle will always be hot, so you can plug a small appliance into it. You may choose to install the lights first and then connect to power, but before you open the receptacle box, ⠿➤ **be sure to shut off power at the service panel. Test several times to verify that power is off, as shown on pp. 8–9. For double protection, use electrician's tools and work as if the wires were hot.**

1 DRILL ACCESS HOLES. Determine where you want the fixture and mark for a hole that the cable will travel through. Also cut a hole above the receptacle so you can reach in for running cable into the box. Here, the wall is plaster so we drilled a hole; if your walls are drywall, you may choose to cut out a triangle instead, as shown on p. 193. To drill holes, use a hole saw, as shown, rather than a spade bit.

2 RUN CABLE INTO THE RECEPTACLE BOX. ⠿➤ With power shut off, pull out the receptacle. Follow the steps on p. 180 for removing a knockout and running cable into the box. For a metal box, secure the cable with a cable connector. If you have a plastic box, poke the cable into the box so it is secured by the opening's flap.

3 WIRE THE SWITCH-RECEPTACLE. Disconnect wires from the receptacle. Snip and restrip the wires if they are long enough. Wire the switch-receptacle so the outlet is always hot and the switch controls the cable running to the fixture (see p. 209). Do not remove the connecting tab. Here, the receptacle was

mid-run, so a pigtail is used to connect to the hot wire leading to downstream receptacles.

Just Changing Fixtures

If you already have switched undercabinet lights and want to replace them—say, by changing from fluorescents or halogens to LEDs—doing so will not be difficult. If possible, choose new fixtures that will cover up the holes in walls and cabinets left by the old ones. ⠿➤ **Shut off power, open the old fixtures, and disconnect the wire splices.** Open up knockouts in the new fixtures, run the cable and wire into them, make the same connections, and drive screws to attach the new fixtures to the underside of the cabinets.

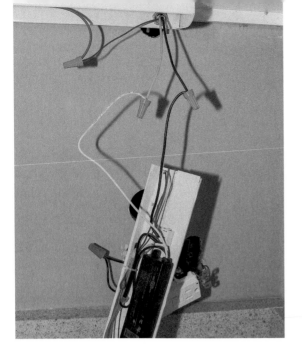

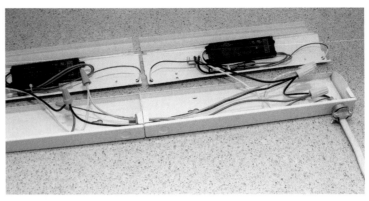

CONNECTING FOR DOWNSTREAM FIXTURES. If there will be more fixtures controlled by the same switch, wire them as shown. If the fixtures are separated, you will need to run cable from fixture to fixture. You may staple the cable to the underside of the cabinet, or cut more holes and hide the cable inside the wall.

4 **WIRE THE FIXTURE.** Connect cable to the fixture's housing with a cable connector. Splice ground, neutral, and hot wires to the fixture's leads.

6 **TEST, AND PATCH WALLS.** Restore power and test that the light works. Replace wall cutouts and apply joint compound in several coats, sanding between coats, until the wall is smooth. Prime and paint.

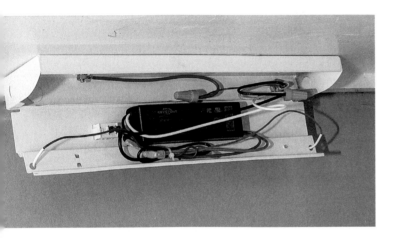

5 **TUCK WIRES AND ASSEMBLE THE FIXTURE.** Carefully push wires in as you fold the fixture onto the housing. Make sure you do not trap any wires as you do this.

Two more wiring options

If you would rather have a standalone switch controlling the undercabinet lights, the wiring is not any more complicated. If the framing is exposed, you will probably want to choose one of these two options. If the wall is finished, you will have to enlarge a hole and replace a box, or cut a new hole for a new box.

SWITCH IN SAME BOX AS RECEPTACLE. In this arrangement, the switch for the lights shares a box with a receptacle. On a mid-run receptacle, the feed wire splices to two pigtails, so it connects to one terminal of the switch, one terminal of the receptacle, and the cable leading to the other receptacles.

SWITCH IN A SEPARATE BOX

If you'd rather have a separate box for the switch, connect the switch's hot wire to power in the receptacle box (here, using pigtails because the receptacle is mid-run). Run power through the switch and on to the fixture.

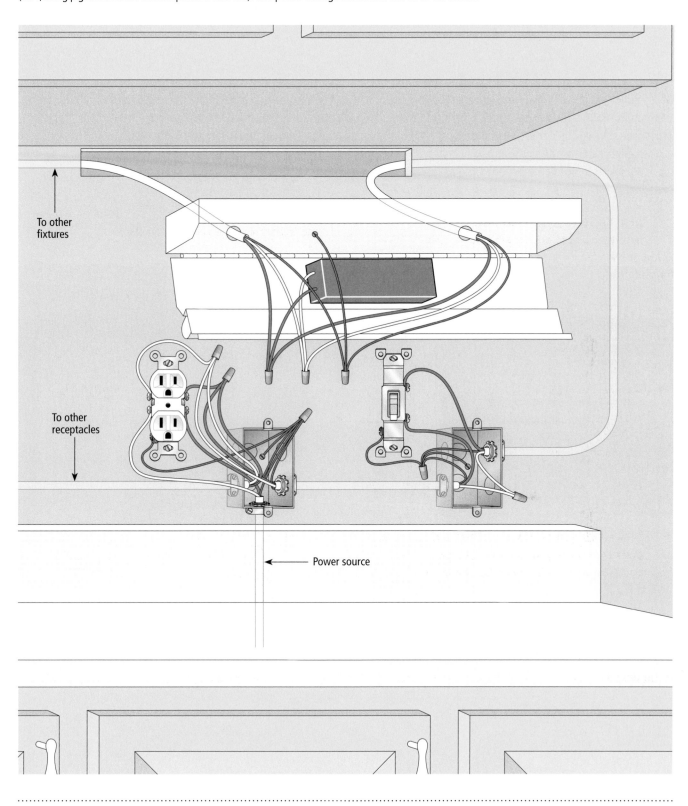

To other fixtures

To other receptacles

Power source

Recessed Canister Lights

These visually unassuming lights, also called pot lights or can lights, are housed inside hollow openings in the ceiling. Thin LED fixtures that look like recessed cans are also available, but they are actually more difficult to install because you have to install a ceiling box for each fixture. Recessed canisters have their own integral boxes, so you just need to string cable from light to light, and in most cases, you can use LED bulbs with them.

These lights come in a wide variety of styles and are typically 4 in. to 8 in. in diameter. Once the basic can fixture is installed, you can finish with the trims of your choice: simple lenses, black or white baffles for various effects, swivel "eyeball" trims that can be directed at a work of art, and moisture-proof trims for showers.

One of the most popular lighting projects is installing recessed canisters in a room with finished ceilings. As the following steps show, this can usually be done without needing to patch the ceiling afterward. If you have an existing switched ceiling fixture you can remove its box, cut a hole for a recessed light, and then string cable from light to light. Or leave the existing light in place and run cable from its box to the canister locations.

Of course, you can also run wiring to a new wall switch (or two, if you want a three-way setup) and have the canisters controlled separately from any existing ceiling fixture. See pp. 211–212 for the most common ways to install multiple lights controlled by one or multiple switches.

Canister Light Placement

Measure the ceiling and make a drawing showing where you want to place the lights. It often works well to space lights 5 ft. or 6 ft. apart. However, be aware that ceiling joists will very likely force you to move some lights over by as much as 8 in. You may also want to determine where furniture will be positioned and place the lights accordingly, as shown here.

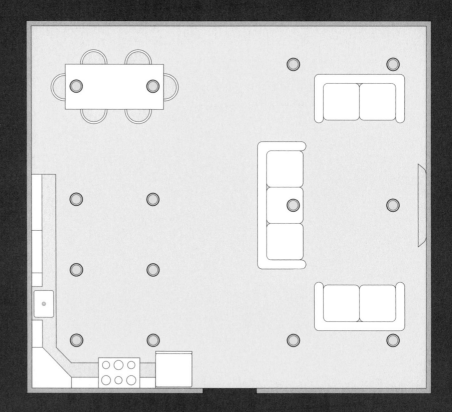

Installing canister lights in a finished ceiling

It's usually easiest to cut the holes for the canisters first, then run cable, and finally make the electrical connections. Before you make any connections, ➠ **be sure to shut** off power at the service panel. Test several times to verify that power is off, as shown on pp. 8–9. For double protection, use electrician's tools and work as if the wires were hot.

1 **MARK FOR CENTERS.** Use a stud detector or wall scanner to find joist locations. Canisters may need to be moved over so they do not bump into joists. Figure your desired layout and use a framing square and tape measure to mark the centers of the lights. Where the lights are in a row, use a string line to make sure the row is straight.

2 **MAKE SURE THERE ARE NO OBSTRUCTIONS.** Bend a wire so one leg is equal to the radius of the lights you will install. Drill a hole at the center mark, insert the wire, and spin it around to make sure there is nothing in the way.

3 **CUT THE HOLES.** Canister lights typically have small flanges that rest against the ceiling, so the holes need to be cut with a fair amount of precision. You could use the supplied template (shown here) to draw circles and then cut with a jab saw, but the going will be slow and it's easy to make mistakes. Instead, purchase a hole-cutting tool, which has a wide-cutting bit and a plastic tray that captures most of the dust created by drilling (above right). Adjust the cutter to match the hole. Make a test cut on a scrap piece of drywall and check that a canister light will fit—not too tight, but snug enough so the flange rests against the drywall. Cut the hole, holding the tool upright at all times so you don't spill any dust. Continue cutting all the holes.

4 **DRILL THROUGH JOISTS.** If a cable run is parallel to joists there should be no obstructions, so you can have a helper push the cable through one hole while you reach into another hole to grab the cable. But if the cable runs perpendicular to joists, you will have to run it through holes in the joists. To make the holes, use a long fishing bit as shown. In most circumstances, it can drill through two joists.

5 **PULL CABLE BACK THROUGH HOLES.** Pull the fishing bit through the next hole, and clip on the mesh cable grabber. Insert the cable into the grabber; when you pull, it will squeeze the cable firmly. Pull the cable back through the holes.

TIP If the cable comes loose from the mesh grabber while you pull, wrap the cable and mesh tightly with electrician's tape to improve the connection.

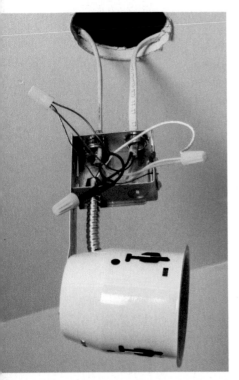

6 **WIRE THE FIXTURE.** The light has an electrical box attached. Remove its cover, strip cable and wires, and make electrical connections. The example shown is perhaps the most common: hot and neutral wires are spliced to the fixture's leads and also to the cable that runs to the next fixture.

7 **ATTACH THE FIXTURE.** Carefully slip the fixture's box, then its body, up into the hole. (You may need to slide mounting hardware back into the body before you can do this.) Press the fixture up firmly, so its flange is tight against the ceiling. Slide or push the three mounting brackets, which grab the drywall from the other side, and clamp the fixture to the ceiling.

Aim the Bit by Bending

You want the holes to be near the centers of joists, or at least 2 in. above their bottoms. Depending on how far away the joist is, you may need to grab the fishing bit firmly and slightly bend it. Poke the bit's tip into the joist, remove your hand, and drill the hole.

8 **INSTALL TRIM AND BULB.** Depending on the type of trim, you may need to screw in the bulb first, or you may need to first attach the trim, then the bulb. The trim attaches via some type of mounting springs or clips.

MOISTURE-RESISTANT FIXTURE. Here is another type of fixture, one with a trim and lens that seal tightly, making it suitable for a wet situation such as above a bathtub.

Installing canister lights in exposed framing

Where the ceiling is unfinished you can install new-work recessed fixtures, which pivot from side to side for exact positioning.

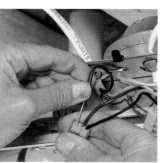

1 **WIRE THE FIXTURE.** Run cable into the fixture's box and make connections, which is usually a simple matter of splicing grounds, hot wires, and neutrals together. Fold the wires back into the box and replace the box's cover.

2 **ATTACH THE FIXTURE.** To fasten the fixture, slide its arms out until they span between joists. The fixture's hardware will automatically drop it ½ in. below the joists, so it will be flush to the finished drywall. Drive four nails or screws to secure the fixture.

3 **ADJUST THE POSITION.** To position several lights in a straight row, stretch a string line that is parallel with a nearby wall. Slide the fixture over until it aligns perfectly. Now you can install the drywall and add the trim.

240-Volt Receptacles

Some heavy-use appliances, such as electric heaters, ranges (or ovens and cooktops), water heaters, and large air conditioners, require 240-volt current (which may be referred to as 220-volt or 250-volt current). If you are installing a new 240-volt appliance, you will need to run cable of the correct size to the service panel, where you will install and connect to a new double-pole 240-volt circuit breaker.

Different 240-volt appliances use specific receptacles and wire sizes. Receptacles will be labeled for safe capacity and should tell you which size wires and breaker to use. For example:

- Many electric clothes dryers use 30 amps; four 10-gauge wires and a 30-amp double-pole breaker are needed for this. Some models require 40 amps.
- A 240-volt window air conditioner may, depending on its size, use 20 amps; only 12-gauge three-wire cable is needed, as well as a double-pole 20-amp breaker (see step 4 on the facing page).
- An electric range or oven is supplied by a 120/240-volt receptacle. The 120-volt service is for timers, clock, and sensors, and 240 volts is needed for heating elements. Ranges are often 50 amps, which requires 6-gauge wires.

Three- and Four-Wire Dryer and Range Receptacles

Prior to the year 2000, electric clothes dryers and ranges usually used three-wire receptacles and cords, meaning there were three wires—two hots and one neutral/ground—and, correspondingly, three prongs plugging into three receptacle slots. Since then, four-wire receptacles and cords have been required. These have red and black hots, a white neutral, and a green ground. The newer receptacles are differently configured so that you cannot plug an older three-prong cord into a newer four-slot receptacle. If you are replacing an old dryer with a newer one, you will need to run four wires (either in conduit or Greenfield or in a cable) and install a new four-prong dryer receptacle.

⏵ **It's extra-urgent that you shut off power and test to verify that power is off when working with 240-volt power, which can certainly kill a human being. Wire the receptacle or appliance first. Before you start to run wires into the panel or attach a new breaker, shut off the main breaker and test that there is no power in the panel. Provide yourself with temporary lighting so you can work without power in your house.**

1 RUN CONDUIT OR GREENFIELD. Run conduit or Greenfield from the receptacle location to the service panel. You'll need ¾-in. conduit for running four 6-gauge or 8-gauge wires. Open a knockout and connect the conduit to the service panel.

2 INSTALL A RECEPTACLE. Here we show a floor receptacle for a dryer, which requires drilling a 1-in. hole in the floor. You can also install a wall receptacle, which will need a box. Be sure to choose the right receptacle for your appliance.

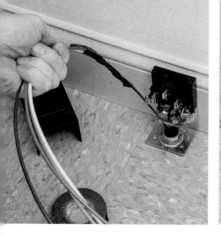

3 RUN WIRES AND CONNECT TO THE RECEPTACLE. For most high-voltage receptacles, strip the wire ends, poke them into the correct terminal holes, and tighten setscrews. Screw the receptacle body to the floor or wall, and snap on the cover.

4 CONNECT IN THE SERVICE PANEL.
⟹ Shut off the main breaker in the service panel. Route the wires neatly around the perimeter of the service panel. Strip wire ends, and connect the ground and neutral wires to the neutral/ground bus bar. Route the hot wires, strip their ends, and poke them into the two terminals of the correct double-pole breaker. Snap the breaker onto the bus bar. Restore power and test.

Receptacles for a Washer and Dryer

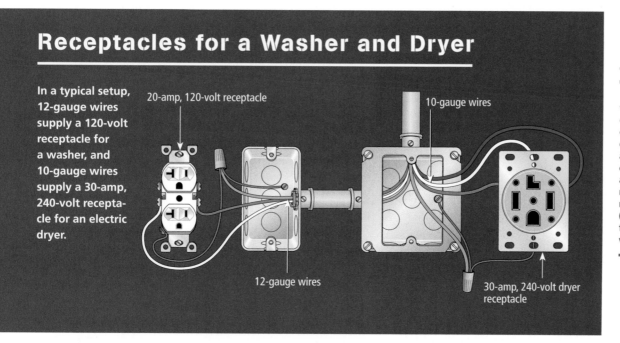

In a typical setup, 12-gauge wires supply a 120-volt receptacle for a washer, and 10-gauge wires supply a 30-amp, 240-volt receptacle for an electric dryer.

20-amp, 120-volt receptacle

10-gauge wires

12-gauge wires

30-amp, 240-volt dryer receptacle

TIP On these pages we show running cable through conduit. Local codes may well allow you to run cable instead for an air-conditioner receptacle and may also allow (very thick) cable for other 240-volt wiring as well.

Upgrading a Service Panel

This is not a project recommended for do-it-yourselfers, but it is often necessary when upgrading a home's wiring. It's a good idea to understand your needs and the options available. Of course, you should call in a professional electrician (or two) to assess your situation. But you may want to be informed about the decision, and these pages will help you with that.

When planning to add significantly to the electrical usage in your home, first determine (1) if there are enough slots for new circuit breakers to supply your new circuits, (2) if your existing service panel has enough total amperage to handle the load, and (3) in the event you do need a new panel with higher amperage, whether you need new, thicker service wires coming from the utility.

Enough slots?

If your service panel has only a couple of unused circuit breaker slots—or no vacant slots at all—you may not be able to add any circuits and may need a new service panel with more slots. An exception: If allowed by codes, you

HALF-THICKNESS BREAKERS. This tandem breaker can supply two circuits while taking up only one slot in the service panel. Most tandems supply two circuits of the same amperage. Be sure this solution is permitted in your area.

may be able to install "skinny" breakers that take up only half a slot each, or "tandem" breakers that supply two circuits in the space of one breaker.

Before installing skinnies or tandems, however, first make sure they are available for your brand of service panel. Check with your building department to see if they are allowed in your area. Many inspectors frown on half-size breakers and consider them less reliable than the standard full-thickness size.

Do you need more total amperage?

If you have a panel that supplies less than 100 amps and you have a medium-size home with normal electrical requirements, you almost certainly need to upgrade to a panel of at least 100 amps—and 150 amps is a safer choice. Nowadays many people find they need 200 amps for a home, and many electricians recommend that level of power as a matter of course. If you plan to add high-usage elements like central air-conditioning, you probably need at least 200 amps. You can do some calculations to get a better idea.

To find your total electrical needs, you could start by adding up all the wattages and amperages of your fixtures and appliances, but that would be very tedious—and unnecessary. In addition, you would find that the total of all electrical users will add up to far more—perhaps more than twice as much—amperage than the rating of your service panel. All your users are not running at the same time, however, so your service panel does not need to have the capacity to match that. See the table at right for figuring service panel needs.

CALCULATING ESTIMATED ELECTRICAL LOAD

There is a method, recommended by the National Electrical Code (NEC), to determine the total electrical load for a house. Let's do this by example. Say you have 2,000 sq. ft. of living space, three small-appliance circuits, a garbage disposal rated at 600 watts, a refrigerator rated at 720 watts, an electric water heater rated at 5,200 watts, and central air-conditioning rated at 4,800 watts:

First, figure the load for general lighting and receptacles by multiplying the total square feet of living space times 3 watts.	2,000 sq. ft. × 3 watts = 6,000 watts
Next, add 1,500 watts for each 20-amp small-appliance circuit. There are typically two of these in a kitchen, and there may be one in a laundry room or a workshop.	3 × 1,500 = 4,500 watts.
Then look at the plates on all major appliances—electric water heater, dryer, dishwasher, electric range, and others—to find the wattage pulled by each. (Remember, watts = amps × volts. So on a 120-volt circuit, 1 amp equals 120 watts, and on a 240-volt circuit, 1 amp = 240 watts.) Add up the total for all these large appliances.	6,520 watts (not including central air-conditioning)
Add together the three totals you got from the above.	17,020 watts
Subtract 10,000 watts from the total, and multiply the result by 0.4 (that is, to determine 40 percent). Then add 10,000 watts to that number.	(17,020 – 10,000) × 0.4 = 2,808 + 10,000 = 12,808 watts
Add to that number the wattage of your air-conditioning or heating, whichever is largest. This gives you the total estimated load.	12,808 + 5,200 = 18,008 watts
Divide the total estimated load by 240 volts to get the service panel size you need.	18,008 ÷ 240 = 75 amps
In this case, a 100-amp panel would be sufficient for your current needs. But to leave open the possibility of adding significant service in the future, it might be prudent to install a panel of at least 150 amps.	

TIP As a very general rule, if you have a 100-amp service panel and the amperage of all your breakers adds up to more than 160 amps, you likely need a new 200-amp (or at least 150-amp) service panel.

What to do if you need more power

If adding new circuits will not overload the total capacity of your service panel and the only problem is that you need more slots for circuit breakers, it may make sense to install a subpanel, which adds new slots but does not increase total power available for the house. Contact an electrician to see if this is an option.

If you need a service panel to deliver more amps, the panel will need to be replaced. The first question then is this: Are the service wires from the utility thick enough for a higher-amperage panel? It is important that you consult with your building department on this matter. In most cases, the wires are not thick enough and need to be replaced. Replacing service wires is, of course, something that only the utility company can do. The building depart-

ment and the utility company will almost certainly require that a licensed electrician be involved.

Replacing a service panel

Here, we'll show the steps involved in replacing a service panel. Again, this is something you will probably not do, but it's useful to be informed about the process and what to expect.

In most cases, the utility company will come and disconnect the power lines leading to the house. If you need thicker wires, they will install those. They will coordinate with a licensed electrician to schedule a reconnect. During the time that the panel is being replaced, there will be no power in your home. An electrician will likely have a portable generator to supply lights while he or she works.

1 SHUT OFF POWER TO THE HOUSE. At a minimum, removing the electric meter will shut off power to the house, as shown. Once the meter is off, the cover—which contains hot wires—must be safely sealed so nobody can access it.

2 LABEL WIRES. ➠ Test to be sure there is no power in the box. If you have an index indicating which breakers control which electrical users, use it as a reference for when you will reinstall the breakers in the new panel. Use pieces of tape and a permanent marker to label each hot wire with its location in the panel. The panel shown was installed in a disorganized way, with too-long wires, a confusing situation that makes labeling especially important.

3 LOOSEN CONNECTORS. Use a hammer and screwdriver, as shown, to loosen and unscrew nuts for cable or conduit connectors. Pry other types of connectors out from the panel.

6 MAKE CABLE HOLES IN THE NEW PANEL. Determine the easiest route for each of the cables to enter the new panel. In most cases you can remove a knockout. Occasionally you may need to drill a new hole, using a hole saw that is precisely the correct size.

4 DISENTANGLE AND PULL WIRES OUT. Loosen screws on the neutral and ground bus bar and pull out those wires. Carefully tease the wires apart and keep them organized as you pull them out of the panel. Take care not to scrape the wires as you pull them, which could damage insulation. (If you have cables attached to the panel, this will be fairly easy. If there is conduit, it can be more difficult.)

5 REMOVE THE OLD PANEL. Disconnect the service wires. Pull the panel out carefully so as not to damage any wire insulation.

7 START RUNNING WIRES, AND ATTACH THE PANEL. If one does not already exist, firmly attach a piece of ¾-in. plywood, larger than the size of the panel, to the wall. Start running wires in, again taking care not to damage insulation as you slide wires into holes. Position the panel where you want it and drive screws to attach it to the plywood.

8 CONNECT THE SERVICE WIRES. Your service wires—two hots and one neutral—may come through the top, side, or rear of the panel. Route the thick wires neatly around the panel, insert the stripped ends into the terminals, and tighten the screws firmly.

TIP You can fasten setscrews with a screwdriver, but the work will be slow and tedious. A drill with screwdriver bit is faster, but be sure to turn its power down—so something like "3" on a scale of 10—so you do not overtighten, especially when fastening to breakers.

9 CONNECT BREAKERS. Using the index, snap circuit breakers of the correct sizes into slots. Run all or most of the wires into the box, and attach the cables and/or conduit with connectors in the knockout holes.

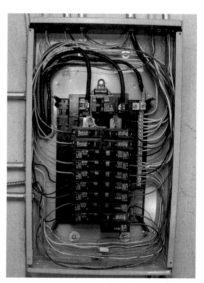

10 ROUTE WIRES AND CONNECT TO TERMINALS. Route wires neatly around the perimeter of the panel and cut them to length. Strip their ends.

11 CONNECT WIRES. Insert neutral and ground wires into the neutral/ground bus bar. Tighten the setscrews to fasten them. Insert each hot wire into its designated breaker and tighten the setscrews to firmly fasten them.

12 RESTORE POWER AND TEST. With all the breakers turned off, have the power to the house restored (probably by the utility). Turn on the main breaker, then the individual breakers, and make sure all power has been restored.

Fans and Heaters

APPLIANCES AND FIXTURES that change indoor climate for the better include attic fans, exhaust fans for the kitchen and bath, wall heaters, and radiant heat. All are covered in this chapter.

Whenever installing a fan, the first order of business is to figure where the air will go. Attic vent fans should be positioned where they can easily suck up air and push it to the outside. Vent fans need venting that is smooth and as short as possible, so air can easily move through it and to the outside.

The heating installations shown here are modest in size and will probably have the role of providing supplemental heat or heating a small area. Still, they will use a fair amount of power, so make sure the heaters will not overload a circuit.

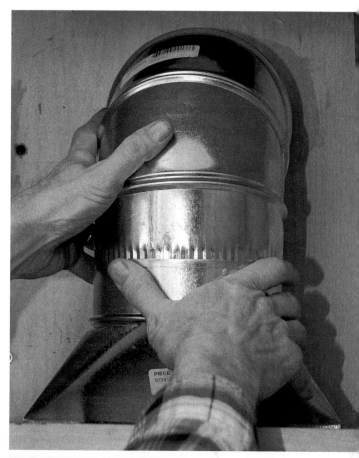

Installing a Range Hood

Wiring for a range hood is usually straightforward; venting is often the more complicated job. But as long as you can connect the existing vent to the new hood unit in the same way, the project should go smoothly.

Here, we show installing a standard 30-in.-wide under-cabinet range hood with a vent that runs up into the cabinet above and then out the wall. If you want a large professional-duty model, it's often best to hire a pro. The company that sells the hood may also offer installation.

Many people are disappointed with their range hoods, so be sure to understand what a standard residential range hood will actually do: Even if it is relatively high powered and installed properly, it usually will not suck out spattered grease; it takes a very powerful fan (one that goes "vroom" rather than "hmmm") to do that. A properly installed home range hood will remove gases, odors, smoke, and steam. But grease is just too heavy; only a commercial-quality range hood will do that.

If your hood will be no more than 20 in. above a 30-in.-wide cooktop and if the vent is made of smooth (rather than corrugated) metal no longer than 4 ft., then a hood rated at 100 cfm (cubic ft. per minute) will do the job. If a hood is higher, is above an island, or if vents are long and/or corrugated, you should get one rated at 125 cfm or 150 cfm. The more power the hood delivers, the louder it will be, but you should be able to turn the power up or down when you use it.

TIP If venting to the outside looks like a daunting challenge, you may choose to skip running vents and install the range hood so it recirculates air through a filter. Many people like the smell of cooking and find they need to suck out smoke only very occasionally, so recirculating works fine for them. On the other hand, many feel that venting to the outside is essential. Although some inspectors may insist on outside venting, national code does allow for recirculating instead.

If there is not already a line for power, run cable that is approved by local codes (armored cable may be required) to the location shown by the range hood's instructions. Make sure it can run into the hood's electrical box without getting trapped when you install the hood. Depending on how much power the hood draws, you may be allowed to place it on a receptacle circuit, or it may share a circuit with a countertop receptacle or other elements in the kitchen.

▶ Be sure to shut off power at the service panel. Test several times to verify that power is off, as shown on pp. 8–9. For double protection, use electrician's tools and work as if the wires were hot.

Vent Options

If venting does not already exist, plan the venting route carefully. The path your vent takes will depend on where you can reasonably reach the nearest access to the outside. To maximize venting efficiency, plan for the shortest route possible with minimal bends and, if you can, use solid rather than flexible corrugated ducting. Ridges impede airflow. Run ducts up rather than sideways as much as possible because heat wants to go up. That said, the most common arrangement is to run the ducting straight horizontally through the wall, or to have it go up into the cabinet above and then over and out the wall. If there is no floor above, the roof may offer the shortest venting path. However, a roof vent cap is tricky to install in a way that produces no leaks, so hiring a roofer for this task is recommended.

Vent Assembly and Cutting Holes

It usually works best to partially assemble vents and cut holes in cabinetry and walls (or the roof) as you go. Start assembly, and then measure and cut the cabinet if needed. For an up-and-over vent like the one shown on pp. 231–232, you may want to attach the first vertical vent piece, then hold it in place to measure for cutting the hole in the cabinet. Wire and attach the range hood, then cut the hole through the wall. Finally, install the rest of the vent and the vent cap.

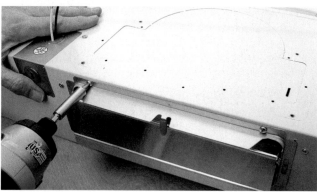

1 **ATTACH THE VENT STARTER.** Determine which direction the vent will run and which opening in the range hood you will use for running your vent. Remove the large knockout by first inserting a screwdriver into a slot and bending back and forth, and then bend the piece out. Attach the vent starter of your choice (which should come with the range hood) by driving sheet-metal screws. Be sure to install correctly, so the adapter's flap (if any) will close when the fan is off.

2 **ATTACH VENT PIECES, AND SEAL WITH FOIL TAPE.** Attach the vent pieces of your choice. Here, we use an adapter to switch from a rectangular to a round vent, which is commonly done. After the vent piece is attached with screws, use aluminum foil tape (not regular duct tape) to tightly seal the joints. Peel off the tape's backing and carefully fold pieces in place. At corners, cut flaps and apply short pieces to make the seal complete at all points.

3 **CHECK FOR FLAP OPERATION.** Throughout the installation, periodically push on any flaps to make sure they can open and close freely. If not, you may need to disassemble and reassemble the venting. There may be a flap near the range hood, and another on the end cap (step 7 on p. 232) to prevent cold air from entering the kitchen. However, some people prefer only one flap, to ensure smooth outward airflow.

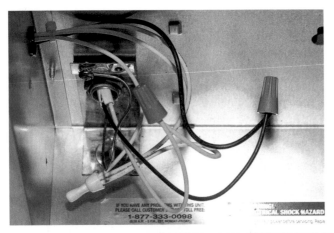

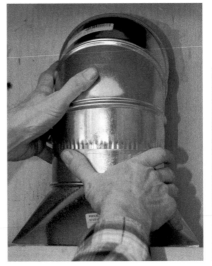

4 **WIRE THE HOOD.** Run cable into the hood's electrical knockout and secure it with a cable connector. Wiring is usually a matter of connecting grounds, splicing white to white and black to black. Tuck the wires up and install the cover, which usually attaches with a single screw.

5 **CUT A PATH TO THE OUTSIDE.** Use a reciprocating saw or jigsaw to cut holes in cabinetry and the inside wall. Use a drill with a long bit to bore locator holes on the outside of the house. Cut out the opening using a reciprocating saw or jigsaw.

TIP If your house is brick or block, cutting the hole for the vent can be a pretty large project. (This is especially true for pre-WWII homes, which have double or even triple thicknesses of brick.) Use a long masonry bit to drill locator holes and chip away the brickwork with a hammer and cold chisel.

TIP Don't use an end cap made for a dryer vent. Instead, get a solid end cap that will remain stable. It should have wire mesh inside to keep critters out of the vent.

6 **CUT VENT PIECES.** Here we switch from a side vent to a top vent to show more options. Measure for cutting vent pipe that reaches to the outside of the house. Use a pair of tin snips to cut the vents. It will take concentration to make straight cuts. Wear gloves, because the cut ends of the pipe are very sharp.

7 **RUN THE VENT OUTSIDE.** It usually works best to install the last section of venting along with the vent cap. Attach the cap with foil tape. Apply a thick bead of caulk around the hole, press the cap into the caulk, and drive screws to fasten.

Installing a microwave/range hood

Space-saving microwaves that double as range hoods include a light that shines on the range and a vent fan. They are usually 16 in. tall, so will limit cabinet size above the unit, but for most people this is a minor tradeoff. Venting options are much the same as for a standard range hood. In our example, a flexible, insulated vent from the previous range hood is repurposed for the microwave unit.

Although wiring and venting are not much different from a range hood, attaching the unit calls for different hardware, because it is much heavier. It attaches via machine screws that come down through the cabinet above, as well as a mounting plate at the back.

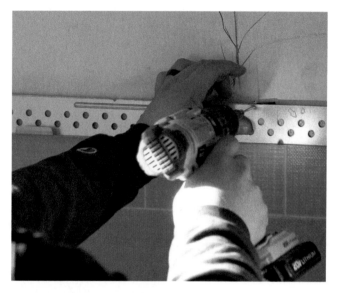

2 INSTALL THE REAR BRACKET. Measure down from the underside of the cabinet below and install the bracket that will do most of the work supporting the microwave. Drive screws into every available stud for a very firm connection.

1 PREP THE OPENING. A unit like this usually plugs into a receptacle that is installed in the cabinet above. Run cable and install a receptacle; make sure the microwave will not overload the circuit that the receptacle is on. Also provide for a vent (see pp. 230–232).

3 MARK FOR HOLES. Hold the template provided by the manufacturer in place on the underside of the cabinet. If you are working alone, tape it in place. Mark for cutting the vent hole, as well as the holes for the machine screws that will attach the microwave to the cabinet, and mark for a hole for running the cord to the receptacle.

4 CUT THE VENT HOLE. To cut out for the vent, first drill holes with a spade bit, then use a jigsaw or reciprocating saw to cut the hole. Also drill holes for the machine screws.

5 INSTALL AND SEAL THE VENT ADAPTER. Position the vent adapter, which makes the transition from rectangular to round in the hole, and drive screws to attach it. Seal the opening with foil tape (not regular duct tape).

6 INSTALL THE MICROWAVE. This is best done with a helper. Slip the back of the unit onto the rear bracket and lift it up against the underside of the cabinet. Drive the machine screws down through the holes in the cabinet and into the threads on the microwave. Tighten the machine screws. Attach the ductwork (see p. 231). Plug in the microwave.

Installing a Bathroom Vent Fan

A bathroom vent fan sucks out humid air, making the bathroom a more comfortable place. Here are some options:

- If you already have plenty of light, you can buy a fan-only unit, which will most likely be controlled by a separate switch. Or you could install it wired in the same way as a second light fixture controlled by the same switch, as shown on p. 207.
- It's more common to install a fan/light combo. This can be wired with a single switch so the fan comes on at the same time as the light. However, most people prefer to have the fan and light controlled separately, because a bathroom often does not need venting.
- You can also purchase a unit that combines a fan, a light, and a heating element. The heater can pull plenty of power, so it may need to be on a separate circuit.

TIP To pull in fresh air efficiently, the bathroom door should have a gap of at least ⅝ in. at its bottom. If the gap at the threshold is smaller than that, take the door off its hinges and cut its bottom.

The right amount of power

Choose a fan with enough power—calculated in cubic ft. per minute, or cfm—to clear the air in a timely manner. If you have an 8-ft.-high ceiling, the fan's cfm rating should be slightly greater than the floor's square footage. For instance, a bathroom that is 8 ft. by 10 ft. has a floor of 80 sq. ft.; the fan should be rated at 100 cfm. If the bathroom has a higher ceiling, add about 10 percent per foot of height to the cfm requirement. For more precise calculations, you can find calculators online.

Be aware, however, that efficient moisture removal depends just as much on the ductwork as on the fan's power. If your ducts are not solid and smooth, or if they are more than 8 ft. long, add another 10 to 20 percent to the needed cfm rating. If the ductwork is seriously clogged, then no amount of fan power will dry out your bathroom.

➡ **Be sure to shut off power at the service panel. Test several times to verify that power is off, as shown on pp. 8–9. For double protection, use electrician's tools and work as if the wires were hot.**

Wiring a Bathroom Fan/Light

It's a good idea to control the light with a standard switch and the fan with a timer so the fan can be left on for 15 minutes or so after someone leaves the bathroom. To wire a fan with light so that each element is controlled separately, run power into the switch box and run three-way cable to the fixture box. Connect the grounds and splice the neutrals in each box. In the switch box, connect the feed wire to both switches and connect the red and black wires to the other terminals. In the fixture box, connect one hot wire to the fan and one to the light. To wire for a fan/light/heater, see step 4 on p. 237.

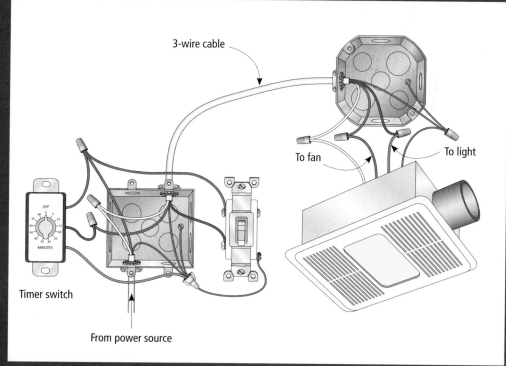

3-wire cable

To fan

To light

Timer switch

From power source

Venting a Bathroom Fan

If possible, run a straight vent directly out through the nearest wall. Run ductwork between joists if there is no insulation and the run is parallel to joists. Otherwise, run the duct above the joists and/or insulation. If a roofline is in the way, venting out the eave may be your best solution.

If you have access to the space above and work carefully, you may not need to patch the ceiling afterward. Here, we show replacing an existing light fixture with a fan/light, but you can also install a new fixture in a new location. If you do not have access from above, see the sidebar on p. 238.

2 **CUT OUT FOR THE FAN.** Place the fan's body where you want it to go and trace around it. The hole must be smaller than the outline you traced; cut about ⅜ in. inside the lines, using a jab saw.

1 **CUT OUT AN EXISTING FIXTURE.** To remove an existing fixture box, ⮕shut off power and test that power is off. Use a reciprocating saw with a metal-cutting blade to cut through the nails or screws that attach the box to the framing and pull the box out.

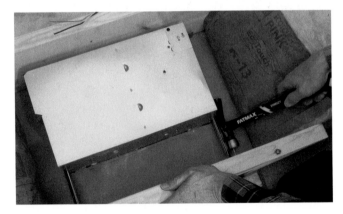

3 **ATTACH THE FAN.** Slide out the fan's mounting bars and drive nails or screws to attach it to a joist on each side. Make the attachment strong, because the fan will do a lot of vibrating over the coming years.

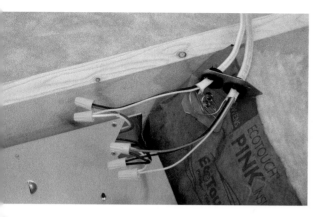

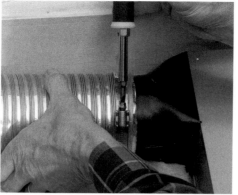

4 **WIRE THE FAN.** Here we show wiring for a fan/light/heater; there are three switches in the switch box, one for each element. Wiring is like that shown on p. 235, but with an extra cable for controlling the heater.

5 **RUN THE VENT.** Bathroom vents tend to run in tight spots, so a flexible vent is often needed. The type shown here creates little wind resistance, and so is much better than the type made of coiled wire and a plastic cover. The vent cap should have a flap that closes to keep cold air out and should have wire mesh that keeps critters out as well. Run it through the house's siding and attach with screws and caulking.

6 **ASSEMBLE THE WORKINGS.** At this point, some assembly will be required, such as adding a housing for the fan and making push-on electrical connections. The connections are typically idiot-proof, with parts that can connect only in the correct way.

7 **ADD THE TRIM.** Finish by snapping on the fan trim, which should neatly cover the hole in the ceiling. The light socket and its trim also snap into place. Restore power and test.

Installing from Below

If you do not have access from above, it will be difficult to install a bathroom fan without opening up the ceiling. The fan must be attached very firmly, so you need to drive fasteners into joists on each side. Cut an ample-size hole, so you have plenty of room to work. Patching a larger hole will be virtually the same amount of work as patching a smaller hole.

Cut an opening that spans from joist to joist. (Don't try to cut in the middle of a joist's thickness.) Run ductwork to the fan and attach the fan securely to the joist on each side [A]. Drive screws to attach 2× nailers to the sides of the joists [B], their bottoms flush with the bottoms of the joists. Now you can cut drywall to fit around the fan [C] and screw it to the nailers. Apply mesh tape and a coat of joint compound, allow to dry, and sand. Repeat two times until the patch is nice and smooth, and then prime and paint.

Smoke and Carbon Monoxide Alarms

Carbon monoxide and smoke alarms are essential safety devices in a home. Codes require that homes have one or more per story. Check with local codes to learn more about just where they should be installed.

Carbon monoxide, or CO, is a dangerous gas produced by boilers, furnaces, and other fire-burning appliances. If they are installed correctly, the CO they produce will be safely carried out of the house via flues, vents, and chimneys. But if something goes wrong—if, say, a heating unit develops a gas leak, or if flues or chimneys get clogged—then CO will escape and ultimately enter living areas. You cannot smell it, which makes it all the more dangerous. And CO can rise through ceilings and floors, so that upper floors of a house can be infiltrated as easily as the room where the leak originated. Smoke detectors, of course, let you know when fire is present in your home.

In many areas, it is required, at least for new construction, that smoke and CO detectors be hardwired, with battery backup. The hardwiring is so they operate even when people neglect to change worn-out batteries. Battery back-up is important because often in a fire the wiring gets damaged, effectively turning off the alarm.

Newer alarms have batteries that last ten years or more, so that hardwiring is not considered as urgent as it was before. Still, hardwiring is often considered the safest way to go.

To wire a smoke detector, install a standard electrical box (usually on the ceiling, but it can also be on the upper part of a wall). Supply power from an unswitched source using a two-wire cable. A hardwired smoke detector typically has a black, a white, and a red lead, which is capped. If you are wiring for only one location, leave the cap on the red lead and wire only the black and white wires to the black and white leads. If you want to wire other alarms as well, uncap the red lead and run three-wire cable to the other alarm's box. In addition to connecting the blacks and whites, also connect the reds in both boxes.

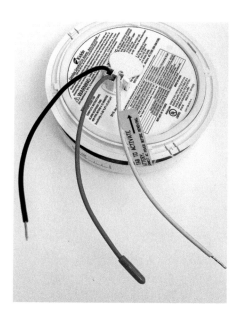

WIRING TWO ALARMS

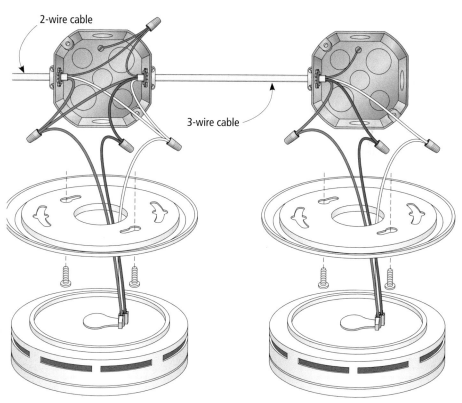

2-wire cable

3-wire cable

Electric Wall Heaters

In most of the country, gas is more efficient than electric heat, but often electric wall or baseboard heaters can effectively supplement heat in a room that tends to be cold. In the case of a small room—say an unheated powder room—an electric heater can supply all the heat that's needed.

Heaters pull pretty large amounts of power, so make sure that yours will not overload the circuit that you put it on (see pp. 154–155). The wall and baseboard heaters shown on the following pages both pull 240 volts, but there are plenty of 120-volt models available. For a 240-volt unit you will probably need to run cable in a home run and install a new double-pole circuit breaker (see p. 222–223). See pp. 196–203 for running cable inside finished walls.

▸ **Before you connect to power, be sure to shut off power at the service panel. Test several times to verify that power is off, as shown on pp. 8–9. For double protection, use electrician's tools and work as if the wires were hot.**

Installing a wall heater

Wall heaters have built-in blowers, which increase their heating power. The amount of heat needed of course depends on how well the room is insulated and how cold it gets, as well as its size. In normal circumstances, a 1,500-watt unit can heat a room of about 150 sq. ft. When in doubt, buy a unit (or configure it; see the tip below) that is a bit more powerful than you need, because you can always turn down the thermostat.

The wall heater shown here has a built-in thermostat, so it can be wired simply, without a switch. If yours does not have a thermostat, see p. 242 for wiring to control it with a wall-mounted double-line thermostat switch.

TIP Some wall heaters allow you to choose the amount of power they will use—and the temperature of the heat that they deliver. The manufacturer's instructions will tell you how to snip a wire or two to lower the heat.

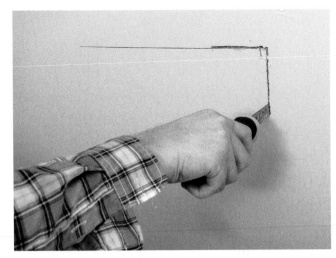

1 CUT A WALL OPENING. Cut a hole in the wall surface of the size required for your heater. Many wall heaters are 14½ in. wide, so they span from stud to stud in a normally framed house. Use a stud finder to locate the wall studs, and choose a location where they are 16 in. on center, if possible. Draw a level line and cut with a jab saw toward a stud until you feel you've hit it. Use the side of the stud as a guide for cutting vertically.

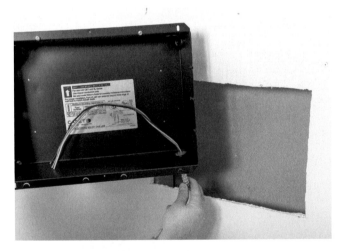

2 RUN CABLE INTO THE HOUSING. Test that the housing will fit into your opening. Run cable with correctly sized wires (for example, 12-gauge wire for a 20-amp unit) into the opening. Here we show only one cable for a heater with its own thermostat; if you're installing a wall thermostat, see p. 242. Strip plenty of insulation so the ground and other wires can travel where they need to go (see step 4). Connect the cable to the housing with a cable connector.

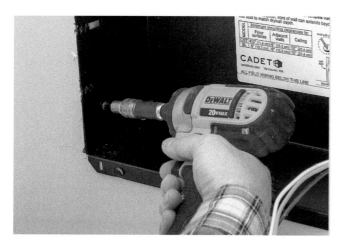

3 **ATTACH THE HOUSING.** Press the housing into place so its flange snugs against the wall surface. Drive at least four screws to attach the housing to studs on each side.

TIP Wall heaters have fans that vibrate slightly, so they should be solidly attached. If your wall heater does not fit nicely between two studs, install framing in the wall so you have a strong surface to attach it to on each side—or on the top and bottom.

4 **WIRE THE HEATER.** Connect the cable to a double-pole circuit breaker at the service panel as shown on p. 223, but leave the breaker turned off. Connect the ground(s). ➠ Test to be sure power is off. For a unit with its own thermostat, wire with the black and the white-marked wire attached to the two heater leads.

5 **ASSEMBLE THE HEATER.** Tuck wires away so they don't get trapped and slip the heater unit into the housing. Attach it firmly. This one mounts via slots at the bottom and two screws at the top.

6 **COVER AND TEST.** Slip on the cover and mount with screws. Restore power at the service panel and test by turning on the thermostat.

Wiring a Wall or Baseboard Heater

A heater thermostat should have an OFF position, so it can be completely shut down. These units are often wired like a 240-volt air conditioner (p. 118). In the service panel, install a double-pole 240-volt breaker of the correct amperage for your unit (usually, 15 amps or 20 amps). Run two-wire cable of the correct wire size to a switch box and two-wire cable to the heater. Mark the white wire black in all three places. Connect the grounds. Connect wires that come from the power source to the "line" side of the thermostat; connect wires leading to the heater to the "load" side.

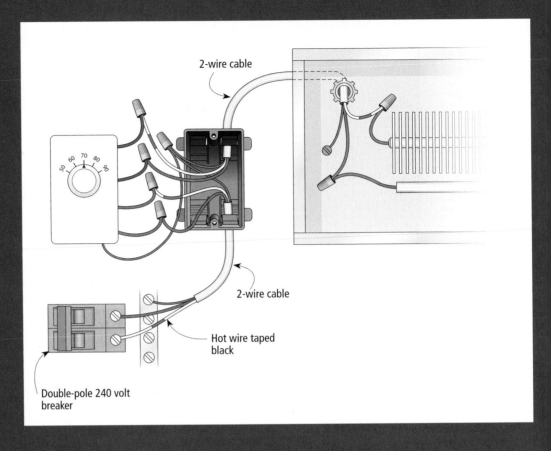

2-wire cable

2-wire cable

Hot wire taped black

Double-pole 240 volt breaker

Installing a baseboard heater

Baseboard heaters are easily reached by youngsters, and so rarely have their own thermostat controls. You will need to install a wall-mounted thermostat. A simple thermostat works for a 120-volt unit, but you'll need a double-line thermostat if the heater is 240 volts.

1 MARK FOR THE CABLE HOLE. Choose a convenient knockout for running the cable into the heater. Usually this should be on a flat spot on the baseboard molding. (It should be at least 1½ in. above the floor, or you will run into the framing's base plate.) Use a stud sensor to make sure your cable hole will not be at a stud location. Remove a knockout, position the heater where you want it, and scribe a line for the cable's hole.

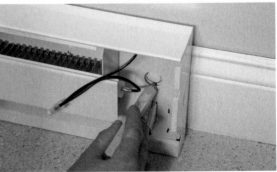

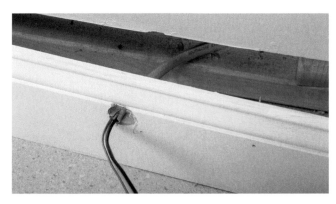

2 **DRILL A HOLE AND RUN CABLE.** ⟾ Turn power off and keep it off until wiring is finished. Drill a hole in the baseboard large enough for the cable connector you will use (see next step). Pull away the baseboard. Run cable from the service panel to a switch box, and then run cable to the baseboard location, as shown on the facing page.

3 **STRIP AND CLAMP THE CABLE.** Strip enough sheathing so the wires can reach where they need to go. Attach the cable to the fan's housing with a cable connector (see pp. 180–181).

4 **WIRE THE HEATER.** Some models have connection boxes on each side, which let you connect to additional baseboard units. To make a connection, first snip two leads (top), and then strip their ends. Connect the ground wire, then splice the black and the white-marked-black wire to the heater's leads.

5 **ATTACH AND TEST.** Replace the cover plate. Drive screws to attach the heater to the baseboard or to the wall. Wire the switch and connect to a double-pole 240-volt breaker in the service panel. Turn on power and test.

Hooking Baseboard Heaters Together

If you want more than one baseboard heater controlled by the same thermostat switch, start at the end of the first heater that is not connected to the thermostat switch. Run two-wire cable and strip and connect the cable to each heater. Snip the leads as shown in step 4 above. Connect the grounds. Mark the white wires black and splice the wires to the heaters' leads.

Radiant Heat

In recent years, electric radiant heat has become more affordable to install and more energy efficient as well. Electric current runs through heating cable that is embedded in a mesh of some sort in a serpentine pattern, making it easy to lay out. The heating cable may be thick or thin, depending on the type of flooring you will install, the existing subflooring, and the amount of heat required. Some products are made to go under luxury vinyl, carpeting, or a floating engineered floor, whereas others will first get covered with mortar, then ceramic or stone tiles.

Companies such as WarmlyYours sell a variety of products tailored for various situations. Some require only 120-volt service, whereas others require 240 volts. Some are very straightforward to install, making them suitable DIY projects. Others are best installed by experienced professionals. Consult with the manufacturer to be sure you won't be getting in over your head. Usually, if you tell a dealer your room's dimensions and your desired floor finish, they will recommend products and create a drawing that shows how to install them.

Wiring is usually straightforward, though you will probably need to install a new circuit. Run cable from the new breaker to a switch box, where it will connect to a thermostat. The power cable from the heating mats also connects to the thermostat.

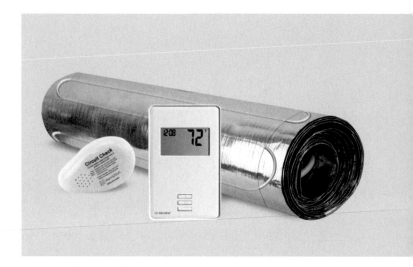

ALL YOU NEED. Companies like WarmlyYours provide a kit with the mat and thermostat, as well as wiring to the thermostat. The product shown here is suitable for small areas and uses only 120 volts. A "circuit tester" may be provided to ensure the wiring is correct and free of shorts before you start installing the flooring.

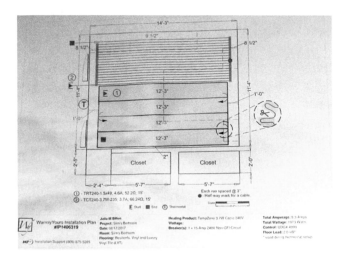

A CLEAR PLAN. In this plan, two types of mats will be installed in a 14-ft. by 11-ft. bedroom. Heavy-duty 240-volt heating mats are used, but the system pulls only 8.3 amps.

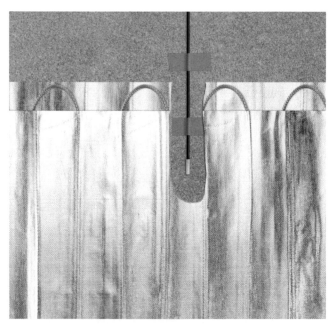

FLEX ROLLS. A product like this is used under carpeting, laminate, or floating wood floors. It comes in wide sheets, to quickly cover a large area, and can be easily configured in different directions. Here, it is installed on top of cork sheeting, which is recommended for concrete subfloors. The sensor leads to the wall, where it travels up to a thermostat.

FOR UNDER TILE OR HARDWOOD. This product, with thicker heating cables, is designed for installing under thick flooring like ¾-in.-thick hardwood or ceramic or stone tiles. Once the mats are placed and the electric hookups are made and tested, the mats are covered with thin mortar or self-leveling compound. Once that sets, you're ready to apply thinset and tile or to install wood flooring without fasteners.

THERMOSTAT CONTROLS. Controls for radiant heating are typically sophisticated, allowing you to plan a warming schedule that suits your life. Many thermostats can be controlled remotely on your cell phone via an app.

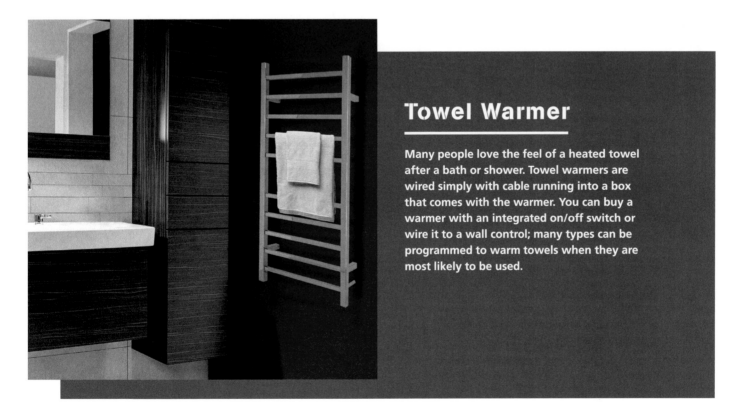

Towel Warmer

Many people love the feel of a heated towel after a bath or shower. Towel warmers are wired simply with cable running into a box that comes with the warmer. You can buy a warmer with an integrated on/off switch or wire it to a wall control; many types can be programmed to warm towels when they are most likely to be used.

Cable, Data, and Smart Home Wiring

MOST HOMES TODAY have a high-speed Internet connection and WiFi capabilities that work with a growing variety of devices, like TVs, thermostats, lights, music hubs, security systems, and more. A device that is "smart" is simply one that can be programmed or controlled with the home's local password-protected Internet network using a computer, a smartphone, or a central hub (more about that in the Smart Home section on p. 255).

Though your provider will supply the basics—cable entering the house leading to a modem or cable running to a TV, for instance— the cables won't be run in an attractive way. If you want your cables hidden, or routed exactly the way you want them, you may need to run them and make connections yourself. This chapter will show the basics of running coaxial and ethernet (Cat5e or Cat6) cables and creating connections.

In addition, we'll show many of the smart home devices available today and ways to control them. Whether you install the exact products we show or similar products, this chapter will help you choose and prioritize your options and give you a good idea of how these things are uploaded and used.

Cable and Ethernet Connections

Your Internet service provider (ISP) will provide a strong signal that can be used for data and audiovisual elements (mostly computers and TV) throughout your home. Nowadays many of these devices use wireless connections. But coaxial cable and ethernet cable is still commonly run throughout homes, for stronger signals.

The ISP usually does not deal with running ethernet cables. Old-fashioned running of cables, stripping, and connecting to terminals is still required. The following pages show how to make some of the most common connections.

The basics

The Internet signal enters the home from the ISP via a coaxial cable that connects to a modem. The modem connects to a router that will have its own network name and password, which you choose. The password keeps your network safe from other Internet users, so that only your devices will use your local network. The router then distributes the signal throughout the home. Your smartphone, computer, or other WiFi-enabled device will see your router's network name; to connect you simply select that network and enter the password. Sometimes the Internet company provides a combination modem/router unit (or you can buy one).

A typical router has four ports for four ethernet cables. Each cable has a plug on either end that clicks into a port. One end plugs into the router, and the other end into a computer or other WiFi-enabled device. A larger home may need more than one router or at least an extender (a wireless solution) to ensure the signal is strong enough on all levels. Devices that are heavy users in your home, like the TV, your home's hub, or a security system with cameras, will work best with (and may require) a wired ethernet cable connection, as opposed to WiFi.

ROUTER AND MODEM. For data distribution, the ISP sends a signal to a modem via a coaxial cable that it runs into the house. The modem connects to a router, which has four ports for ethernet cables. In a small home, or one with only one or two floors, the router may not be needed.

TV Connections

For a television, it's common for the cable or satellite company to connect one or two coaxial cables to your home's DVR box to bring you access to hundreds of channels. The DVR box connects to the TV typically through three color-coded RCA cables. There are a variety of ways to connect a TV to the Internet so that you can stream programs from Hulu, Netflix, YouTube, etc. You can connect a computer to the TV via an HDML cable, but it's also possible to use Roku, a gaming box, or a DVD player with WiFi capabilities. For a house with multiple TVs, a simple splitter can send the DVR signal to other rooms.

In this example, coaxial cable (far left) runs to the cable (or satellite) company's box, three color-coded RCA cables run from the box to the TV, and an HDMI cable runs from a WiFi-enabled DVD player (on top of the cable box) to the TV. (The two smaller cables provide power.)

LV BOX. When running low-voltage (LV) cables into a wall plate, you could use a standard electrical box, but a low-voltage box like this is easier. This one is installed onto a finished wall; other types are used in exposed framing.

CONNECTOR KITS. Consult with a salesperson when choosing tools to go along with your cables and connectors. Here are two kits, one for coaxial and one for ethernet cable, that work for many of the most common types of cables and connectors. Before you buy a kit, be sure it will work for your components.

Running cables

Use the methods shown in Chapter 7 to route cables and wires through finished walls or exposed framing. Running these cables is easier, because they are so thin and flexible, but be sure to protect them from nails as you would electrical cable—by running through holes in the centers of studs or protecting with nailing plates where they are closer than 1¾ in. from the finished wall or ceiling surface.

Connection for coaxial cable

There are two basic types of coaxial cable. RG-6 is the most common choice today, because its shielding and wire are superior to the older RG-59. If you already have RG-59 cable and only need to make a connector, there is no reason to replace all your cable with RG-6 unless you think your signal is weak. There are various sizes of cable, so be sure to buy cable and connectors that match in type; follow the label on the connector packaging.

The steps on pp. 250–251 show installing the most common type of coaxial end fitting, an F-type male connector. Once installed, the cable can be plugged into almost any plug. There are three ways to make the connection:

• A twist-on connection is the easiest to install, because you need no special connecting tools, but it is also the least reliable, so we do not recommend it.

• A compression connection calls for a special tool that is somewhat expensive, but it makes a very secure connection easily.

• A crimp connection calls for an inexpensive tool and is only slightly more difficult than a compression connection. We show the last two types in the pages that follow.

Compression connection

A compression connection is the most foolproof method for making an F-type connection. That's why it's the most commonly used by cable installers. (It's also called a crimp connector, but we'll use "compression" to differentiate it from the following method.)

3 PEEL BACK THE BRAIDING. Use your finger to gently strip the outer metal braiding—but not the metal sheathing that clings tightly to the white plastic dielectric insulation—and pull it back.

4 INSERT THE CONNECTOR. Insert the stripped cable end into a fitting made for your size and type of cable. Push until you can see the white dielectric meeting up against the bottom of the fittings cup and the center wire poking past the end of the fitting just slightly.

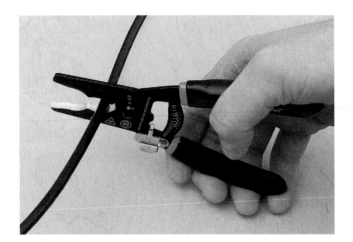

1 CUT TO LENGTH. Cut the cable so you have some slack for pulling out and servicing the TV. A special coaxial cutter like the one shown has scalloped cutting edges for easy cutting. It also keeps you from crimping the end of the cable (as can happen when cutting with side cutters).

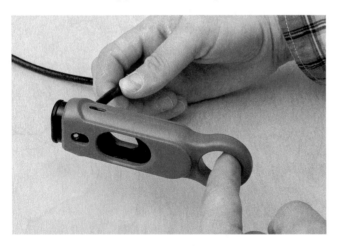

2 STRIP BOTH INSULATIONS. Coaxial has a thin outer jacket and a thicker inner plastic "dielectric" insulation that is covered with metal braiding. This tool strips both at the same time. Open the tool's jaws, insert the cable so its end is flush with the outside of the tool, release the jaws so they bite into the cable, and rotate three times. The insulations will be automatically stripped to the correct lengths.

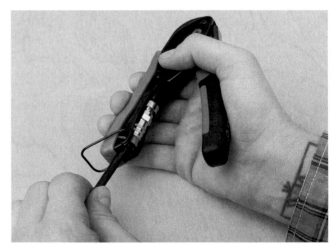

5 COMPRESS FIRMLY. Slip the fitting and cable into the compression tool's slot and push on the cable to be sure the fitting does not slide out. Squeeze the tool with good pressure until you feel the connection is firmly made.

Using a crimp tool

This method uses a lower-tech tool and calls for a bit more concentration on your part. It will also take a minute or two longer.

1 **STRIP BOTH INSULATIONS.** The crimp tool has slots for stripping the inner insulation, the outer jacket for RG-59, and the outer jacket for RG-6. First, insert the cable so ¼ in. protrudes. Squeeze and rotate to strip off ¼ in. of outer and inner insulations and reveal the center wire.

2 **STRIP THE OUTER JACKET.** Insert into the correct hole for your type of cable so ¼ in. of the outer jacket shows. Squeeze and twist to strip it off. Measure to see that you have very close to ¼ in. of both types of insulation stripped.

3 **PUSH ON THE CONNECTOR.** Grasp the cable with the end of the tool and firmly push the correct fitting onto the stripped wire end. You should see the white dielectric insulation pressing against the fitting's cup.

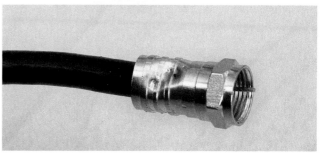

4 **CRIMP AND TEST.** There are three rings on the shaft of the fitting. Grab the fitting with the crimper between the second and third rings and squeeze until you crimp. Rotate the fitting a half turn and do the same between the first and second rings. Tug on the fitting to make sure it is firmly attached and check that the center wire protrudes just slightly past the fitting's end.

Making Network Fittings

Though cable types vary, there are two basic options: Cat6 cable delivers the cleanest signal because its wires are thick and it has a plastic insulator running through its center to separate the wires and prevent crosstalk. However, it is fairly expensive. Cat5e cable has slightly thinner wires and no center insulator—just a thin nylon string in its middle. Though not as good as Cat6, Cat5e is generally considered good enough for most residential use. Predictably, Cat5e is also less expensive. Cat5 and other types are not recommended, but if you already have Cat5, it's fine to use it—installing fittings made for it, of course.

These connections are somewhat challenging, but probably not as difficult as they appear. Use the right tools and pay close attention. You'll need good close-up vision.

Making a male RJ45 connector

Be sure to choose fittings that match your type of cable. Here we show a male RJ45 connector (the part that plugs in).

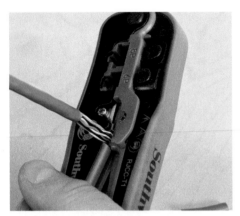

1 **STRIP THE SHEATHING.** Use the cutting slot of the tool to cut the cable to length. Insert about 1¼ in. of the cable end into the correct stripping slot, squeeze gently, and pull outward to remove the outer sheathing. It's very important that all the wire insulations are in sound condition. Look closely at all the wires: If you see any damaged insulation or bare wire, cut the cable and start again, perhaps squeezing less tightly.

2 **CUT THE CENTER INSULATION OR STRING.** Here we show Cat6, which has a black plastic insulator. Cut it off as far back as you can, taking care not to damage any of the wires. If you have Cat5e, cut off the nylon string.

3 **SEPARATE THE WIRES.** The wires are in four twisted-together pairs. Pull the wires out, untangle them, and work to make them fairly straight.

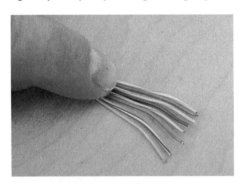

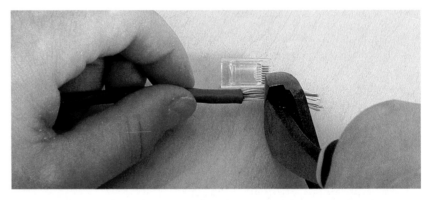

4 **ARRANGE IN THE RIGHT ORDER.** Straighten the wires even more as you arrange them in the following order: white and orange, solid orange, white and green, solid blue, white and blue, solid green, white and brown, solid brown. Press the wires down on a table firmly, to help them stay in line.

5 **CUT TO LENGTH.** Hold the cable with the arranged wires against the fitting you will use and measure for cutting to length. The cable sheathing should enter the fitting far enough so it can be captured when the fitting is crimped, and the wire ends should be long enough to poke all the way into the fitting's tiny metal sheaths. Alternately, cut off ½ in. of the exposed wires, or as much as recommended by the connector manufacturer.

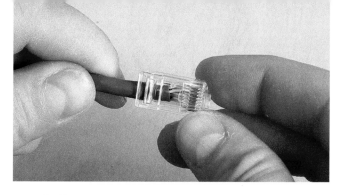

6 PUSH THE WIRES INTO THE SLOTS. Keeping the wires in the correct order, slide them into the fitting. They will slip into their separate sheaths, probably more easily than you expect. Check again that they are in the correct order.

7 CRIMP. Slip the fitting into the correct opening in the crimping tool and squeeze to crimp. Tug to make sure the connection is firm, and check again that the wires are in the correct order and are all slipped into the metal sheaths.

Connecting jacks

Jacks, or female fittings, connect differently from male plugs. Again, make sure the fitting is made for the cable you are using.

An Older Connection

Older Cat5 female connections sometimes worked in this simple way: Strip the sheathing, then just poke each wire into the correct color-coded slot. The fitting's slots pierce the wire insulations, making good connections. Just be sure every wire is inserted all the way.

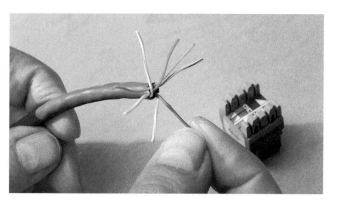

1 STRIP SHEATHING, SEPARATE WIRES. Carefully strip about ½ in. of sheathing and check that the wire insulation did not get nicked during the stripping. Untwist the wires and pull them apart in the correct order.

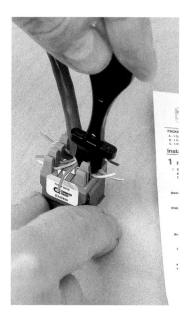

2 PUSH THE WIRES INTO THE SLOTS. There is no need to strip wire insulation. Press the cable down so its sheathing will be captured when you install the cover (step 4). Use the punch-down tool provided with the jack to push each wire into its correct slot. Be sure to push each wire down all the way.

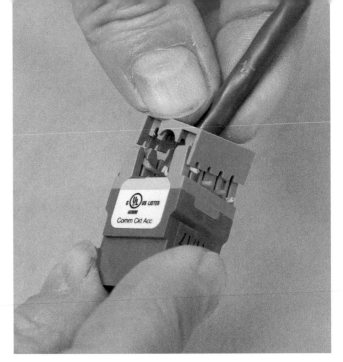

3 **TRIM THE WIRES.** Use side cutters or heavy-duty scissors to cut the wires near the jack. Take care not to loosen the wires as you cut.

4 **ADD THE COVER.** Snap the dust cover in place to complete the jack. The cover should grab the sheathing firmly.

Jacks and Cover Plates

For a neat look and firm connections, install LV or standard boxes and run the cables into them. A variety of plates are available, to house one or more jacks of different types.

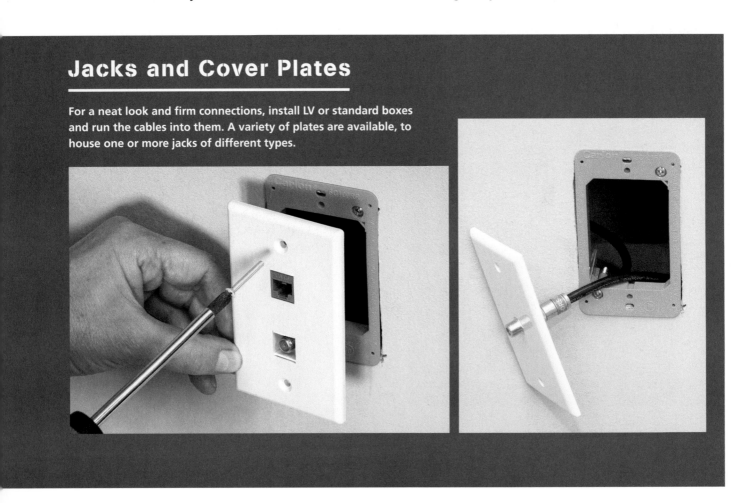

The Smart Home

Smart home technology is a rapidly evolving field with a fun future. A lot of features work well individually, but there are still issues to resolve with overall coordination. For instance, the ability to use voice commands to coordinate and control all the WiFi-enabled devices in your home is not yet working, or at least not without some kinks. On the other hand, a lot of new devices are coming on the market, and manufacturers are working to make them easier to use. It is possible, for instance, using a central hub, to program your smart home so that when you use a digital passcode lock to open the door, it can trigger lights to go on and the thermostat to go up. A basic level of coordination is beginning to work well, and things are bound to improve.

Hubs

A smart home hub uses WiFi to "talk" to all the smart devices in your home. A hub is an unassuming disk with several ports that coordinates the communication between your home's smart devices so that you can control them with a single app provided by the hub manufacturer. In a simple system, the lights may be programmed to go down at night and the coffee pot to turn on in the morning. In a more complex arrangement, devices may be programmed to work together. For instance, using motion sensors in rooms, you can program lights to turn off and on as people move through the home.

TEMPERATURE FLEXIBILITY. One of the more popular smart home upgrades is the digital thermostat, which can be controlled by your computer or phone, even when you're away, and programmed to automatically adjust on schedule. Utility companies often offer incentives because homes with these devices use less energy.

HUBS FOR MUSIC. At a basic level, hubs can be used for controlling music selections, either from your own library or from an Internet site like Spotify, and the quality of the built-in speakers is ever improving. Several manufacturers offer mini-hubs (like the one above) that connect to the main hub via WiFi that you can place in other rooms in your home so you can listen to music there, too, or use voice commands.

TIP Tech experts advise that you choose your hub first, then, as you shop for smart devices, make sure you buy what's compatible with your hub. Compatibility issues can be a headache, and hub apps can also be less than user-friendly. Be sure to do some research and read reviews.

Voice commands

For the most part, voice commands for music and Internet-related tasks are solid features of hubs, and most people report being impressed with the quality of voice recognition software. For instance, using a voice command, you can make phone calls to Uber or restaurants, or ask for information from the Internet and get a read-outloud report of news, weather, sports scores, or traffic. With voice helper software like Amazon's Alexa, you can use a voice command to tell the hub where you parked your car and ask it to remind you later. It will be interesting to see how voice-helper capabilities grow and improve.

The kinks appear when connecting a plethora of WiFi-enabled devices, like those discussed in the sidebar below, to the hub; then voice commands may not always work seamlessly.

Setting up a hub

Typically, a hub needs to be hardwired to your home's router with an ethernet cable and plugged into a standard outlet. (It will usually have several hours of battery backup.) Once it's connected and boots up, you'll need to

download the hub app with a smartphone or tablet and create an account. Then you'll need to pair the hub and the app. Some hubs may use geofencing (a GPS function that locates where the phone is) to sense when you are home or away. Once the app is up and running, you're ready to pair your home's devices. This is where things may slow down, because hub apps are often not as user-friendly as users would like.

Compatibility issues

A good question to ask is whether the hub works with third-party devices, meaning does it support the wireless protocols of the smart devices in your home? Protocols are the different "languages" used for wireless communication. For instance, your thermostat and smart bulbs may be built with different protocols, and your hub needs to be able to interact, or be compatible, with these. A hub that is compatible with a large number of third-party devices and supports most of the major wireless protocols relied on by smart devices is a better choice.

User-friendliness of the hub app

If you'd like hub setup to be easy right out of the box, check reviews. For instance, often hub apps have nested categories—e.g., basic icons, then subcategories that may be five levels deep that you need to wade through to set up a new device. It can be confusing to find the right subcategory for the particular feature you want to control. In addition, the app may not have a "home" or "back" button to easily get back to the main menu.

Smart thermostats

The digital thermostat is a popular smart home upgrade that is a straightforward installation project for a do-it-yourselfer. You replace your existing thermostat by connecting a new smart thermostat to the same wires (though check with the manufacturer first to make sure the device you're interested in is compatible). Then connect it to the Internet.

Setting up a smart thermostat

With the Nest thermostat, once the device is installed you need to download an app, set up a Nest account, and connect your device to your home's WiFi network. Then you can begin programming it. Newer thermostats have a learning feature that remembers your choices—for example, for turning down the heat at night or while you're away—and makes it easy to set up a schedule tailored to your preferences. It's also possible to add a sensor to a particular room, like a young child's room, to ask that the heat level be warmer in that room. Some utility companies offer a rebate, because these types of devices save energy.

Temperature sensors

Your digital thermostat is also your home's main temperature sensor, and the fact that it is in only one place can be frustrating. Sensors in different rooms in the home—for instance, in a bedroom that tends to be warm at night or a kitchen that heats up when the afternoon sun is strong—offer some flexibility. Using sensors, you can program the thermostat to obey the sensor in another room rather than the main sensor at the times you select. (If your heating system is zoned—with several areas of the house controlled by different thermostats—then multiple temperature sensors are probably not needed.)

Sensors are much cheaper than the thermostat itself, so it may make sense to buy several. Simply place one on a shelf

or on a wall in a problematic room and pair the sensor with the thermostat app. Then you should be able to use the thermostat app to make the changes you would like.

Smart plugs

If you have a hub, you may also want to get some smart plugs. You can connect a smart plug to just about any electrical device in your home. You simply insert the plug in the outlet and plug your electrical device into the plug, which you can then program.

For instance, if you tend to forget to turn off your basement horticultural LED grow lights at night, you can use a smart plug to automatically do that. If this is the only type of smart device you're interested in, you don't need a hub. Simply use the app supplied by the manufacturer to control the plugs with your phone or tablet. Either way, smart plugs are easier to program with an app than an old-fashioned manual timer.

Smart switches

For lighting, you can use smart bulbs, typically with a hub or smart switches. With a switch, you're using ordinary bulbs and automating the on/off switch itself using your home's WiFi.

CONSIDERATIONS FOR SMART SWITCHES. Smart switches are a good choice if your fixture uses nonstandard bulbs in size, shape, or style. Even if the light is manually switched off, your programmed choices may still work with a smart switch. Some smart switches have dimming capabilities, though this will probably cost more. For more information about smart switches, see p. 100.

Smart bulbs

You can replace your home's standard incandescent bulbs with smart bulbs, which let you control them from your phone or your home's hub. Smart bulbs use LEDs and digital technology to work, so they are more expensive, but they also use less energy and last longer.

Mood

For establishing a warm and comfortable mood in your home, pay attention to color temperature, which is measured in K, or Kelvins. This has nothing to do with actual temperature; rather, it's a measure of the warmth or coolness of the light. The higher a bulb is on the Kelvin scale, the bluer or cooler the light. Higher temperatures, like 8,500K, tend to feel harsh in a home but are useful to keep you awake at the office. Lower temperatures, like 2,500K, translate to a redder, warmer light, which most people find inviting and relaxing at home.

Smart security

A smart security system typically uses both WiFi and a cloud service to protect your home. It's a little more complicated to install a system with so many components—sensors for doors and windows, cameras for outdoors or inside, a security hub, and a fob for doorway entry. Wiring

BRIGHTNESS. Many smart bulbs are interchangeable with a standard 60-watt incandescent bulb, but brightness can vary quite a bit. The more lumens, the brighter. But the way the light disperses is also a factor to consider. For instance, light can disperse in an intense narrow beam or be more evenly distributed. It may be hard to assess this when buying, so you may want to check reviews beforehand.

is needed for many of these components, so do some research and ask questions to see whether you are up to the challenge. If you're content with a smaller security upgrade, a doorbell with camera is an easier project.

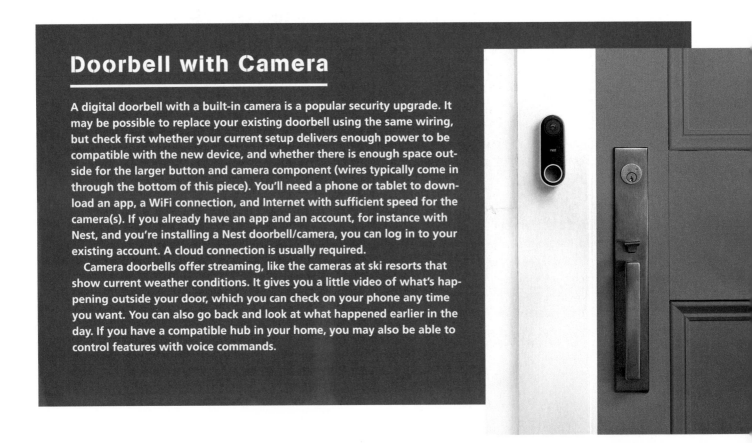

Doorbell with Camera

A digital doorbell with a built-in camera is a popular security upgrade. It may be possible to replace your existing doorbell using the same wiring, but check first whether your current setup delivers enough power to be compatible with the new device, and whether there is enough space outside for the larger button and camera component (wires typically come in through the bottom of this piece). You'll need a phone or tablet to download an app, a WiFi connection, and Internet with sufficient speed for the camera(s). If you already have an app and an account, for instance with Nest, and you're installing a Nest doorbell/camera, you can log in to your existing account. A cloud connection is usually required.

Camera doorbells offer streaming, like the cameras at ski resorts that show current weather conditions. It gives you a little video of what's happening outside your door, which you can check on your phone any time you want. You can also go back and look at what happened earlier in the day. If you have a compatible hub in your home, you may also be able to control features with voice commands.

PASSCODE LOCK. A digital lock uses a passcode for unlocking a key-free deadbolt. The lock will typically connect to your home's WiFi and to the app that controls it through the cloud.

INDOOR CAMERA. There are a number of uses for indoor cameras, such as keeping an eye on a sleeping baby, children on another floor of the house, or a pet. They can bring peace of mind. If you're installing a security system with cameras on the outside of your home, it's easy to add additional cameras inside as well.

WHOLE-HOUSE SECURITY SYSTEMS. Home security systems are a little more complicated because there are more components. For instance, the Abode starter kit has its own hub called a Gateway (a disk with a number of connection ports), a door or window sensor, a remote key fob, and a motion sensor. The Gateway hub can also connect to your home's lights, locks, thermostats, garage door openers, and other compatible devices, letting you control them, too.

Credits

All photos by Steve Cory and Diane Slavik except for those noted below. All drawings by Mario Ferro except for those noted below.

Introduction

p. 2: photo courtesy Nest

Chapter 1

p. 18: drawing by Trevor Johnston
p. 31: drawings by Trevor Johnston

Chapter 3

p. 56: photos courtesy Tech Lighting (top and bottom)
p. 57: photos courtesy Tech Lighting (top left, bottom left, top right, center right, and bottom right); photo by Loftus Design (center right)
p. 58: photo courtesy Kohler/Robern (top left); photos courtesy Tech Lighting (bottom left, top right, and bottom right)
p. 59: photos courtesy Tech Lighting (top left, bottom left, top right, and bottom right)
p. 83: photos courtesy Minka Aire (top left and bottom left); photos courtesy Hunter Fan Company (top right and bottom right)
p. 92: drawing by Trevor Johnston

Chapter 4

p. 98: photos courtesy Inter IKEA Systems B.V. (bottom left, top right, top center right, bottom center right, bottom right)
p. 99: photo courtesy Inter IKEA Systems B.V. (top right)
p. 115: drawings by Trevor Johnston

Chapter 6

p. 154: photo by Patrick McCombe, courtesy *Fine Homebuilding* magazine, © The Taunton Press, Inc.
p. 156: drawing by Trevor Johnston
p. 158: photo by Loftus Design
p. 163: photo by Loftus Design
p. 164: photo by Doreen Schweitzer
p. 165: photo courtesy diamondLife

Chapter 8

p. 207: top drawing by Trevor Johnston
p. 212: top drawing by Trevor Johnston

Chapter 9

p. 244: photos courtesy WarmlyYours (bottom left, top right, and bottom right)
p. 245: photos courtesy WarmlyYours (top right and bottom left)

Chapter 10

p. 246: photo courtesy Nest
p. 255: photos courtesy Nest (left and center); Google (right)
p. 257: photos courtesy Wemo (top and bottom)
p. 258: photos courtesy LIFX (top); Nest (bottom)
p. 259: photos courtesy Nest (top left, bottom left, and bottom right); photo top right courtesy Wemo

Index